Books and pamphlets by R.C. Churchill

DISAGREEMENTS
HE SERVED HUMAN LIBERTY
A SHORT HISTORY OF THE FUTURE
SHAKESPEARE AND HIS BETTERS
THE POWYS BROTHERS
THE FRONTIERS OF FICTION
A BIBLIOGRAPHY OF DICKENSIAN CRITICISM

THE ENGLISH SUNDAY
ART AND CHRISTIANITY
ENGLISH LITERATURE AND THE AGNOSTIC

ENGLISH LITERATURE OF THE EIGHTEENTH CENTURY
ENGLISH LITERATURE OF THE NINETEENTH CENTURY
(ed) POPE'S EPISTLE TO DR ARBUTHNOT
(with George Sampson) THE CONCISE CAMBRIDGE HISTORY OF
    ENGLISH LITERATURE

SIXTY SEASONS OF LEAGUE FOOTBALL
ENGLISH LEAGUE FOOTBALL
(ed) OFFICIAL RULES OF SPORTS AND GAMES

MRT

A Bibliography
of
Dickensian Criticism
1836-1975

Compiled and Edited by
R. C. Churchill

Garland Publishing, Inc., New York & London

1975

Copyright © 1975

by R. C. Churchill

Library of Congress Cataloging in Publication Data

Churchill, Reginald Charles.
  A bibliography of Dickensian criticism, 1836-1975.

  (Garland reference library of the humanities ; no. 12)
  Includes index.
  1. Dickens, Charles, 1812-1870--Bibliography.
I. Title.
Z8230.C47 [PR4581]   016.823'8   75-5119
ISBN 0-8240-1083-3

Printed in the United States of America

TABLE OF CONTENTS

TABLE OF CONTENTS, cont.

A complete bibliography of Dickensian criticism, from his
own time to the present day, would take many volumes.   The
present volume is, I believe, the most comprehensive yet
attempted.

The accent throughout is on chronological order.   I have
tried to do justice to all periods of Dickens criticism,
not merely the Victorian period and the modern period, both
of which have been much anthologized in recent years, but
also the early twentieth century, from Swinburne and
Chesterton and Quiller-Couch to my own first writing on
Dickens in 1937.   So much that is currently regarded as
"modern" was first pointed out many years ago, as is
evident from the quotations I make in this book from
such critics as Swinburne, Chesterton, Stephen Leacock,
Quiller-Couch, H.C.Dent, and myself.   It was Chesterton
who first pointed out the symbolic nature of Dickens's
literary and moral art in Bleak House; it was Quiller-Couch
who first insisted that as a _novelist_ - and the emphasis
was his own - Dickens was the greatest in English and
"among the greatest of all the greatest European novelists";
it was Stephen Leacock who wrote that "the works of Charles
Dickens represent the highest reach of the world's
imaginative literature... the world's supreme achievement
in art"; it was H.C.Dent who first pointed out that Dickens,
like Shakespeare, "sums up in his work most of the

characteristics of his predecessors and who transcends them
all by the universality of his genius"; it was the present
writer in 1937 who first pointed out the inseparable nature
of Dickens's literary art and the best of his social criticism
from Oliver Twist to Hard Times and Little Dorrit and who
insisted on the central importance of his dramatic use of
the English language.

This book, then, is an attempt to do justice all round,
to emphasize the value of the Dickensian criticism of the
early twentieth century, while not denying the equal value
of the best of the work done in the Victorian age and in the
modern period from Orwell, Wilson and House to the scholarly
and sophisticated present. A mini-anthology as well as a
bibliography, this book presents the evidence, and the
reader can judge for himself.

From copyright works, my quotations have had to be brief,
but fair, I trust, to their immediate context. I have
occasionally indulged myself in a longer quotation from a
work out of copyright. In regard to quotations from critics
of the Victorian age, I have relied mainly on the extracts
quoted by Charles Dickens the Younger in his introductions
to the Macmillan edition and by Philip Collins in his
excellent contribution to the Critical Heritage series.
In regard to quotations from the early twentieth century
critics, I have usually consulted the originals, but have

PREFACE, cont.

also made use of the anthologies and selections which have
appeared in recent years, in particular the admirable
Penguin volume edited by Stephen Wall. Mostly it will be
found that I have indicated the source of my quotations
where I have not gone to the originals - by such references
as "qu Wall 1970 p 99" or "qu Collins 1971 p 100" - but where
I do not make any particular reference, the reader will know
that my quotation has either been quoted many times before
or (in the case of modern works) comes from a review by
myself or some other reviewer.

To Philip Collins's Dickens Bibliography (from NCBEL 1969)
and to the work done by Madeline House, Graham Storey and
their associate editors in the truly magnificent Pilgrim
Edition of Dickens's letters - the third volume of which
I had the privilege of reviewing last year - I owe the
considerable debt shared by all who have profited by their
scholarly labours.

For assistance of various kinds, in my own Dickensian
labours in recent years, I am grateful to my former
colleague Mr R.E.Kellett; to my friend Mr Maurice Hussey;
to Mr Keith Brace, Literary Editor of The Birmingham Post;
and to Ifor Evans, Lord Evans, Professor Emeritus in the
University of London.

                                              R.C.C.
St Leonards, Sussex
March 1975
                          xi

ABBREVIATIONS

abr (abridged); anon (anonymous); ao (and others); appx
(appendix); Archiv (Archiv für das Studium der neueren
Sprachen)

BCB (British Council Booklet, Writers & Their Work series);
bibliog (bibliography); bk (book)

CBEL (Cambridge Bibliography of English Literature); cf
(compare, contrast); ch (chapter); CHEL (Cambridge History
of English Literature); col (column); CQ (Critical Quarterly)

DNB (Dictionary of National Biography); DS (Dickens Studies);
DSA (Dickens Studies Annual); DSN (Dickens Studies Newsletter)

EC (Essays in Criticism); ed (edited by); edn (edition);
EL (Everyman's Library); ELH (Journal of English Literary
History); EML (English Men of Letters)

FL (Fontana Library); fwd (foreword by)

HC (Harper Classics); HLQ (Huntington Library Quarterly)

ibid (same source as last entry); illustr (illustrated by);
intn (introduction by); incl (includes, included, including)

JEGP (Journal of English & Germanic Philology)

Mag (Magazine); MLN (Modern Language Notes); MLQ (Modern
Language Quarterly); MLR (Modern Language Review); MP
(Modern Philology)

NCBEL (New Cambridge Bibliography of English Literature);
NCF (Nineteenth-Century Fiction); nd (no date); no (number);
ns (new series)

OP (Oxford Paperbacks); OPUS (Oxford Paperbacks University
Series); op cit (in the work cited)

p (page); pp (pages); para (paragraph); pbd (published);
pbn (publication); PB (Penguin, Pelican, Peregrine Books);
PEL (Penguin English Library); PGEL (Pelican Guide to English
Literature); PMLA (Publications of the Modern Language
Association of America); PQ (Philological Quarterly); pref
(preface, preface to, preface by); pst (posthumously);
pt (part)

qu (quoted in, quoted by, quoting, quotation)

ABBREVIATIONS, cont.

ref (referring to, reference found in); REL (Review of English
   Literature); RES (Review of English Studies); Rev (Review,
   Reverend); rp (reprinted, reprints, reprinting); rv
   (revised, revised by, revision of); rt (retitled)

SC (Signet Classics); SEL (Studies in English Literature);
   SP (Studies in Philology)

TLS (Times Literary Supplement); tr (translated by); trn
   (translation)

UP (University Paperbacks)

vol (volume)

WC (World's Classics)

Publication in London (or London and New York) unless

   otherwise stated

ERRATA

p 5 line 17: for "Priestly" read "Priestley"

p 8 line 19: for "Nesbit" read "Nisbet"

p 17 line 26: for "1924" read "1926"

p 20 line 9: for "1939" read "1929"

p 21 line 9: for "1912" read "1915"

p 28 line 16: for "chartier" read "Chartier"

p 30 line 15: for "1943" read "1953"

p 47 line 27: for "deit" read "diet"

p 51 penultimate line: for "Wllers" read "Wellers"

p 66 line 6 from bottom: for "Wther" read "Whether"

p 69 line 30: for "reviwers" read "reviewers"

p 71 line 8 from bottom: for "sprining" read "springing"

p 72 line 18: for "illustraots" read "illustrators"

p 75 line 3: for "William" read "Charles"

p 96 line 13 from bottom: for "Drmatic" read "Dramatic"

p 107 line 28: for "Englisj" read "English"

p 110 line 22: for "A Structure" read "Structure"

p 115 penultimate line: for "The Singular" read "Singular"

p 153 line 12: for "1920" read "1923"

p 197 line 16: for "set" read "sent"

p 199 line 3 from bottom: for "left" read "felt"

p 212 line 15: for "1853" read "1855"

p 214 line 24: for "Manichaen" read "Manichean"

p 293 line 6 from bottom: for "Grahame" read "Graham"

INTRODUCTION

Bibliographies

Kitton, Frederic G. Dickensiana: A Bibliography of the
Literature relating to Charles Dickens and his Writings.
1886; rp 1971 fwd K.J.Fielding.

Dibelius, Wilhelm. Charles Dickens. Leipzig 1916; rv 1926.
Incl comprehensive bibliog.

Darton, F.J.Harvey. Charles Dickens in vol 3 CBEL ed F.W.
Bateson. Cambridge 1940; rv Philip Collins NCBEL 1969
ed George Watson. Concise CBEL ed Watson 1958; rv 1965.

Miller, W. The Dickens Student and Collector: A List of
Writings relating to Charles Dickens and his Works 1836-1945.
Cambridge Mass 1946.

Fielding, K.J. Charles Dickens. BCB 1953; rv 1960, 1963.
Incl select bibliog.

Nisbet, Ada. Charles Dickens. Victorian Fiction: A Guide to
Research, ed Lionel Stevenson, Cambridge Mass 1963.

Bateson, F.W. Charles Dickens. A Guide to English Literature,
1965.

Collins, Philip. A Dickens Bibliography. 1970. From NCBEL
1969 above.

Journals

Slater, Michael (ed). The Dickensian: A Magazine for Dickens
Lovers. From 1905; vols 1-64 1905-68 rp 1970. Journal of
the Dickens Fellowship founded 1902, originally monthly, now
thrice-yearly. Former eds incl B.W.Matz, Walter Dexter and
Leslie C.Staples. Annual bibliog: The Year's Work in Dickens
Studies.

Peyrouton, Noel C.(ed). Dickens Studies: A Journal of Modern
Research and Criticism. Boston 1965-70. Succeeded by:

Partlow, Robert B.jr(ed). Dickens Studies Annual. Carbondale
Ill from 1971.

Stevenson, Lionel (ed). Dickens Studies Newsletter.

1

Duane DeVries of Polytechnic Institute of New York
succeeded Lionel Stevenson as ed Dickens Studies Newsletter
from vol 5 no 3 issue (Oct 1974).

Biographies

Mackenzie, Robert Shelton. Brief Autobiography of Boz.
   Durham Advertiser 26 Jan 1838. Reply by Dickens 9 Feb
   saying "Dr Mackenzie...knows as much of me as of the meaning
   of the word autobiography. "

Anon. Visit of Boz: Sketch of his Life. Bunker-Hill Aurora
   & Boston Mirror 29 Jan 1842. Reply by Dickens 5 Feb saying
   it contained statements about his and Mrs Dickens's birth and
   parentage which were "entirely new" to him.

Dickens. 1847. Autobiographical fragment qu Forster 1872 below
   bk 1 chs 1-2; cf Copperfield chs 4, 11.

Anon. Dickens: A Critical Biography. Our Contemporaries
   series 1858.

Mackenzie, Robert Shelton. Life of Charles Dickens.
   Philadelphia 1870.

Taverner, H.T. and J.C.Hotten. Dickens: The Story of his Life.
   1870; rp with Speeches by Dickens 1873.

Sala, George Augustus. Charles Dickens. 1870; rp 1971.

Hammond, R.A. The Life and Writings of Charles Dickens.
   Intn Elihu Burritt. Toronto 1871.

Forster, John. The Life of Charles Dickens. 3 vols 1872-4;
   rv 2 vols 1876; 2 vols in one nd c1890; abr 1903 ed George
   Gissing; 2 vols 1911 ed B.W.Matz; 2 vols EL 1927 ed G.K.
   Chesterton; 1 vol 1928 ed J.W.T.Ley; 2 vols EL 1966 ed A.J.
   Hoppé. This, the classic Life, bears same relation to
   succeeding Lives as Boswell to succeeding Lives of Johnson.
   See R.C.Churchill, Dickens's Boswell, Birmingham Post 25 Jun
   1966 and Sylvère Monod, Forster's Life of Dickens and Literary
   Criticism, English Studies Today 4 Rome 1966.

Clarke, Charles and Mary Cowden. Recollections of Writers.
   1878. Keats, Lamb, Hunt, Dickens...

Ward, A.W. Dickens. EML 1882.

Langton, Robert. The Childhood and Youth of Charles
    Dickens. Manchester 1883; rv 1891, 1912.

Dickens, Mary. Charles Dickens: by his Eldest Daughter.
    1885; rt My Father as I Recall Him, 1896.

Marzials, Sir Frank. Life of Charles Dickens. 1887.

Stephen, Sir Leslie. Charles Dickens in DNB 1888.
    "He should have passed it on to somebody else. It attempts
    to be fair, with very little success..." (Fielding 1953).

Du Pontavice de Heussey, R.Y.M. Un maître du roman
    contemporain: l'inimitable Boz. Paris 1889.

Kitton, Frederic G.(ed). Charles Dickens by Pen and Pencil.
    1890; rv 1890, 1891.

Kitton, Frederic G. Charles Dickens: His Life, Writings and
    Personality. 2 vols Edinburgh 1902; 1 vol nd c1904.

Chesterton, G.K. and Frederic G.Kitton. Charles Dickens.
    Bookman Biography series 1903. Booklet of 44pp not to
    be confused with Chesterton 1906 below.

Fitzgerald, Percy. The Life of Charles Dickens as Revealed
    in his Writings. 2 vols 1905.

Chesterton 1906: see below under "General Criticism:
    Twentieth Century".

Shore, W.T. Charles Dickens. 1910.

Moses, B. Charles Dickens. 1912.

Whipple, Edwin P. Charles Dickens: The Man and his Work.
    2 vols Boston 1912.

Dibelius 1916: p 1 above.

Ley, J.W.T. The Dickens Circle: A Narrative of the
    Novelist's Friendships. 1918.

Dark, Sidney. Charles Dickens. 1919.

Nicoll, Sir William Robertson. Dickens's Own Story:
    Sidelights on his Life and Personality. 1923.

Dickens, Sir Henry Fielding. Memories of My Father. 1928.
By his youngest son (1849-1933).

Straus, Ralph. Dickens: A Portrait in Pencil. 1928;
rt A Portrait of Dickens 1938.

Wagenknecht, Edward. The Man Charles Dickens: A Victorian
Portrait. Cambridge Mass 1929; rv Norman Okla 1966.
"...fundamentally sound and much better documented than
anything that had appeared before" (Fielding 1953).

Stonehouse, John Harrison. Green Leaves: New Chapters in
the Life of Charles Dickens. 1931.

Darwin, Bernard. Charles Dickens. Great Lives series 1933.

Leacock, Stephen. Charles Dickens: His Life and Work. 1933.
One of the best, but also one of the most neglected in
recent years. See further below under "General Criticism:
Twentieth Century".

Dent, H.C. The Life and Characters of Charles Dickens.
Fwd Laton Blacklands. 1933; rp Odhams edn Dickens's Works
nd c1935.

Kingsmill, Hugh (H.K. Lunn). The Sentimental Journey: A Life
of Charles Dickens. 1934.

Wright, Thomas. The Life of Charles Dickens. 1935.
See further below under "Dickens and Ellen Ternan".

Straus, Ralph. Dickens: The Man and the Book. 1936.

Dybowski, R. Dickens. Warsaw 1936. Incl bibliog Polish
trns. See further below under "Dickens and Conrad".

Storey, Gladys. Dickens and Daughter. 1939. Author close
friend of Kate Dickens, Mrs Perugini (1839-1929).

Pope-Hennessy, Una. Charles Dickens: 1812-1870. 1945.

Lemonnier, Léon. Dickens. Paris 1946; tr 1947. See further
below under "Dickens in France".

Aldington, Richard. Four English Portraits: 1801-1851. 1948.
Dickens; Disraeli; Charles Waterton; the Prince Regent.

Pearson, Hesketh. Dickens: His Character, Comedy and Career.
1949.

Lindsay, Jack. Charles Dickens: A Biographical and Critical Study. 1950.

Symons, Julian. Charles Dickens. 1951; new edn 1969.

Johnson, Edgar. Charles Dickens: His Tragedy and Triumph. 2 vols New York 1952, London 1953; rv 1965. The fullest biography since Forster.

Fielding, K.J. Dickens since Forster. TLS 9 Oct 1953.

Fielding 1953: p 1 above.

Bowen, W.H. Charles Dickens and his Family. Cambridge 1956.

Adrian, Arthur. Georgina Hogarth and the Dickens Circle. Oxford 1957.

Fielding, K.J. Charles Dickens: A Critical Introduction. 1958; rv 1965. "The best brief introudction to the work and life" (Nisbet 1963).

Katarsky, Ivan M. Dickens. Moscow 1960. See further below under "Dickens in Russia".

Priestly, J.B. Charles Dickens: A Pictorial Biography. 1961.

Wagenknecht, Edward. Charles Dickens and the Scandal-mongers. Norman Okla 1965.

Hibbert, Christopher. The Making of Charles Dickens. 1967. The early years to 1836.

Fido, Martin. Charles Dickens: An Authentic Account of his Life and Times. 1970.

Collins, Philip. Dickens in 1870. TLS 4 Jun 1970.

Letters

Hogarth, Georgina and Mary Dickens (ed). The Letters of Charles Dickens: edited by his sister-in-law and eldest daughter. 3 vols 1880-2; rv 2 vols 1882; rv 1 vol 1893.

Hutton, Laurence (ed). Letters of Charles Dickens to Wilkie Collins: 1851-70. Selected by Georgina Hogarth. 1892.

Baker, George P.(ed). Charles Dickens and Maria Beadnell.
St Louis 1908.

Lehmann 1912: see below under "Dickens the Journalist".

Dexter, Walter (ed). The Unpublished Letters of Charles
Dickens to Mark Lemon. 1927.

Dexter, Walter (ed). Dickens to his Oldest Friend: Letters
of a Lifetime from Charles Dickens to Thomas Beard. 1932.

Dexter, Walter (ed). Mr and Mrs Charles Dickens: His Letters
to Her. Fwd Kate Dickens, Mrs Perugini. 1935.

Dexter, Walter (ed). The Love Romance of Charles Dickens:
Told in his Letters to Maria Beadnell. 1936.

Dexter, Walter (ed). Letters of Charles Dickens. 3 vols
1938. In Nonesuch edn of Dickens 23 vols 1937-8.

Johnson, Edgar (ed). The Heart of Charles Dickens. New York
1952; London 1953 rt Letters from Charles Dickens to Angela
Burdett-Coutts 1841-65.

Dupee, F.W.(ed). Selected Letters of Charles Dickens.
New York 1960.

House, Madeline and Graham Storey (ed). Associate ed: W.J.
Carlton, Philip Collins, K.J.Fielding, Kathleen Tillotson.
The Letters of Charles Dickens: Vol I 1820-39. Oxford 1965.
The authoritative Pilgrim edn planned by Humphry House
(1908-55) in 1949. To be completed in 12 vols.

House, Madeline and Graham Storey (ed). Associate ed:
Kathleen Tillotson. The Letters of Charles Dickens: Vol II
1840-41. Oxford 1969. See above.

House, Madeline, Graham Storey and Kathleen Tillotson (ed).
Associate ed: Noel C.Peyrouton. The Letters of Charles
Dickens: Vol III 1842-43. Oxford 1974. See above.
Preface tells us that "the total of letters known..has
risen...to 13,074."

Tomlin 1974: see below under "Dickens in France".

Selections, Anthologies, Symposia, etc.

Philip, Alexander J. A Dickens Dictionary. Gravesend 1909;
  rv W.Laurence Gadd 1928.

Smith, M.S.C.(ed). Studies in Dickens. New York 1910.

Bentley, Eric (ed). The Importance of Scrutiny. New York
  1948; Gotham Lib edn New York 1964. Incl Churchill 1937-42
  qv below under "General Criticism: Twentieth Century".

Wagenknecht, Edward (ed). An Introduction to Dickens.
  Chicago 1952.

Allott, Miriam. Novelists on the Novel. 1959. Incl
  Thackeray, Flaubert, Bennett and E.M.Forster on Dickens.

Clark, William Ross (ed). Discussions of Dickens. Discussions
  of Literature series Boston 1961.

Butt, John (ed). A Dickens symposium, REL 2 1961.

Ford, George H. and Lauriat Lane jr (ed). The Dickens Critics:
  1841-1960. Ithaca NY 1961. From Poe to Trilling.

Gross, John and Gabriel Pearson (ed). Dickens and the
  Twentieth Century. 1962. Recent criticism by John Bayley,
  William Empson, John Wain, Angus Wilson, Arnold Kettle ao.

Peyrouton, Noel C.(ed). Dickens Criticism: Past, Present and
  Future Directions. Symposium with George H.Ford, J.Hillis
  Miller, Edgar Johnson and Sylvère Monod. Cambridge Mass
  1962.

Hardwick, Michael and Mollie (ed). The Charles Dickens
  Compendium. 1965.

Price, Martin (ed). Dickens. Twentieth-Century Views series
  1967.

Dyson, A.E.(ed). Dickens. Modern Judgements series 1968.
  Criticism by Humphry House, Angus Wilson, Lionel Trilling,
  Edgar Johnson, C.B.Cox, Dorothy Van Ghent ao.

Slater, Michael (ed). Dickens and Fame 1870-1970: Essays on
  the Author's Reputation. Dickensian 66 1970. By K.J.
  Fielding, George H.Ford, Sylvère Monod, Philip Collins.

Wall, Stephen (ed). Charles Dickens: A Critical Anthology.
  Penguin Critical Anthologies series 1970. From 1836 to 1968.

Selections, etc cont.

Tomlin, E.W.F.(ed). Charles Dickens: 1812-1870. 1970.
  Essays by J.B.Priestley, Ivor Brown, Edgar Johnson,
  Christopher Hibbert, Harry Stone, Emlyn Williams and
  Nicolas Bentley.

Slater, Michael (ed). Dickens 1970. 1970. Centenary essays
  by Walter Allen, Margaret Lane, Pamela Hansford Johnson,
  C.P.Snow, Barbara Hardy, Raymond Williams, John Holloway
  and Angus Wilson.

Collins, Philip (ed). Dickens: The Critical Heritage. 1971.

Anon. Dickens: Views of the Victorians. TLS 5 Mar 1971.
  Review of Collins 1971 above.

Partlow, Robert B.jr (ed). Dickens the Craftsman. 1971.
  Essays by Philip Collins, K.J.Fielding, A.W.Brice, James R.
  Kincaid, Harry Stone, Richard J.Dunn, Sylvère Monod ao.

Watt, Ian (ed). The Victorian Novel: Modern Essays in
  Criticism. 1971.

Kettle, Arnold (ed). The Nineteenth-Century Novel: Critical
  Essays and Documents. 1972.

Nesbit, Ada and Blake Nevius (ed). Dickens Centennial Essays.
  1973. From NCF centenary issue 1970.

Hardwick, Michael and Mollie (ed). The Charles Dickens
  Encyclopaedia. Reading Berks 1973.

Hobsbaum, Philip. A Reader's Guide to Charles Dickens.
  Reader's Guide series 1973.

GENERAL CRITICISM: NINETEENTH CENTURY

Period 1836-1839

Maginn, William. Fraser's Mag Aug 36. "...Boz the
magnificent (what a pity it is that he deludes himself
into the absurd idea that he can be a Whig.'..."

Fonblanque 1836: see below under "Sketches by Boz".

Anon. Morning Advertiser 25 Oct 36. On Dickens's future
prospects. "We sincerely hope that our youthful author
may long be spared to contribute to the entertainment
of the public..."

Anon (Abraham Hayward). Quarterly Rev Oct 37. On Dickens's
future prospects. "The fact is, Mr Dickens writes too often
and too fast... If he persists much longer in this course,
it requires no gift of prophecy to foretell his fate –
he has risen like a rocket, and he will come down like
the stick".

Ainsworth 1837: see below under "Dickens's London".

Anon. Some Thoughts on Arch-Waggery and in Especial on the
Genius of Boz. Court Mag Apr 37; rp Dickensian 4 1908.

Lewes 1837: see below under "Pickwick".

Mahony, Francis Sylvester. A Poetical Epistle from Father
Prout to Boz. Bentley's Miscellany Jan 38.

Hunt, Leigh. Letter to Dickens Jul 38. "If you are a master
now (as undoubtedly you are) you will be a still greater
one by and by. What rejoices me particularly in your having
so much heart (not always the accompaniment of wit) is that
it makes me anticipate a Shakespearian lot for you..."
(qu House 1965: p 6 above; pp 685-6. See further below
under "Dickens and Shakespeare").

Smith, Sydney. Letter to Sir George Philips Sep 38.
"Nickleby is very good. I stood out against Mr Dickens
as long as I could, but he has conquered me" (Letters of
Sydney Smith vol 2 p 671.)

Anon (Thomas H. Lister). Edinburgh Rev Oct 38. "...the truest
and most spirited delineator of English life, amongst the
middle and lower classes, since the days of Smollett and
Fielding".

Talfourd, Thomas Noon. Sonnet to Dickens "on perusing the
    completed Oliver Twist". Dated Xmas 38; pbd with other
    verses in Talfourd's Tragedies 1844.

Wilkie, Sir David. Speech at dinner to celebrate completion
    of Nickleby 5 Oct 39, "all about the reality of Dickens's
    genius, and how there had been nothing like him issuing
    his novels part by part since Richardson issued his novels
    volume by volume, and how in both cases people talked about
    the characters as if they were next-door neighbours or
    friends, and how as many letters were written to the author
    of Nickleby to implore him not to kill poor Smike as had
    been sent by young ladies to the author of Clarissa to
    'save Lovelace's soul alive'" (Forster 1872 bk 2 ch 4;
    qu Churchill 1937-42; see further below under "Reading
    Public", "Serial Novelist", "Characters" and "Dickens
    and Richardson".)

The Eighteen-Forties

Anon. Dickens and his Works. Fraser's Mag Apr 40.

Anon. New Zealand Gazette, Port Nicholson, Wellington,
    16 May 40. Announced formation of Pickwick Club of New
    Zealand: "it tends to prove that in this remote region of
    the globe - this land of savages - Englishmen relish the
    inimitable works of Boz" (qu House 1969: p 6 above; p 161n;
    cf Copperfield ch 63.)

Townshend, Rev Chauncy Hare. Sonnet "to the Author of
    Oliver Twist, Nicholas Nickleby, etc", c1840; pbd Sermons
    in Sonnets and Other Poems 1851. Begins: "Man of the genial
    mind!..." and ends: "I thank thee in the name of human
    kind!" (qu House 1969 p 112n.)

Landor, Walter Savage. 1841. Recorded by Crabb Robinson
    as declaring that Dickens was "with Shakespeare the
    greatest of English writers, though indeed his women are
    superior to Shakespeare's. No one of our poets comes near
    him" (qu House 1969 from Henry Crabb Robinson on Books and
    their Writers ed E.J.Morley 1938; see further below under
    "Dickens and Shakespeare".)

Smith, Sydney. Letter to Dickens 17 Apr 41. "We are constant
    readers here of all you write. You have many attributes -
    but I love your humour most..."

Anon. Caledonian Mercury Edinburgh 26 Jun 41. "...the
Shakespeare of his day..." (full qu House 1969 p 315n;
cf Landor 1841 above.)

Sterling 1841: see below under "Dickens and Thackeray".

Poe 1841: see below under "Barnaby Rudge".

Parley's Penny Library vol 1 Dec 41. Dedicated to Dickens
as "the living Shakespeare" (cf Caledonian Mercury above.)

Marx 1841-2: see below under "Dickens in Germany".

Jeffrey 1841-7: see below under "Old Curiosity Shop",
"Christmas Carol", "Chimes" and "Dombey and Son".

Janin 1842: see below under "Nickleby".

Thackeray 1842: see below under "Dickens in France"

Wordsworth 1842: see below under "Reading Public".

Collins, Dr Stephen. Charles Dickens. Miscellanies,
Philadelphia 1842. "He confers honour on his country and
his species... genius in union with virtue..."

W.W.(Walt Whitman). Boz and Democracy. Brother Jonathan
New York 26 Feb 42; rp Rivulets of Prose, New York 1928.
Defends low-life scenes in the novels and speaks of
Whitman's "love and esteem" for Dickens's writings. See
further below and under "Radical and Reformer" and "Dickens
and Walt Whitman".

Whitman, Walt. Dickens and Democracy. Aurora New York 2 Apr
42. Defends Dickens against criticism in April Democratic
Rev that the "bad characters" in the novels are "atrociously
exaggerated".

Felton, Cornelius Conway. Charles Dickens: His Genius and
Style. North American Rev Jan 43.

Forgues, Paul Emile Daurand. Revue Britannique Paris Apr 43.
See further below under "Dickens in France".

Brindley, Thomas Bardel. The Omnipotence of the Deity and
Other Poems. 1843. Dedication to Dickens speaks of his
"mind of so gigantic an order" and his "profound knowledge
of human life" (qu House 1974 p 515.)

The Eighteen-Forties, cont.

Horne, Richard Henry. Charles Dickens. A New Spirit of the
Age, 1844; WC edn 1907. See K.J.Fielding, Dickens and R.H.
Horne, English 9 1952.

Belinsky 1844-8: see below under "Dickens in Russia".

Douglas Jerrold's Shilling Mag Jan 45. Sonnet to Charles
Dickens. Begins: "Oh, potent wizard: painter of great
skill..." and ends with ref to Christmas Carol as "an
allegory fine" and The Chimes whose "burden...is holy and
benign."

Anon. Boz versus Dickens. Parker's London Mag Feb 45.

Danzel, W. Uber Dickens' Romane. Blätter für Literarische
Unterhaltung 9-13 Aug 45.

Anon. The Writings of Dickens. North British Rev 3 1845.

Thackeray 1847: see below under "Dombey".

Anon (J.Eagles). A Few Words about Novels. Blackwood's Mag
64 1848.

Emerson, Ralph Waldo. English Traits. Lectures at Boston
1848; pbd Boston and London 1856.

Anon (Edwin P.Whipple). North American Rev 69 1849; rp
Literature and Life 1851.

Druzhinin 1849: see below under "Dickens in Russia".

Thackeray 1849: see below under "Copperfield".

The Eighteen-Fifties

Thackeray 1851: see below under "Dickens and Sterne".

Schmidt, J. Dickens: eine Charakteristik. Leipzig 1852.

Skelton, F.W. On the Genius of Dickens. Knickerbocker Mag
New York May 52.

Anon. The Genius and Characters of Charles Dickens.
Working Man's Friend 21 Aug 52.

Talbot, G.F. The Genius of Dickens. Putnam's Monthly Mag
   New York Mar 55.

Taine, Henri (Hippolyte Taine). Charles Dickens: son talent
   et ses oeuvres. Revue des Deux Mondes 1 Feb 56; rv vol 5
   Histoire de la littérature Anglaise Paris 1863-4, tr
   Edinburgh 1871; qu Forster 1872, Leacock 1933, Pope-
   Hennessy 1945, Wall 1970, etc.

George Eliot 1856: see below under "Characters".

Anon (Sir James Fitzjames Stephen). Mr Dickens as a Politician.
   Saturday Rev 3 Jan 57. Light Literature and the Saturday
   Review. 11 Jul 57. Cf Hollingshead 1857 below.

Anon (E.B.Hamley). A Remonstrance with Dickens. Blackwood's
   Mag Apr 57.

Anon (Sir James Fitzjames Stephen). The License of Modern
   Novelists. Edinburgh Rev Jul 57. Criticizes Dickens,
   Charles Reade and Mrs Gaskell. Reply by Dickens, Household
   Words 1 Aug 57 in article ironically titled Curious Misprint
   in the Edinburgh Review (qu Dickens 1892 and Wall 1970 qqv.)

Hollingshead, John. Dickens and his Critics. Train Aug 57;
   rp Essays 1865. Reply to Stephen and others.

Jeaffreson, J.C. Novels and Novelists. 1858.

Bagehot, Walter. Charles Dickens. Review of Cheap Edition
   of the Works of Mr Charles Dickens (1857-8). National Rev
   Oct 58; rp Literary Studies vol 2 1879; EL edn 1911 ed
   George Sampson, II p 164-97.

Masson, David. British Novelists and their Styles. 1859.
   Ch 4. See further below under "Style and Language".

The Eighteen-Sixties

Ruskin, John. The Roots of Honour. Cornhill Mag Sep 60;
   rp Unto This Last 1862; WC edn 1911 p 26n.

Ludwig 1860: see below under "Hard Times".

Anon (G.Turner). Dickens and his Reviewers. Welcome Guest
   1 1860. Cf Hollingshead 1857 above.

Galloway, A.H.   A Critical Dissertation on Some of the
   Writings of Charles Dickens.   Liverpool nd c1862.

Taine 1863: p 13 above.

Williams, S.F.   Dickens: A Series of Criticisms.   Rose,
   Shamrock & Thistle 3-4 1863-4.

McCarthy, Justin.   Westminster Rev ns 26 1864; rp Con Amore
   1868.

Hopkins, Gerard Manley.   Letter to A.W.M.Baillie 10 Sep 64;
   ptd Poems and Prose ed W.H.Gardner PB 1953 p 160.

Gourdault, J.   Les privilégiés et les pauvres gens dans les
   romans de Dickens.   Revue des Cours Littéraires 2 1865.

Arnold, Matthew.   Preface to Essays in Criticism First Series
   1865.   "The English novel was one of Arnold's critical blind
   spots.   The satiric catalogue of typical philistine literatur
   in the Preface...includes - along with The Wide, Wide World
   and Henry Ward Beecher's Sermons - Dickens's Little Dorrit."
   (Bateson 1965: p 1 above; p 151n.)   "Arnold's attitude
   towards Dickens was irritating to many people, and to
   Swinburne intolerable" (Watts-Dunton pref Swinburne 1913 qv).
   Cf De Quincey who thought Dickens's novels showed "want of
   fidelity to human nature" and who once referred to "Albert
   Smith, Dickens, etc" (qu Edward Sackville-West, A Flame in
   Sunlight: The Life and Work of Thomas De Quincey, new edn
   1974 p 330).   But see Arnold 1881 qu below under "Dickens
   and Education".

James, Henry.   Review of Our Mutual Friend.   Nation New York
   21 Nov 65; rp Selected Literary Criticism ed Morris Shapira
   1963; PB edn 1968 pp 31-5.

Anon (Edwin P.Whipple).   The Genius of Dickens.   Atlantic
   Monthly Boston May 67.

Anon (Charles Eliot Norton).   North American Rev Apr 68.

Stott, G.   Contemporary Rev Jan 69.

The Eighteen-Seventies

Friswell, J.Hain. Mr Charles Dickens. Modern Men of
Letters Honestly Criticized, 1870.

Longfellow 1870: see below under "Edwin Drood".

Jowett, Benjamin. Sermon in Westminster Abbey 19 Jun 70.
1870; rp Sermons 1899; qu Forster 1872, Wall 1970, etc.
Dickens died 9 June 1870 aged 58.

Stanley, Arthur Penrhyn, Dean. Sermon preached in
Westminster Abbey 19 Jun 70. 1870; rp Sermons on Special
Occasions 1882.

Anon (G.Fraser). Saturday Rev 11 Jun 70.

Hutton, R.H. The Genius of Dickens. Spectator 18 Jun 70;
rp Brief Literary Criticisms 1906.

Trollope, Anthony. Charles Dickens. St Paul's Mag Jul 70.

Austin, Alfred. Temple Bar Jul 70.

Harte, Bret. Dickens in Camp. Overland Monthly San
Francisco Jul 70; rp Poems Boston 1871.
"And on that grave where English oak and holly
    And laurel wreaths entwine,
Deem it not all a too presumptuous folly -
    This spray of Western pine!'"

Ham, J.P. Parables of Fiction: A Memorial Discourse on
Charles Dickens. 1870.

Buchanan, Robert. The Good Genie of Fiction. St Paul's Mag
Feb 72.

Lewes, George Henry. Dickens in Relation to Criticism.
Fortnightly Rev Feb 72 pp 141-54. "Odious by intolerable
assumptions of an indulgent superiority" (Forster 1872);
"Insolent and idiotic impeachment" (Swinburne 1902).
Some points, however, eminently discussible - and have
indeed been discussed (eg Hutton 1874, Churchill 1937-42
and elsewhere).

Flaubert 1872: see below under "Pickwick".

Hutton, R.H. The Dispute about Dickens. Spectator 7 Feb 74;
rp Criticisms of Contemporary Thought and Thinkers 1894.
Cf Lewes 1872 above.

Butler, Samuel.   The Way of All Flesh, ch 53.   Written c1875;
   pst pbd 1903.

Whipple, Edwin P.   Ints New Illustrated Lib edn New York 1876-'

Dilthey, Wilhelm.   Dickens und das Genie des erzahlenden
   Dichters.   Westermanns Monatshefte 41 1877.

The Eighteen-Eighties

Canning, A.S.G.   The Philosophy of Dickens.   1880.

Watt, J.C.   Great Novelists: Scott, Thackeray, Dickens,
   Lytton.   Edinburgh 1880.

Ruskin, John.   Fiction, Fair and Foul.   Nineteenth Century
   Jun 80-Oct 81; rp On the Old Road 1885; qu Wall 1970 qv.

Ward 1882: p 3 above.

Swinburne, Algernon Charles.   Dickens.   Sonnet pbd Tristram
   of Lyonesse and Other Poems 1882; rp Swinburne 1913 qv.
   Begins: "Chief in thy generation born of men..." and ends
   by comparing Dickens with Shakespeare, Sterne, Fielding and
   Goldsmith.

James, Henry.   The Art of Fiction.   Longman's Mag Sep 84;
   rp Partial Portraits 1888; incl Selected Literary Criticism:
   p 14 above; pp 78-97.

Hennequin, E.   Dickens: étude analytique.   Nouvelle Revue 49
   Paris 1887.

Stephen 1888: p 3 above.

FitzGerald, Edward.   "I for one worship Dickens, in spite of
   Carlyle and the critics..." (qu Pearson 1949: p 4 above;
   ref Letters 1889-1902.)

Hepburn, James (ed).   Letters of Arnold Bennett: Vol II 1889-
   1915.   Oxford 1968.   "He exhibited the advanced taste of his
   time by being thoroughly dismissive about Dickens and George
   Eliot" (TLS 19 Dec 1968; cf Lewes 1872 above where Dickens
   is criticized in implicit favour of George Eliot.   Bennett
   venerated Flaubert and the French novel and thought highly
   of George Moore, who himself criticized Dickens.)

Henley, William Ernest.   Views and Reviews.   1890; rp 1909;
   qu Quiller-Couch 1922 qv.

Howells, William Dean.   Criticism and Fiction.   Boston 1891;
   qu Van Wyck Brooks, The Confident Years 1952 p 85.)

Lang, Andrew.   Dickens.   Essays in Little, 1891.

Dickens, Charles jr (1837-96).   Ints Macmillan edn 1892-1925.
   See particularly ints Bleak House, Little Dorrit, Edwin Drood.

Harrison, Frederick.   Dickens's Place in Literature.   1894;
   rp Studies in Early Victorian Literature 1895.

Howells, William Dean.   My Literary Passions.   New York 1895.

Lilly, W.S.   Four English Humorists of the Nineteenth Century.
   1895.   Dickens, Thackeray, George Eliot, Carlyle.

Saintsbury, George.   Corrected Impressions.   1895; rv
   Collected Essays 1923.   Two essays on Dickens.

Aronstein, P.   Dickens-studien.   Anglia 18 1896.

Saintsbury, George.   A History of Nineteenth Century Literature.
   1896; rv 3rd edn 1901.

Shorter, Clement.   Victorian Literature.   1897.

Kitton, Frederic G.   The Novels of Charles Dickens.   1897.

Lang, Andrew and B.W.Matz (ed).   The Gadshill edn 1897-1908.
   "Nothing could be worse than Lang's introductions... They
   almost deserve the tremendous trouncing they received from
   Mr Swinburne" (Robertson Nicoll, qu Watts-Dunton, Swinburne
   1913 qv below.)

Gissing, George.   Charles Dickens: A Critical Study.   1898;
   Imperial edn 1902; Casket Lib edn 1924.   "By far the best
   extant" (Seccombe 1906); "the best thing on Dickens in
   English" (Edmund Wilson 1939); "the first full-length
   critical study... still one of the best" (Fielding 1953).
   See P.Coustillas, Gissing's Writings on Dickens, Dickensian
   61 1965.

Cross, Wilbur L.   The Development of the English Novel.
   New York 1899.

17

Meynell, Alice.   Dickens as a Writer.   Pall Mall Gazette
   Jan 99.   See further below under "Decade 1900-1909" and
   "Decade 1910-1919".   Mrs Meynell was daughter of Dickens's
   friend Thomas James Thompson.

Henley, William Ernest.   Some Notes on Dickens.   Pall Mall Mag
   Aug 99.

Gissing, George.   Ints uncompleted Rochester edn 1899-1901;
   rp Critical Studies of the Works of Charles Dickens ed T.
   Scott New York 1924 and in Gissing 1925 qv below.

GENERAL CRITICISM: TWENTIETH CENTURY

Decade 1900-1909

Brownell, W.C.   Victorian Prose Masters.   New York 1901.

Gissing, George.   Dickens in Memory.   Literature 21 Dec 01;
   rp Gissing 1925 qv.

G.G.(George Gissing).   Charles Dickens.   Critic New York
   Jan 02.

Swinburne, Algernon Charles.   Charles Dickens.   Quarterly Rev
   Jul 02; rp Swinburne 1913 qv.

Coustillas, Pierre (ed).   Gissing's Writings on Dickens.   1969.
   Incl reviews of Swinburne 1902 and Kitton 1902.

Meynell, Alice.   Dickens as a Man of Letters.   Atlantic Monthly
   Boston Jan 03.

Dickens, Kate, Mrs Perugini.   Charles Dickens as a Lover of
   Art and Artists.   Mag of Art Jan 03.

Chesterton and Kitton 1903: p 3 above.

Tolstoy, Count Leo.   "All his characters are my personal
   friends.   I am constantly comparing them with living persons,
   and living persons with them.   And what a spirit there was
   in all he wrote." (talking of Dickens to Sydney C.Cockerell
   on Cockerell's visit to Russia July 1903, reported to
   Swinburne - see below - and qu Quiller-Couch 1922 and Wall
   1970; see further below under "Dickens in Russia").

Swinburne.   Letter to Cockerell (see above) 5 Aug 03.   "I am
   equally interested and delighted to hear what you tell me.
   I trust you will make it public.   The appreciation of so
   great a man as Tolstoy...does what no other living man's
   could do: it adds a crowning ray of glory to the fame of
   Dickens.   Above all, what a superb and crushing reply to the
   vulgar insults of such malignant boobies and criticasters as
   G.H.Lewes and Co.(too numerous a Co.!) is the witness of such
   a man as this... After all, like will to like - genius will
   find out genius, and goodness will recognize goodness..."
   (qu Quiller-Couch 1922 and Wall 1970 qqv.)

Lord, W.F.   Charles Dickens.   Nineteenth Century Nov 03.

19

Kitton, Frederic G. (ed). Autograph edn 1903-8 with ints
George Gissing, George Saintsbury, Edward Dowden ao.
Uncompleted.

McCarthy, Justin. Portraits of the Sixties. 1903. Ch 2.

Baillie-Saunders 1905: see below under "Radical and Reformer".

Chesterton, G.K. Charles Dickens. 1906; rt Dickens: A
Critical Study, New York 1911, and Charles Dickens: The
Last of the Great Men, int Alexander Woollcott, New York
1942; trn Paris 1909; trn Moscow 1939; ed Teranishi Takeo,
Japanese edn 1932. "...the best essay on that author that
has ever been written" (T.S.Eliot, Tablet 20 Jun 36). See
also Fielding 1953 qu Desmond MacCarthy and R.C.Churchill
Contemporary Rev Jan 74.

Sibbald, W.A. Dickens Revisited. Westminster Rev Jan 07.

Chesterton, G.K. Prefaces EL edn 1907-11; rp Appreciations
and Criticisms of the Works of Charles Dickens 1911; new
edn 1933 rt Criticisms and Appreciations... See R.C.
Churchill, Chesterton on Dickens: The Legend and the
Reality DSN 1974.

Jackson, Holbrook. Great English Novelists. 1908.

Swinburne, Algernon Charles. Essay on Oliver Twist rp
Swinburne 1913 qv. Originally preface to Oliver c1908
in "the large American edition de luxe of Dickens's works
now in course of issue" (Watts-Dunton 1912).

Leffmann, H. About Dickens: Being a Few Essays on Themes
suggested by the Novels. Philadelphia 1908.

Munro, W.A. Dickens et Daudet: romanciers de l'enfant et
des humbles. Toulouse 1908. See further below under
"Dickens and Childhood".

Pugh 1908: see below under "Radical and Reformer".

More, Paul Elmer. The Praise of Dickens. Shelburne Essays,
New York 1908.

Barlow, G. The Genius of Charles Dickens. 1909.

Decade 1910-1919

Mair, G.H. English Literature: Modern. HUL 1911. Ch 9.

Bookman Feb 1912; rp 1914. Dickens Centenary No. Tributes by
  Shaw, Chesterton, Hardy ao.

Jerome, Jerome K. Charles Dickens. Pall Mall Gazette 7 Feb 12.

Escott, T.H.S. Dickens: His Work, Age and Influence. London
  Quarterly Rev 1912.

Nabokoff, Vladimir. Dickens: A Russian Appreciation.
  Dickensian 8 1912.

Powys, John Cowper. Visions and Revisions. 1912. See also
  Autobiography 1934 pp 12, 205, 308, 345.

Jugler 1912: see below under "Characters".

Meynell, Alice. Notes of a Reader of Dickens. Dublin Rev
  Apr 12; rp Hearts of Controversy 1917.

Lightwood, J.T. Charles Dickens and Music. 1912. See also
  below under "Characters".

Canning, A.S.G. Dickens Studied in Six Novels. 1912.

Shaw 1912: see below under "Hard Times".

Whipple 1912: p 3 above.

Calthrop, Dion Clayton and Sir Max Pemberton (ed). The Dickens
  Souvenir of 1912. 1912.

Watts-Dunton, Theodore. Swinburne as a Dickensian. In Editor's
  Preface, dated Dec 1912, to Swinburne 1913 below.

Swinburne, Algernon Charles. Charles Dickens. 1913; pst pbd
  ed Watts-Dunton; rp Swinburne 1902 and 1908 qqv. "A study of
  the foremost novelist of the Victorian Era by one of the
  foremost poets... should influence future criticism..." (Pref.)
  Has in fact been rather neglected but short extract incl Wall
  1970; not discussed in Fielding 1953.

Chesterton, G.K. The Victorian Age in Literature. HUL 1913;
  OPUS edn 1966. See particularly pp 32-7, 51-7.

Saintsbury, George. The English Novel. 1913.

James, Henry. A Small Boy and Others. 1913; rp Autobiography
1957. Reflects (pp122-3) on "the force of the Dickens
imprint...in the soft clay of our generation... He did too
much for us surely ever to leave us free - free of judgement,
free of reaction... he laid his hand on us in a way to
undermine as in no other case the power of detached
appraisement... criticism, round about him, is somehow
futile and tasteless..." James had refused Morley's
invitation to write the vol on Dickens for EML series.

Crotch 1913-20: see below under "Radical and Reformer".

Shaw, Bernard, John Galsworthy, A.C.Benson, Hall Caine ao.
Intns Waverley edn 1913-18.

Shaw, Bernard. On Dickens. Dickensian 10 1914.

Wells, H.G. Boon. 1915. Incl parody of Ford Madox Ford's
admiring attitude to James and Turgenev and patronizing
attitude to Dickens; qu Mizener 1972 qv; cf Pound 1918.

Leacock, Stephen. Fiction and Reality: A Study of the Art
of Charles Dickens. Essays and Literary Studies, 1916.
Proves amusingly, with help from some Dickens characters,
that the so-called "caricature" is an artistic means of
conveying "the real truth - the reality greater than life"
(p 188). Donald A.Cameron points out that Leacock "was
insisting that Dickens was one of the greatest of English
writers...years before Edmund Wilson established that
opinion as critical orthodoxy" (Stephen Leacock: The Boy
Behind the Arras, Journal of Commonwealth Literature Jul 67
p 8). See also Leacock 1933 qv.

Phelps, William Lyon. The Advance of the English Novel.
New York 1916.

Dibelius 1916: p 1 above.

Saintsbury, George. Dickens. CHEL 13 Cambridge 1916;
cheap edn 1932.

Pound 1918: see below under "Dickens and Henry James".

Eliot 1918: see below under "Comedy and Satire".

Burton, R.E. Dickens: How to Know Him. Indianapolis 1919.

Waugh, Arthur. Charles Dickens. Tradition and Change:
Studies in Contemporary Literature, 1919.

Decade 1910-1919, cont.

Anon (Virginia Woolf). Dickens by a Disciple. TLS 27 Mar 19.

Dark 1919: p 3 above.

Grossman 1919: see below under "Dickens in Russia".

The Nineteen-Twenties

Chesterton, G.K.   Charles Dickens Fifty Years After.   1920.

Zweig, Stefan.   Drei Meister: Balzac, Dickens, Dostojewski.
   Leipzig 1920.   See further below under "Dickens and Balzac"
   and "Dickens and Dostoevsky".

Lubbock, Percy.   The Craft of Fiction.   1921; qu Allott 1959,
   Wall 1970 etc.

Santayana, George.   Charles Dickens.   Dial New York Nov 21;
   rp Soliloquies in England 1922, Essays in Literary Criticism
   New York 1957; qu Quiller-Couch 1922, Cecil 1931, Churchill
   1937, Leavis 1948, Priestley 1960, Wall 1970.

Radlov 1922: see below under "Dickens in Russia".

Quiller-Couch, Sir Arthur.   Charles Dickens and Other
   Victorians.   Lectures at Cambridge 1922; pbd 1925 with addnl
   essay on Trollope.   A neglected classic of Dickensian
   criticism as well as a pioneer work on the relation of the
   Victorian novel to Victorian society.   See R.C.Churchill,
   Our Debt to Q, Use of English Spring 1974.

Matz 1922: see below under "Pickwick".

Inge, W.R., Dean.   The Victorian Age.   1922; qu Sampson 1941.

Murry, John Middleton.   "Dickens is a baffling figure.   There
   are moments when it seems that his chief purpose in writing
   was to put a spoke in the wheel of our literary aesthetics...
   That is why people tried to get rid of him by declaring that
   he was not an artist... it did not have the desired effect...
   perhaps because simple people asked why the books of a man
   who was not an artist should have this curious trick of
   immortality... So we are beginning to discover that Dickens
   was an artist, but, of course, only in parts..."
   (Pencillings, 1923, pp 40-1; cf Forster 1927 and see further
   below under "Literary Artist".)

Zweig, Stefan. Charles Dickens. Dial New York Jan 23.
  Cf Santayana 1921: p 23 above.

Whibley, Charles. A Study of Dickens. Dickensian 19 1923.

Moore, George. Conversations in Ebury Street. 1924. Cf
  Bennett 1889-1915: p 16 above under Hepburn. John Eglington
  in Irish Literary Portraits points out that Moore, like
  James and Howells in America, was comparatively indifferent
  to "the vitality and good spirits" of English novels like
  Dickens's, with their "affiliation to drama and poetry
  rather than to the arts of painting and drawing" (qu Van
  Wyck Brooks, New England: Indian Summer, 1940 p 276n.)

Gissing, George. The Immortal Dickens. 1925; pst pbd
  ed B.W.Matz; rp Gissing 1899 and 1901 qv. Int p vii
  expresses gratitude for work of Gissing, Chesterton and
  Quiller-Couch whose "three volumes now form, with Forster's
  life of Dickens, such a quartette of indispensable studies
  as the writings and life of no other novelist have ever
  inspired."

Priestley 1925: see below under "Characters".

Priestley, J.B. The Secret of Dickens. Saturday Rev 26 Sep 25
  Cf Crotch 1919 under "Radical and Reformer" below.

Delattre 1927: see below under "Dickens in France".

Belloc, Hilaire. Dickens Revisited. New Statesman 22 Jan 27.
  Cf Sibbald 1907: p 20 above.

Forster, E.M. Aspects of the Novel. Clark Lectures
  Cambridge 1927; pbd 1927; PB edn 1962. Forster's adverse
  criticism sometimes quoted without his qualifying remarks
  of (reluctant?) admiration. See eg Allott 1959 and TLS
  correspondence Churchill v Slater 1970 qqv.

Eliot, T.S. Wilkie Collins and Dickens. TLS 4 Aug 27; rp
  Selected Essays 1932; rv 2nd edn 1934. See further below
  under "Characters", "Drama and Melodrama" and "Dickens and
  Wilkie Collins."

Maurois, André (E.S.W.Herzog). Un essai sur Dickens. Paris
  1927; rp Etudes Anglaises Paris 1927; rv tr Dickens 1934.

Heuer, H. Romaneske Elemente im Realismus von Dickens.
  Marburg 1927.

Priestley, J.B.   The English Novel.   1927.

Straus 1928: p 4 above.

Wagenknecht 1929: p 4 above.   "I understood Dickens's
    greatness long before Edmund Wilson and his Pied Piper
    followers came along to explain it to me" (1966 rv edn;
    cf Leacock 1916: p 22 above.)

The Nineteen-Thirties

Ford, Ford Madox.   The English Novel.   1930.   Cf Wells 1915
    and Ford 1939 qqv.

Clark 1930: see below under "Radical and Reformer".

Cecil, Lord David.   Early Victorian Novelists.   Lectures at
    Oxford c1931-2; pbd 1934; FL edn 1964 with new pref.
    Both Quiller-Couch 1922-5 and Cecil 1931-4 unfortunately
    ignored by Edmund Wilson 1939-41 qv in his condemnation
    of Oxford and Cambridge for their neglect of Dickens.
    Leacock 1933 makes similar mistake.

Chesterton, G.K.   Charles Dickens.   The Great Victorians,
    ed H.J.and Hugh Massingham, 1932; rp A Handful of Authors
    1953.

Leavis, Q.D.   Fiction and the Reading Public.   1932.
    Concludes (p 158) that Dickens stands "primarily for a
    set of crude emotional exercises", only Copperfield and
    Great Expectations achieving the rank of literature.   Cf
    F.R.Leavis 1947-8 (which adds Hard Times), F.R.Leavis 1962
    (adds Dombey) and F.R.and Q.D.Leavis 1970 (adds Little
    Dorrit).   Cf Canning 1912: p 21 above.

Chancellor, E.Beresford.   Dickens and his Times.   1932.
    See also under "Dickens's London" below.

Sitwell, Osbert.   Dickens.   1932.

Leacock 1933: p 4 above.

Dent 1933: p 4 above.

Wickhardt, W.   Die Forman der Perspektive in Dickens
    Romanen.   Berlin 1933.

Kingsmill 1934: p 4 above.

O'Faolain, Sean. Dickens and Thackeray. The English Novelists
ed Derek Verschoyle, 1936. See further below under "Dickens
and Thackeray".

Lemonnier, Léon. L'actualité de Dickens. Mercure de France
15 Nov 36.

Shaw, Bernard. Fwd Great Expectations. Edinburgh 1937; rp
Novel Lib edn 1947. Discusses Dickens in general as well as
Expectations in particular.

Jackson, T.A. Charles Dickens: The Progress of a Radical.
1937. A Marxist view qu Orwell 1939, House 1941, Hardy 1970.

Waugh, Arthur, Thomas Hatton ao. Nonesuch Dickensiana. 1937.
Prospectus for Nonesuch edn 1937-8.

Churchill, R.C. The Diversity of Dickens. Paper read to the
Doughty Society, Downing College Cambridge, Nov 37. Nucleus
of Churchill 1942 qv.

Dobrée, Bonamy and Edith Batho. The Victorians and After:
1830-1914. Introduction to English Literature series 1938.

Lemonnier, Léon. Génie de Dickens. French Rev 11 1938.

Sitwell, Osbert. Dickens and the Modern Novel. Trio, 1938.
Cf Leavis 1948 below.

Powys, John Cowper. The Pleasures of Literature. 1938.

Ford, Ford Madox. The March of Literature. 1939. Ford's
view of Dickens qu Mizener 1972 qv.

Orwell, George (Eric Blair). Charles Dickens. Dated 1939; pbd
Inside the Whale and Other Essays 1940; rp Critical Essays
London 1946; Dickens, Dali and Others New York 1946; and
The Decline of the English Murder and Other Essays PB 1968.

Christie, O.F. Dickens and his Age. 1939. Cf Jackson 1937
and House 1941 and see further below under "Dickens's
England", "Dickens's London" and "Radical and Reformer".

Wilson, Edmund. Dickens: The Two Scrooges. Addressed "to the
  Students of English 354, University of Chicago, Summer 1939";
  pbd with Wilson 1940 qv in The Wound and the Bow: Seven Studies
  in Literature, Cambridge Mass 1941, London 1942; rv 1952; UP
  edn 1961. "It is the purpose of this essay to show that we
  may find in Dickens's work today a complexity and a depth to
  which even Gissing and Shaw have hardly...done justice - an
  intellectual and artistic interest which makes Dickens loom
  very large in the whole perspective of the literature of the
  West" (p 3 UP edn). "The first critic to do justice to the
  uneasy Dickens, to trace conflict behind a brilliant
  restlessness of creation" (G.W.Stonier, New Statesman 18 Apr
  42); "...no need to feel anything but grateful for it" (F.R.
  Leavis, Scrutiny 11 p 72); "crudely journalistic...wild
  travesties of Dickens's novels and character" (Q.D.Leavis 1970
  qv p 96).

The Nineteen-Forties

Evans, Ifor. A Short History of English Literature.   1940; rv
  1963. Ch 11: The English Novel from Dickens to the Present
  Day.

Orwell 1940: see Orwell 1939 p 26 above.

Maly-Schatter, F. The Puritan Element in Victorian Fiction:
  with especial reference to George Eliot, Dickens and
  Thackeray. Zürich 1940. Cf Taine 1856 and see further below
  under "Dickens and Religion" and "Sex in Dickens".

Wilson 1940: see below under "Edwin Drood".

House, Humphry. The Dickens World. Oxford 1941; rv 1942; OP edn
  1960. "An important assessment" (Fielding 1953); "laid the
  foundations of modern Dickens scholarship" (Wall 1970); but
  condemned by Q.D.Leavis 1970 qv p 38 as ignoring "the surely
  essential and obvious fact that Dickens was a creative
  artist". This itself ignores facts that House deliberately
  treated Dickens "as if he were a journalist more than a
  creative artist" (p 215 OP edn; qu Churchill, Dickens as
  Journalist, review of House Scrutiny 10 p 304) and Mrs
  Leavis's own disparaging opinion of Dickens's artistry in
  Leavis 1932 qu above p 25.

Silman 1941: see below under "Dickens in Russia".

Sampson, George. The Concise CHEL. 1941; 2nd edn with
R.C.Churchill 1961; 3rd edn rv Churchill 1970.

Wilson 1941: see Wilson 1939 p 27 above.

Pritchett, V.S. In My Good Books. 1942.

Churchill, R.C. Dickens, Drama and Tradition. Scrutiny 10
1942; rp Bentley 1948 p 7 above. Revision and expansion
of Churchill 1937 qv.

Stoll 1942: see below under "Characters".

Stevenson, Lionel. Dickens's Dark Novels. Sewanee Rev 51
1943.

Oehlbaum, I. Das pathologische Element bei Dickens. Siebnen
1944.

Rantavaara, I. Dickens in the Light of English Criticism.
Helsinki 1944. Cf Lewes 1872, Peyrouton 1962, Slater 1970,
Tomlin 1970 qqv.

Alain (E.chartier). En lisant Dickens. Paris 1945.

Laird, John. Philosophy in the Works of Dickens.
Philosophical Incursions into English Literature,
Cambridge 1946.

Warner, Rex. On Reading Dickens. The Cult of Power, 1946.
Cf Alain 1945 and Angus Wilson 1960 qqv.

Pritchett, V.S. The Living Novel. 1946.

Lemonnier 1946: p 4 above.

Bowen, Elizabeth. English Novelists. 1946.

Lamm, M. Dickens och hans Romaner. Stockholm 1947.

Liddell, Robert. A Treatise on the Novel. 1947; qu Allen
1954, Allott 1959, Wall 1970 etc.

Leavis 1947: see below under "Hard Times".

Darwin, Bernard, Humphry House, Kathleen Tillotson, H.W.
Garrod, Osbert Sitwell, Dingle Foot, Lionel Trilling,
Margaret Lane, Leslie C.Staples ao. Intns New Oxford
Illustrated edn 1947-58.

Butt, John. Dickens at Work. Durham University Journal
   Jun 48. Nucleus of Butt and Tillotson 1957 qv.

Leavis, F.R. The Great Tradition: George Eliot, Henry James,
   Joseph Conrad. 1948; rv PB edn 1962. (Not to be confused
   with Granville Hicks, The Great Tradition, 1933). Incl appx
   on Hard Times rp Leavis 1947 qv and discussion of Dickens in
   ch 1 (pp 28-31 PB edn) where Dr Leavis gives his reasons for
   "not including Dickens in the line of great novelists". Cf
   Leavis 1970 qv for an almost exactly contrary opinion as to
   Dickens's relative status; and see further below under
   "Dickens and Henry James". Criticism of Leavis 1948 incl
   Churchill 1953, Allen 1954, Pritchett 1954 and Snow 1970 qqv.
   Pritchett justly observes that Leavis "left out half the
   English tradition and tried to rebuild the English novel by
   putting the roof of Henry James on first" (New Statesman 7 Dec
   54). Cf the "most ingenious architect" at the Grand Academy
   of Lagado (Gulliver pt 3 ch 5) and further below under
   "Dickens and Thackeray".

Cruikshank 1949: see below under "Radical and Reformer".

Pearson 1949: p 4 above.

Cooke, J.D. and Lionel Stevenson. English Literature of the
   Victorian Period. New York 1949.

Grisewood, Harman (fwd). Ideas and Beliefs of the Victorians:
   An Historic Revaluation of the Victorian Age. 1949.
   Originally broadcasts on BBC Third Programme by Humphry House ao

Petersen, E.L. Searcher after Truth. If by your Art, ed
   Petersen, Pittsburgh 1949.

The Nineteen-Fifties

Churchill, R.C. Disagreements: A Polemic on Culture in the
   English Democracy. 1950. Written 1947-8. Ch 3 pp 111-13
   discusses relation between Shakespeare and Dickens, "the most
   Shakespearean writer among the Victorians", and importance of
   cultural link between them. See further below under
   "Sentiment and Sentimentality".

Lindsay 1950: p 5 above.

Vines, Sherard.   A Hundred Years of English Literature.   1950.

Wilson, Angus.   Dickens and the Divided Conscience.   Month
  May 50.

Yamamoto 1950: see below under "Style and Language".

Symons 1951: p 5 above.

Churchill, R.C.   English Literature of the Nineteenth Century.
  1951.   Ch 5: The Drama and Dickens.   See further below under
  "Drama and Melodrama" and "Stage and Platform".

Kettle, Arnold.   An Introduction to the English Novel.   2 vols
  1951-3.

Nisbet 1952: see below under "Dickens and Ellen Ternan".

Praz, Mario.   La Crisi dell'Eroe nel Romanze Vittoriano.
  Florence 1952; tr 1956 The Hero in Eclipse in Victorian
  Fiction. See pt 2.

Monod, Sylvere.   Dickens romancier.   Paris 1943; rv tr Dickens
  the Novelist 1969.   Not to be confused with Leavis, Dickens
  the Novelist 1970 qv.

Fielding 1953: p 1 above.

Van Ghent, Dorothy.   The English Novel: Form and Function.
  New York 1953.

Churchill, R.C.   The Relations between Literary History and
  Literary Criticism.   1953.   Pref 1st edn (omitted 2nd edn)
  English Literature of the Eighteenth Century.   Reply to
  critics of Churchill 1951 qv and discussion of treatment
  of Dickens in Leavis 1948 qv.   "...what is Dickens doing
  in an appendix when the theme of the book is the great
  tradition in the English novel?" (p xviii).

Allen, Walter.   The English Novel: A Short Critical History.
  1954; PB edn 1958.   Ch 4: The Early Victorians.

Tillotson, Kathleen.   Novels of the Eighteen-Forties.
  Oxford 1954.   Incl Dombey.

Maugham, W.Somerset.   Ten Novels and Their Authors.   1954;
  PB edn 1969.

The Nineteen-Fifties, cont.

Boege, F. Recent Criticism of Dickens. NCF 8 1954. Cf Gross
1962 below.

Izzo, C. Autobiografismo di Dickens. Venice 1954.

House, Humphry. All in Due Time: Collected Essays. 1955.
Pst pbd ed Madeline House. Incl 5 essays and broadcasts on
Dickens and his times.

Ford, George H. Dickens and his Readers: Aspects of Novel-
Criticism since 1836. Princeton 1955; New York 1965. See
further below under "Reading Public".

Parrot, T.M. and R.B.Martin. A Companion to Victorian
Literature. 1955.

Thalmann, L. Dickens in seinen Beziehungen zum Ausland.
Zürich 1956.

Butt, John and Kathleen Tillotson. Dickens at Work. 1957.
The novelist's MSS, revisions etc. "...gave for the first
time a detailed analysis of how Dickens combined the
exigencies of serial publication with the disciplines of
art" (Wall 1970). Pref describes Dickens studies as having
"hardly passed beyond the early nineteenth-century phase of
Shakespeare studies; while the study of his text seems
arrested in the early eighteenth century". Cf Tillotson
1966 qv and further below under "Serial Novelist".

Fielding 1957: see below under "Hard Times".

Zabel, M.D. Craft and Character in Modern Fiction. 1957.
Begins with Dickens (pp 3-69). Cf Waugh 1919: p 22 above.

Coveney 1957: see below under "Dickens and Childhood".

Fielding 1958: p 5 above.

Cox, C.B. In Defence of Dickens. Essays & Studies ns 11 1958.

Stone, Harry. Dickens and Interior Monologue. SP 55 1958.
Cf Churchill 1937-42 qv and further below under "Style and
Language".

Monod, Sylvère. Charles Dickens. Paris 1958.

Miller, J.Hillis. Charles Dickens: The World of his Novels.
Cambridge Mass 1958.

Ford, Boris (ed). From Dickens to Hardy. PGEL vol 6 1958;
rv 1960, 1963, 1964, 1966 etc. Incl G.D.Klingopulos,
Notes on the Victorian Scene and The Literary Scene; and
R.C.Churchill, Charles Dickens and Three Autobiographical
Novelists, latter incl some comparisons with Dickens.
See further below under "Dickens and Henry Mayhew",
"Dickens and Samuel Butler" and "Dickens and Gissing".

Stang, Richard. The Theory of the Novel in England: 1850-70.
1959. Concludes that while "James's position as the major
theorist of the novel remains unique...many of his statements
were anticipated by earlier critics and novelists". Ref
R.H.Hutton (Spectator), G.H.Lewes (Westminster Rev), W.C.
Roscoe (National Rev) etc in reviews of Dickens, George
Eliot and others. "Mr Stang has done a real service in
bringing to light an almost unknown aspect of mid-Victorian
literature... Even Thackeray and Trollope, he shows, were
not consistent in their 'gentlemanly' attitude to the
writing of novels, while novelists as various as Bulwer-
Lytton, Dickens, Charlotte Brontë and George Eliot are
revealed as having the sort of care for their art more
usually associated with Flaubert or James" (R.C.Churchill,
Spectator 18 Dec 59). See further below under "The
Literary Artist".

Engel, Monroe. The Maturity of Dickens. Cambridge Mass 1959.
Insists that Dickens "can and should be read with pleasure
and no restriction of intelligence by post-Jamesian adults".
Cf Stang 1959 above but see review by Churchill Spectator
Nov 13 59 for limitations of Engel's Jamesian approach.

Quirk 1959: see below under "Style and Language".

Raleigh, J.H. Dickens and the Sense of Time. NCF 13 1959.

Horsman, E.A. Dickens and the Structure of the Novel.
Dunedin 1959.

Miyazaki, K. Dickens's Novels. Tokyo 1959.

Smith, S.M. Anti-Mechanism and the Comic in Dickens.
Renaissance & Modern Studies 3 1959. See further below
under "Dickens and the Railway Age".

Wilson, A.H. The Great Theme in Dickens. Susquehanna
University Studies 6 1959.

The Nineteen-Sixties

Sükösd, M.   Charles Dickens.   Budapest 1960.

Dupee, F.W.   The Other Dickens.   Partisan Rev 27 1960.

Rees, Sir Richard.   Dickens: or The Intelligence of the
Heart.   For Love or Money, 1960.   Cf Orwell 1939 qv.

Wilson, Angus.   Charles Dickens: A Haunting.   CQ 2 1960; rp
Dyson 1968: p 7 above.

Priestley, J.B.   Literature and Western Man.   1960; pt 4
ch 17 (pp 235-41 PB edn 1969).

Seehase, G.   Dickens: zu einer Besonderheit seines Realismus.
Halle 1961.

Hardy, Barbara.   The Change of Heart in Dickens's Novels.
Victorian Studies 5 1961.

Butt, John.   Editing a Nineteenth-Century Novelist: Proposals
for an Edition of Dickens.   English Studies Today 2nd series
Berne 1961.   See Tillotson and Butt 1966 below.

Cockshut, A.O.J.   The Imagination of Charles Dickens.   1961.

Leavis 1962: see below under "Dombey".

Collins 1962: see below under "Dickens and Crime".

Beaumont, G.   Pour l'amour de Dickens.   Nouvelles Littéraires
15 Feb 62.

Reid, J.C.   The Hidden World of Charles Dickens.   Auckland 1962.

Gross, John.   Dickens: Some Recent Approaches.   In Gross 1962:
p 7 above.

Pearson, Gabriel.   Dickens: The Present Position.   Ibid.

Fielding, K.J.   Dickens and the Critics.   Dickensian 58 1962.

Brown, Ivor.   Dickens in his Time.   1963.

Davis, Earle.   The Flint and the Flame: The Artistry of
Charles Dickens.   Columbia Mo 1963; London 1966.

Collins 1963: see below under "Dickens and Education".

The Nineteen-Sixties, cont.

Marcus, Steven. Dickens: From Pickwick to Dombey. New York 1964.

Bodelsen 1964: see below under "Symbolism".

Cockshut, A.O.J. Dickens Criticism. Critical Survey 4 1964.

Garis, Robert. Dickens Criticism. Victorian Studies 7 1964.

Wagenknecht 1965: p 5 above.

Stoehr, Taylor. Dickens: The Dreamer's Stance. 1965.

Hill, A.G. The Real World of Dickens. CQ 7 1965.

Wall, Stephen. Dickens's Plot of Fortune. REL 6 1965.

Garis, Robert. The Dickens Theatre: A Reassessment of the Novels. Oxford 1965. Questions as "seriously misleading" the "misdirected piety" of Edmund Wilson and others. See further below under "Drama and Melodrama" and "Style and Language".

Graham, Kenneth. English Criticism of the Novel: 1865-1900. Oxford 1965.

Lane, Margaret. Purely for Pleasure. 1966. Incl three essays on Dickens. By a former President of the Dickens Fellowship.

Axton 1966: see below under "Drama and Melodrama".

Tillotson, Kathleen and John Butt (ed). The Clarendon edn. Oxford from 1966. "In this edition a critical text is established, a text free from the numerous corruptions that disfigure modern reprints, with an apparatus of variants that will exhibit Dickens's progressive revision" (pref). See further below under "Oliver Twist", "Dombey" and "Edwin Drood".

Summers, Montague. Dickens and the Decadent. Dickensian 63 1967.

Dabney, Ross H. Love and Property in the Novels of Dickens. Berkeley 1967.

Jarmuth, S.L. Dickens's Use of Women in his Novels. New York 1967. See further below under "Sex in Dickens".

Greene, Graham. Collected Essays. 1969. See below under "Oliver Twist".

Smith, Grahame.   Dickens, Money and Society.   1969.

Blount, Trevor.   Dickens: The Early Novels.   BCB 1969.

Pritchett, V.S.   George Meredith and English Comedy.
  Clark Lectures Cambridge 1969; pbd 1970; pp 17-20.

Fluchère, Henri, Sylvère Monod ao.   Dickens Centenary no
  Europe Dec 69.   Paris.   Incl items on Dickens in French
  films and TV and reports on Dickens in Italy, Hungary and
  Bulgaria.   See further below under 1970, under "Dickens in
  France", "Dickens in Italy", "Dickens in Germany" and
  "Dickens in Russia", studies of Dickens pbd Helsinki,
  Stockholm, Zürich, Copenhagen, Budapest, Tokyo etc above
  and below, and specialist works such as Delattre 1927,
  Gummer 1940 qqv.   Briefer studies incl Ian F.Finlay,
  Dickens's Influence on Dutch Literature, Dickensian 53
  1957, and L.Verkoren, Dickens in Holland, ibid 55 1959.

Period 1970-1974

Dyson, A.E.   The Inimitable Dickens: A Reading of the Novels.
  1970.

Wilson, Angus.   The World of Charles Dickens.   1970.   "The
  finest study of Dickens by a novelist since Gissing's"
  (TLS 4 Jun 70).

Tomlin, E.W.F.   Dickens's Reputation: A Reassessment.   In
  Tomlin 1970: p 8 above.

Slater 1970: p 8 above.

Anon.   Dickens 1812-1870.   TLS 4 Jun 70.   Compares 1912 and
  1970 as Dickens centenaries.   A fairer view of 1912 is
  given above p 21.

Snow, C.P.   The Case of Leavis and the Serious Case.   TLS
  9 Jul 70; rp Public Affairs 1971.   Claims Dickens "never
  justly appreciated until our own time" (pp 83-4 1971 rp).
  Rejoinder by R.C.Churchill TLS 23 Jul 70; defence of Snow
  by Michael Slater TLS 7 Aug; reply by Churchill TLS 21 Aug.
  See further Churchill 1973-4 below and this present book
  passim.

Brown, Ivor. Dickens and his World. 1970.

Hardy, Barbara. Dickens: The Later Novels. BCB 1970.

Lucas, John. The Melancholy Man: A Study of Dickens's
Novels. 1970.

Leavis, R.F.and Q.D. Dickens the Novelist. 1970. Incl
rv Leavis 1947 and 1962 qqv. Complete volte-face from
critical position taken up in Leavis 1932 and 1948.

Williams, Raymond. The English Novel. 1970.

Sucksmith, Harvey Peter. The Narrative Art of Charles
Dickens: The Rhetoric of Sympathy and Irony in his Novels.
Oxford 1970.

Wing, George. Dickens. Writers and Critics series 1970.

Daleski, H.M. Dickens and the Art of Analogy. 1970.

Hardy, Barbara. The Moral Art of Dickens. 1970.

Churchill, R.C. Second Thoughts About Dickens. Humanist
Jan 71. Review of Leavis 1970 and Lucas 1970.

Gomme, A.H. Dickens. Literature in Perspective series 1971.

Welsh, Alexander. The City of Dickens: Studies in History,
Theme and Allegory. Oxford 1971.

Keating, P.J. The Working Classes in Victorian Fiction.
1971. From Dickens to Morrison.

Kincaid, James R. Dickens and the Rhetoric of Laughter. 1972.

Mizener, Arthur. The Saddest Story: A Biography of Ford
Madox Ford. 1972. Incl pp on Ford's disparagement of
Dickens and his much exaggerated version of the contempt
for Dickens expressed by .some members of the Pre-
Raphaelite circle of artists and poets he had known in his
youth. Contrast the lifelong Dickensian enthusiasm of
Swinburne, intimate friend of Rossetti and the other
Pre-Raphaelites, and the opinion of Shaw 1937 qv that
"the Pre-Raphaelites and the aesthetes...were all
Dickens worshippers..." (qu Wall 1970 p 289.)

Gold 1974: see below p 203.

Carey, John. The Violent Effigy: A Study of Dickens's Imagination. 1974. Cf Cockshut 1961.

Churchill, R.C. Dickens in Perspective: The Continuity of Dickensian Criticism. Fwd Ifor Evans. Written 1973-4. Not yet published.

CRITICISM OF PARTICULAR WORKS

Sketches by Boz

Hogarth, George (Dickens's future father-in-law). Morning
Chronicle 11 Feb 1836. "...evidently the work of a person
of various and extraordinary intellectual gifts". Compares
A Christmas Dinner with Washington Irving and praises the
"terrible power" of A Visit to Newgate. Cf House 1969 below.

Anon. Court Journal 20 Feb 1836. "Boz is a kind of Boswell
to society - and of the middle ranks especially". Cf
Blackwood's Mag Jun 1855 qu below under "Radical and Reformer"

Anon. Atlas 21 Feb 1836. "...sometimes falls into that
manner of caricature...which...appears to us to be sheer
vulgarity..."

Anon. Morning Post 12 Mar 1836. "...a close and accurate
observer of events. The graphic descriptions...invest all he
describes with amazing reality."

Poe, Edgar Allan. Southern Literary Messenger Richmond Va
Jun 1836. Highly favourable review; cf Poe on Old Curiosity
Shop and Barnaby Rudge qqv below.

Fonblanque, Albany. 1836. "I remember still with what hearty
praise the book was first named to me by my dear friend
Albany Fonblanque, as keen and clear a judge as ever lived
either of books or men" (Forster 1872 bk 1 ch 5). Fonblanque
(1793-1872) was ed Examiner 1830-47 and was known for his
satirical wit. Dickens called him "another Swift". He was
caricatured as "Mr Fonnoir" in Rosina Bulwer's novel
Cheveley (1839).

Anon. New Moral World 18 Jul 1840. "Who can more ably develop
the vital truth, that circumstances make, or mar, the man,
than the inimitable Dickens? The society which he so clearly
depicts cries aloud for change" (qu House 1969 p 100n; see
further below under "Radical and Reformer").

Forster 1872: p 2 above. Forster goes on (after qu Fonblanque
1836 above) to give his own opinion of the Sketches which he
felt Dickens himself "decidedly underrated" in later life.
"He gave, in subsequent writings, so much more perfect form
and fullness to everything it contained, that he did not care
to credit himself with the marvel of having yet so early
anticipated so much" (bk 1 ch 5; cf Swinburne 1902 and
Saintsbury 1916 below.)

Sketches by Boz, cont.

Benignus, S. Studien über die Anfänge von Dickens.
Esslingen 1895. See further below under "Dickens in
Germany".

Swinburne 1902: p 19 above. "No one could have foreseen what
all may now foresee in the Sketches...not only a quick and
keen-eyed observer...but a great creative genius" (p 2 1913
edn.)

Saintsbury 1916: p 22 above. "The best of them are real
studies for the finished pictures of the novels... There are
not many things more curious in critical enquiry...than the
way in which Our Parish shows the future novelist" (p 309
1932 edn; cf House 1941 below.)

Quiller-Couch 1922: p 23 above; pp 2-3.

Dent 1933: p 4 above; pp 115-9 1935 edn.

Darton, F.J.Harvey. Dickens: Positively the First Appearance:
A Centenary Review. 1933. Celebrates centenary of Dickens's
first story A Dinner at Poplar Walk (Monthly Mag Dec 1833).
Cf Forster 1872 bk 1 ch 4 para 3. Darton incl bibliog of
Sketches which were favourably reviewed (besides those
mentioned p 38 above) by William Jerdan in The Literary
Gazette and by The Sun, Sunday Times, Sunday Herald,
The Satirist and The Athenaeum. See Walter Dexter,
Contemporary Opinion on Dickens's Earliest Work and The
Reception of Dickens's First Book, Dickensian 31-2 1935-6.

Dexter, Walter. The Genesis of Sketches by Boz. Dickensian 30
1934.

House 1941: p 27 above. Compares Sketches with Dombey, Bleak
House, Our Mutual Friend and Drood as instances of Dickens's
hatred of "any charity that had a stigma" (pp 78-9).

Priestley, J.B.(ed). Scenes of London Life: from Sketches by
Boz. 1947. See further below under "Dickens's London".

Hill, T.W. Notes on Sketches by Boz. Dickensian 46-8 1950-2.
Detail of contemporary ref manners and customs 1830s.

Carlton, W.J. The Third Man at Newgate. RES ns 8 1957.

Butt and Tillotson 1957: p 31 above; ch 2.

Cox, C.B. Comic Viewpoints in Sketches by Boz. English 12
1959.

Sketches by Boz, cont.

Browning, R. In Gross 1962: p 7 above.

House 1969: p 6 above. Notes (p 268) that some English (but not
  American) reviewers in the 1830s claimed to have found evidence
  for influence on both Sketches and Pickwick of Washington
  Irving's Sketch-Book of Geoffrey Crayon (1820) which Dickens
  certainly knew well. Cf House 1941 (p 24) qu Quarterly Rev
  Oct 1837 and further below under "Dickens and Christmas" and
  "Dickens and the Stage-Coach".

Miller 1970: see below under "Oliver Twist".

Grillo, Virgil. Charles Dickens's Sketches by Boz: The End
  in the Beginning. Boulder Colo 1974. Cf Forster 1872 and
  Saintsbury 1916 qu above.

Sunday Under Three Heads

This pamphlet pbd 1836 under pseudonym Timothy Sparks was
  directed against Sir Andrew Agnew's Sabbath Observance Bill.
  See further below under "Dickens and Religion" and "Dickens
  and Sport". It was the first of Dickens's works to be
  illustrated by Hablot K. Browne who in the same year succeeded
  Seymour and Buss as illustrator of Pickwick: Phiz to Dickens'
  Boz. See "Dickens and his Illustrators" below.

House 1941: p 27 above. Ch 5 pp 123-5 is best modern account.
  For contemporary reviews see Dickensian 32 1936. Following
  critics have made other observations:

Dent 1933: p 4 above. "...a most interesting piece of work...
  reveals...a Dickens in dead earnest, hard, bitter, cynical,
  without a jest on his lips, a fierce defender of the scanty
  rights of the poor" (p 135 1935 edn; see further below under
  "Radical and Reformer").

Johnson, Edgar. Dickens and the Bluenose Legislator. American
  Scholar 17 1948.

Churchill 1958: p 32 above under Ford. Compares pamphlet with
  Little Dorrit ch 3. "...proves how early Dickens attained
  some of his leading ideas" (pp 123-4; cf Churchill 1937-42
  and House 1941 p 123).

The Pickwick Papers

For full details of the extensive Pickwickiana 1836-1967, incl
Bibliographies, Extra Illustrations, Imitations and Sequels,
Dramatizations etc, see NCBEL 1969 (p 1 above under Darton)
or Collins 1970 cols 787-90. Most of these have only a
marginal critical interest.

Macaulay 1836. His adverse criticism of Hard Times is always
remembered, but it is sometimes forgotten that in 1836 he
praised Pickwick judiciously, observing that with the creation
of Sam Weller "something new and great had come into English
literature" (qu Leacock 1933 p 33).

Lewes 1837. Similarly, the 1872 article by George Henry Lewes
(p 15 above) is always remembered for its severe criticism of
Dickens as a literary artist, but it is sometimes forgotten
that Lewes's praise of Pickwick (National Mag Dec 37) led to
a meeting between the two men and that the critic was
henceforth "my good friend Mr Lewes", as Dickens describes
him in the preface to Bleak House.

Forster, John. Examiner 2 Jul 1837. Ref Mr Pickwick in the
Fleet prison: "the author has achieved his masterpiece...
Every point tells..."

Carlyle. Letter to John Sterling 28 Jul 1837. "Thinner wash,
with perceptible vestige of a flavour in it here and there,
was never offered to the human palate".

Southern Literary Messenger Richmond Va Sep 1837. Review by
Poe (according to NCBEL 1969) or by Tucker (House 1969 p 142
n5) praising inset tales for their "considerable power" (cf
Wilson 1939 below) but accusing main body of book for its
"absurd caricature" and "impossible incidents happening to
beings that have no existence in nature".

Reynolds, G.W.M. Pickwick Abroad. Monthly Mag Dec37-Jun38;
rp book form 1839, 1864, 1905 with pref defending imitation.
See W.Miller, G.W.M.Reynolds and Dickens, Dickensian 13 1917.
This was most famous of many Pickwick imitations which incl
Pickwick in America (1838-9), Pickwick in India (Lighthouse
mag Madras 1839-40) and in Germany Stolle's Deutsche
Pickwickier and Hesslein's Berliner Pickwickier. See W.
Miller, Imitations of Pickwick, Dickensian 32 1936; Ellis
Gummer, Dickens's Works in Germany (1940); Louis James,
Fiction for the Working Man 1830-50 (1963; qu Wall 1970 pp
472-8). Leacock 1933 pp 36-7 cites first of Pickwick
imitations on the stage (written and performed before Dickens
had completed the original) and further information is given
in Malcolm Morley, Pickwick Makes his Stage Debut, Dickensian
42 1946 and in notes to House 1969.

Irving, Washington. Letter to Dickens 26 May 1841. "Old
Pickwick is the Quixote of commonplace life, and as with
the Don, we begin by laughing at him and end by loving him"
(qu House 1969 p 269n). Comparison with Cervantes must
have gratified Dickens from such a source: Irving had been
diplomatic attaché in Madrid and was shortly to become
Minister to Spain (1842-5). See further below under
"Dickens and Cervantes".

Forster, John. Did not altogether maintain his initial
enthusiasm (p 41 above). Though continuing to praise the
prison scenes, where "the comedy gradually deepens into
tragedy" (Forster 1872 bk 2 ch 1; cf Blount 1968 p 15),
on the whole he did not think Pickwick "comparable to the
later books".

Flaubert, Gustave. Letter to George Sand 12 Jul 1872. "I've
just read Pickwick by Dickens... Some bits are magnificent;
but what a defective structure! All English writers are
like that. Walter Scott apart, they lack composition.
This is intolerable for us Latins" (qu Allott 1959 p 232).

Fitzgerald, Percy. The History of Pickwick. 1891. Incl
bibliog. Fitzgerald also wrote Pickwickian Manners and
Customs (1897) and Pickwickian Studies (1899).

Harrison 1894-5: p 17 above. "The glory of Charles Dickens
will always be in his Pickwick, his first, his best, his
inimitable triumph" (p 143.)

Gissing 1899: p 18 above. "The same kind of power went to
the shaping of Mr Pickwick's man-servant as to the bodying
forth of Mercutio - power which...we indicate by the one
word genius" (p 48 1925 edn). See further below under
"Comedy and Satire" and "Dickens and Shakespeare".

Chesterton 1906: p 20 above. "It is, first and foremost, a
supernatural story... Pickwick...is the fairy prince...
the abstract wanderer and wonderer, the Ulysses of comedy
..." (pp 90-1).

Swinburne 1908: p 20 above; p 4 1913 edn.

More 1908: p 20 above.

Barlow 1909: p 20 above. Cf Harrison 1894.

The Pickwick Papers, cont.

Mair 1911: p 21 above. "In the Preface to Pickwick he
answers those who criticized the novel on the ground that
Pickwick begins by being purely ludicrous and develops into
a serious and sympathetic individuality, by pointing to the
analogous process which commonly takes place in actual
human relationships..." (p 229; Wall 1970 qu the Dickens
preface Mair refers to: pp 82-3 is para Mair had in mind;
see further below under "Characters".)

Dibelius, Wilhelm. Zu den Pickwick Papers. Anglia 35 1912.

Saintsbury 1916: p 22 above. "There is no book like Pickwick
anywhere; it is almost...worth while to read the wretched
imitations of it in order to enjoy the zest with which one
comes back to the real, though fantastically real, thing"
(p 311 1932 edn; cf p 319n and see further above p 41
under "Reynolds").

Matz, B.W. The Inns and Taverns of Pickwick. 1922. By ed
Dickensian. See further below, for books in this field,
under "Dickens's England" and "Dickens's London".

Leacock 1933: p 4 above. "...seems to have groped his way
into the book as Mark Twain did into Huckleberry Finn, the
prospect opening before him as he moved on" (p 32; see
further below under "Dickens and Mark Twain").

Dent 1933: p 4 above. Points out (p 151 1935 edn) significance
of "deeper note" in The Stroller's Tale in ch 3 and compares
(pp 153-4) Fleet Prison scenes with prison scenes in
Copperfield and Little Dorrit. "Like Shakespeare, he began
with a comedy of manners, and like him, quickly found himself
absorbed by the humanity of which manners is but the cloak"
(p 157.)

Betjeman, John, with Alfred Noyes, Ralph Straus, James Agate,
Hugh Kingsmill ao. A Pickwick Portrait Gallery: From the
Pens of Divers Admirers... 1936. Celebrates centenary which
was also honoured by special nos of Dickensian 1936-7, by
A Handbook to Pickwick Papers (L.Clendening, New York 1936),
by A Centenary Bibliography (W.Miller and E.H.Strange 1936)
which rp early reviews, and by a number of Pickwick
Exhibitions in London, Melbourne and elsewhere.

Churchill 1937: see below under Pearson 1949.

Orwell 1939: p 26 above; pp 34-5, 37, 45-7 1946 edn.

The Pickwick Papers, cont.

Wilson 1939-41: p 27 above.   Points out importance (for his
argument) of the inset tales (pp 9-13 UP edn; cf Soutnern
Literary Messenger 1837 and Dent 1933 above and comment in
Wall 1970 p 319; see further Robert L.Patten, The Interpolate
Tales in The Pickwick Papers, DS 1 1965, and replies by H.M.
Levy and W.Ruff DS 3 1967.)

Hill, T.W.   Notes on the Pickwick Papers.   Dickensian 44-5 1948

Pearson 1949: p 4 above.   "Sam was the making of the book,
but most modern readers feel that ne comes near to unmaking
it.   No famous comic character in fiction is less funny
except Touchstone..." The TLS reviewer (9 Sep 49) comments:
"He who finds Sam a bore has surely...a most imperfect
sympathy with his creator".   Cf Churchill 1937-42: "One
monologue by Mrs Gamp is worth a whole chapter of Wellerisms"
(p 361).

Maclean, H.N.   Mr Pickwick and the Seven Deadly Sins.   NCF 8
1954.

Auden, W.H.   "After Cervantes, as a writer who combines
literary talent and a mythopoeic imagination, comes Dickens
and of his many mythical creations Mr Pickwick is one of the
most memorable... the real theme of Pickwick Papers...is the
Fall of Man..." (Dingley Dell and the Fleet.   The Dyer's Han
and Other Essays, 1962.   Cf Irving 1841 and Chesterton 1906
above.)

Killham, J.   In Gross 1962: p 7 above.

Axton, W.F.   Unity and Coherence in the Pickwick Papers.
Studies in English Literature 5 1965.

Marcus 1965: p 34 above.   "...the novel in which Dickens
achieved the very thing we tend to think is the exclusive
right of only the greatest, most mature, most fully
consummated artists: he achieved transcendence...a
representation of life which...extends our awareness of the
limits of our numanity" (p 17).

Colwell, M.   Organization in the Pickwick Papers.   DS 3 1967.

Hardy, Barbara.   The Triumph of Dingley Dell.   London Rev
no 2 1967.   Cf Auden 1962 above.

The Pickwick Papers, cont.

Leavis 1970: p 36 above. "...the callow Pickwick Papers..."
(p 280).

Vann, J.Don. Pickwick in the London Newspapers. Dickensian
Jan 1974.

The SC edn has Afterword by Steven Marcus; the PEL edn 1972
is ed Robert L.Patten.

Oliver Twist

Anon (T.H.Lister). Edinburgh Rev Oct 1838. "One of the
qualities we most admire in him is his comprehensive spirit
of humanity. The tendency of his writings is...to excite
our sympathy in behalf of the aggrieved and suffering in
all classes; and especially in those who are most removed
from observation...the orphan pauper - the parish apprentice
- the juvenile criminal... His humanity is plain, practical
and manly. It is quite untainted with sentimentality".

Victoria, Queen. Found Oliver "excessively interesting",
"liked it so much" and defended it against the opinion of
Lord Melbourne who thought it "low" (Diary 30 Dec 38, 3 Jan
39, 7 Apr 39; qu House 1969 p 26n and Collins 1971 p 44.)

Ikey Solomons Junior (W.M.Thackeray). Catherine. Fraser's
Mag May39-May40. Parody of "the Newgate novel" where
Thackeray writes that Dickens's power was "so amazing"
that the reader was led "to have for Bill Sikes a kind of
pity and admiration, and an absolute love for the society
of the Dodger". And this in turn led the public to want
"something more extravagant still, more sympathy for
thieves, and so Jack Sheppard makes his appearance."
Ainsworth's novel was coupled with Oliver by several other
critics, one critic linking them as "the gallows-school of
novelists". Dickens replied in pref 1841 edn. See further
below under "Dickens and Crime".

Anon (Richard Ford). Quarterly Rev Jun 1839. Praised
revelation of London life - "one half of mankind lives
without knowing how the other half dies" - but criticized
the satire on the poor-law and workhouse system as unfair
and "exaggerated". Review qu more fully in Collins 1971
pp 81-6.

Anon (John Forster). Examiner 25 Sep 1841. Cf Forster 1872
bk 2 ch 3.

Bagehot 1858: p 13 above. "Mr Sykes is the character most approaching to a coherent man...to be found in Mr Dickens's works...Miss Nancy is a still more delicate artistic effort. Criticism is the more bound to dwell on...these delineations because no artistic merit can make Oliver Twist a pleasing work" (pp 184-5 EL 1911).

Collins, Wilkie. "The one defect in that wonderful book is the helplessly bad construction of the story. The character of Nancy is the finest thing he ever did. He never afterwards saw all sides of a woman's character - saw all round her. That the same man who could create Nancy created the second Mrs Dombey is the most incomprehensible anomaly that I know of in literature" (note in copy of Forster 1872 reported Pall Mall Gazette 20 Jan 1890 and qu Wall 1970 p 222.)

Gissing 1899: p 18 above. Cf Gissing 1898 for view of Nancy and cf Bagehot and Collins above.

Chesterton 1907-11: p 20 above. Compares Oliver, Bleak House and Hard Times as similar expressions of Dickens's moral attitude to Victorian society. "He disliked a certain look on the face of a man when he looks down on another man..." After displeasing Sir Leicester Dedlock in Bleak House "he displeased Mr Rouncewell in Hard Times...by calling him Mr Bounderby... When Dickens found that after a hundred economic arguments...the fact remained that paupers in modern workhouses were much too afraid of the beadle...then he struck.. This is what makes the opening chapters of Oliver Twist so curious and so important" (pp 46-7 1933 edn; cf Churchill 1937-42 pp 371-5 and see further below under "Radical and Reformer".)

Swinburne 1908: p 20 above. "...a dramatic fiction or poem, such as all true creative work in the form of narrative must be... not merely a success, but a triumph... On the literary and sentimental side of his work Dickens was but a type of his generation and his class: on the comic and the pathetic, the tragic and the creative side, 'he was not of an age, but for all time'" (pp 3-5, 9 1913 edn.)

Saintsbury 1916: p 22 above. "...it is doubtful whether, in good judgments, it has ever been or ever will be put in the first class of Dickens's work" (p 316 1932 edn; cf Collins and Swinburne above.)

Oliver Twist, cont.

Santayana 1921: p 23 above. Ref Bumble and "the eye of the
law" in ch 51: "We must go back for anything like it to the
very greatest comic poets, to Shakespeare or to Aristophanes...
This is high comedy; the irresistible, absurd, intense dream
of the old fool, personifying the law in order to convince
and to punish it..." (pp 546-7; cf Churchill 1937-42 pp 366-7,
373-4 and see further below under "Comedy and Satire").

Leacock 1933: p 4 above; pp 42-8 qu below under "Radical and
Reformer".

Churchill 1937-42: p 26 above. "It was the particular genius
of Dickens that he could always put his finger on the social
evil which hurt the sufferer the most. He was always
'seeing people', thinking in terms of flesh and blood rather
than in ideas or institutions, and such a bent of mind, it
will be agreed, is essentially the novelist's. He saw the
Workhouse Board not as an institution but as so many
individuals anxious to assert their authority at someone
else's expense... He was aware of the fact that the petty
regulation...was not only the one that hurt the pauper most
keenly but the one the Board got the most pleasure out of
inflicting. The exaggeration here is simply the necessary
exaggeration of art, the necessary 'fine excess'" (p 373;
cf Chesterton 1907-11 above and see further below under
"Radical and Reformer").

House 1941: p 27 above. Dickens's attitude to New Poor Law
(pp 92-105). Cf House 1947 (p 28 above) where it is pointed
out that the deit of Oliver and his fellow-paupers was "a
telling caricature of the Commissioners' recommended
dietaries" (p xiii 1949 intn; see also House 1955: p 31 above)

Brogan, Colm. Oliver Twist Re-examined. Listener 26 Aug 1948.

Hill, T.W. Notes on Oliver Twist. Dickensian 46 1950.

Johnson 1950: see below under "Dickens and Religion".

Greene: p 34 above. The Young Dickens. The Lost Childhood
and Other Essays, 1951; rp Collected Essays 1969. Greene
emphasizes what he sees as the Manichean atmosphere of the
novel: "This world of Dickens is a world without God... In
this Manichean world we can believe in evil-doing, but
goodness wilts into philanthropy, kindness, and those
strange vague sicknesses into which Dickens's young women
so frequently fall and which seem in his eyes a kind of
badge of virtue..." (pp 55-7 1951 edn; see further below
under "Dickens and Religion" and "Dickens and Crime".)

Oliver Twist, cont.

Kettle 1951-3: p 30 above.

Auden 1953: see below under "Dickens and Mark Twain".

Pritchett, V.S. Books in General. 1953. Discusses
    significance of original illustrations: "Cruikshank...
    upsets all the weary pieties of realism which lie between us
    and a comprehension of Dickens" (qu Churchill 1942 from New
    Statesman c1941 comparing Pritchett's observation on
    Cruikshank and Oliver with Phiz and Chuzzlewit: p 361n.
    See further below under "Dickens and his Illustrators".)

Lucas, A. Oliver Twist and the Newgate Novel. Dalhousie Rev
    34 1954. Cf Thackeray 1839-40 qu p 45 above.

Bishop, J. The Hero-Villain of Oliver Twist. Victorian
    Newsletter no 15 1959. Cf Greene 1951 above.

Tillotson, Kathleen. Oliver Twist. Essays & Studies ns 12 19:
    Cf Tillotson 1966 below.

Bayley, John. Oliver Twist: Things as they Really Are in Gros:
    1962: p 7 above. "...what brings Sikes and Nancy to life is
    the gap between what they look like and what they are like:
    between their appearance as Dickens insists we shall have it
    and the speech and manner with which another convention
    requires him to endow them. They rise, as it were, between
    two stools; they achieve their real selves by being divided
    between two modes of artifice... The Sikes in grey cotton
    stockings is the same man who goes to murder like Macbeth...
    (pp 63-4; cf Bagehot 1858 and Collins 1872 above.)

Hollingsworth, K. The Newgate Novel 1830-47: Bulwer, Ainsworth
    Dickens and Thackeray. Detroit 1963. Cf Thackeray, Forster
    Greene, Bayley above and see further below under "Dickens an
    Crime".

Chaplin, Charles. My Autobiography. 1964. Incl childhood
    experience of Lambeth workhouse in 1890s comparable on some
    points to Oliver's 60 years before. Useful footnote to
    Churchill 1937 and House 1941 above.

Tillotson, Kathleen (ed). The Clarendon edn. Oxford 1966.
    See p 34 above. Best scholarly edn. Incl glossary of early
    Victorian thieves' cant.

Dabney 1967: p 34 above. Love and property in Oliver.

Miller, J.Hillis. The Fiction of Realism. Lecture at
    University of California 1970; rv Miller and Borowitz 1971:
    see below under "Dickens and his Illustrators".

Wall 1970: p 7 above. Qu Kettle, Greene, Marcus, Cockshut and
    Miller on Oliver Twist to prove diversity of modern approach
    to Dickens who "has become a mine with many levels" (p 321).

The PEL edn ed Peter Fairclough has intn by Angus Wilson.

Nicholas Nickleby

Anon (John Forster). Examiner 1 Apr 1838. Cf Forster 1872
    bk 2 ch 4 where he develops his view of "the secret and form
    of his art" in making "these creations so real" comparing
    Dickens in this respect with Jane Austen whose "art" was
    "carried to exquisite perfection on a more limited stage...
    I told him, on reading the first dialogue of Mrs Nickleby
    and Miss Knag, that he had been lately reading Miss Bates in
    Emma, but I found that he had not at this time made the
    acquaintance of that fine writer" (para 3; see further below
    under "Dickens and Jane Austen").

Smith, Sydney. Letter to Dickens 11 Jun 1839 saying his friends
    "have not the smallest objection to be put into a number, but
    on the contrary would be proud of the distinction; and Lady
    Charlotte, in particular, you may marry to Newman Noggs"
    (qu Forster 1872; cf Pearson 1949 who confirms that it was
    Nickleby which first made Dickens a favourite in high society
    (pp 73-4); also, we know, in university circles, where the
    future Cardinal Newman was known to his intimate friends as
    "Noggs").

Anon. Sun 4 Jul 1839. "...this admirable tale...nothing in
    Fielding better than this..." (qu House 1965 p 562n; see
    further below under "Dickens and Fielding".)

Wilkie 1839: p 10 above.

Anon. Fraser's Mag Apr 1840. Cf Thackeray 1842 below.

Guess. Scenes from the Life of Nickleby Married. 1840.
    One of several imitations and sequels. Cf Reynolds 1837:
    p 41 above.

Janin, Jules. Journal des Débats 31 Jan 1842. "Picture to
yourself a mass of childish inventions in which everything
that is horrible alternates with everything that is simple:
here pass, in a flood of tears, people so good that they are
absolutely silly: further on...are all sorts of robbers,
crooks, thieves and paupers, so repulsive that one cannot
conceive how any society containing them can last for twenty
four hours. It is the most sickening mixture you can imagin
...this last book of Dickens" (qu Leacock 1933 pp 182-3; see
Thackeray below.)

Thackeray 1842: defence of Dickens against Janin's criticisms.
See below under "Dickens in France". An inscribed copy of
A Christmas Carol in 1843 probably expresses Dickens's
gratitude for this "witheringly sarcastic answer" to the
French critic (House 1974 pp 399n, 608n; cf Leacock p 183
who takes a less flattering view of Thackeray's defence,
speaking of its "calm insular superiority" and "the form of
reproof...scarcely happy".)

Watson 1887: see below under "Dickens's England".

Gissing 1899: p 18 above.

Saintsbury 1916: p 22 above. "...Dickens, whose portrayal of
the weakness of the stage...makes one of the most delightful
features of the book...put beside the Crummleses...a stage-
acting and stage-speaking hero in Nicholas; a stage-heroine
in Kate; a stage-villain in Ralph...almost all these, moreov
being of a very inferior stage kind" (p 317 1932 edn; cf
Quiller-Couch 1922 p 47 and see further below under "Drama
and Melodrama" and "Stage and Platform").

Playfair, Nigel (director). When Crummles Played. 1927.
Revival at Lyric Theatre Hammersmith of George Lillo's
famous melodrama The London Merchant or The History of Georg
Barnwell (1731). "Mr Harvey Darton has preserved for us...
the essential Dickensian flavour of that production" (John
Hampden, intn Eighteenth-Century Plays, EL 1928 p xvi ref
F.J.H.Darton, Vincent Crummles: His Theatre and his Times,
1926). Cf Malcolm Morley, Where Crummles Played, Dickensian
58-9 1962-3.

Leacock 1933: p 4 above; pp 51-2, 182-3. See under Janin and
Thackeray above.

Churchill 1937-42: p 26 above; p 365. Cf Saintsbury 1916.

Hill, T.W. Notes on Nicholas Nickleby. Dickensian 45-6
1949-50.

Pearson 1949: p 4 above. Cf Sydney Smith 1839.

Clinton-Baddeley, V.C. Benevolent Teachers of Youth.
Cornhill Mag 1957 pp 361-82. On the Yorkshire schools,
originals of Dotheboys Hall. See further below under
"Dickens and Education".

Bergonzi, Bernard. In Gross 1962: p 7 above.

Blount 1968: p 35 above. "In my view it is one of his great
novels..." (pp 18-21, 36-8).

Slater, Michael (ed). Scholarly edn pbd Menston Yorks 1973.
"Dr Slater's detailed account of its composition and serial
publication immediately and decisively established itself
as the most comprehensive, sound and cogent introduction
to the novel" (TLS 22 Jun 73). See further below under
"Serial Novelist".

Master Humphrey's Clock

Thackeray. 1840. "The new Boz is dull but somehow gives
one a very pleasing impression of the man: a noble tender-
hearted creature, who sympathizes with all the human race"
(letter qu House 1969 p 13n). Cf Santayana 1921: "a vast
sympathetic participation in the daily life of mankind".

Anon (Thomas Hood). Athenaeum 7 Nov 1840. "The main fault
of the work is in its construction... the author is rather
too partial to one of the most unmanageable things in life
or literature, a Club..."

Reynolds, G.W.M. Master Timothy's Book-Case. 1842; rp 1847,
1886. One of several imitations. Reynolds also reviewed
the original (Teetotaler 4 Jul 1840) but Dickens alas did
not give us his temperate or intemperate opinion of The
Book-Case.

Anon. Times 27 Dec 1845. Thought resuscitation of the
Wllers in the Clock the first sign that Dickens's
"creative faculty" was "on the decline".

Dickens. 1848. Self-criticism in pref cheap edn Old Curiosity
Shop. Confessed that as early as March 1840 he had "been mac
uneasy by the desultory character" of the Clock and that he
believed his readers shared this feeling. Cf Monthly Rev
May 1840 qu House 1969 p viii(n).

Wells, H.G. "...I find all the novels of Dickens, long as
they are, too short for me. I am sorry they do not flow into
one another more...as Shakespeare ran the glorious glow of
Falstaff through a group of plays. But Dickens tried this
once when he carried on the Pickwick Club into Master
Humphrey's Clock. That experiment was unsatisfactory, and
he did not attempt anything of the sort again" (The Scope of
the Novel, talk given to Times Book Club 1911, rv 1914, rp
Henry James and H.G.Wells ed Leon Edel and Gordon N.Ray 1958
p 137). It might be said, though, that a few of the later
characters are unconscious imitations of the earlier: "...a
weakness of these last novels is a tendency for Dickens to
repeat his effects. Dora of Copperfield had been successful
changed into Flora, but what can we say of Flora's father bu
that he is a weak imitation of Mr Pecksniff? He is describe
almost in the same language..." (Churchill 1958 p 139).

Chesterton 1913: p 21 above. Contrasts Dickens with Trollope
and Thackeray in their "love of following characters and
kindred from book to book and from generation to generation.
Dickens very seldom tried this latter experiment, and then
(as in Master Humphrey's Clock) unsuccessfully; those magnes
blazes of his were too brilliant and glaring to be indefinit
prolonged" (p58 OPUS edn.)

Saintsbury 1916: p 22 above. "...it taught him never to
reintroduce his characters - a proceeding successful enough
with some other authors, but which the very stuff and substa
of his own form of creation forbade" (p 319 1932 edn.)

Leacock 1933: p 4 above. "...all true lovers of Pickwick
insist on believing that he did not really visit Master
Humphrey" (p 53.)

Blount 1968: p 35 above. Points out influence of Goldsmith's
miscellany The Bee, which Dickens had read as a boy (p 21;
cf House 1965 and see further below under "Dickens and
Goldsmith".)

The New Oxford Illustrated edn has intn Derek Hudson. Vol als
incl A Child's History of England qv below.

The Old Curiosity Shop

Hood 1840: p 51 above. Describes "the Child, asleep in her
little bed" as "like an Allegory of the peace and innocence
of childhood in the midst of Violence, Superstition and all
the hateful or hurtful Passions of the world".

Anon. Scotsman Edinburgh 13 Feb 1841. "It is surely no common
pen that can enlist the sympathies of so many thousands in
behalf of two such unobtrusive and harmless wanderers as
Nell and her grandfather".

Latimer, Thomas. Western Times Exeter 6 Mar 1841. Praised
novel for "breadth of humour, depth of pathos" but considered
it showed a lack of "fixedness of purpose in the mind of the
author" - a criticism Dickens replied to in a letter to
Latimer 13 Mar 41 (House 1969 pp 232-4; see further below under
"Serial Novelist" and for a related instance see Grubb 1953
below.)

Anon. Metropolitan Mag Mar 1841. "The heroine, little Nelly...
deserves a better fate than to die so prematurely."

Jeffrey, Lord. March 1841. "...nothing so good as Nell since
Cordelia" (qu Forster 1872 bk 2 ch 10). This was probably
the first time any of Dickens's characters had been compared
with Shakespeare's, though about the same time Landor
compared Nell with Juliet and Desdemona (Forster, Life of
Landor vol 1 p 449) and Capt Basil Hall RN wrote to Dickens
that Nell was "a sort of blood relation to Ariel" (House 1969
p 245n.) See further below under "Dickens and Shakespeare".

Anon (Edgar Allan Poe). Graham's Mag Philadelphia May 1841.
"...chaste, vigorous, and glorious imagination..." but Poe
regretted Nell's death as leaving "too painful an impression".
Cf Metropolitan Mag above.

Robinson, Crabb. 1841. Thought the "pathetic parts" of the
novel "among the best things" Dickens had written (qu House
1969 from Morley 1938). Cf view of Edward FitzGerald who
wrote of "Boz's sham pathos" in treatment of Nell (ibid from
FitzGerald Letters 1960). FitzGerald's 1846 essay Little
Nell's Wanderings is rp in A FitzGerald Medley 1933.
See further below under "Sentiment and Sentimentality"
and "Dickens and Childhood".

The Old Curiosity Shop, cont.

Anon. Christian Remembrancer Dec 1842. "...we do object most
strongly to the way in which her dying and her death are
worked up... The whole matter is one tissue of fantastic
sentiment... We have great doubts as to the propriety of this
incessant working up of our feelings by pictures of
consumption" (qu House 1969 below; cf FitzGerald above).

Belinsky, Vissarion. Read first Russian trn 1843 and "conclude
that Dickens's 'immense talent' had gone into a decline"
(Henry Gifford, Dickens in Russia, qu Wall 1970 p 516; cf
Dostoevsky below.)

Dostoevsky, Fedor. c1846-8. "...would appear at this stage
to be engaged more with The Old Curiosity Shop than any other
novel by Dickens... The image of Nell...prompted Dostoevsky t
create his own Nelly and endow her with a grandfather named
Smith...in The Insulted and Injured which marks his return to
social themes..." (Gifford above pp 516-7; cf Phelps 1916:
p 22 above; pp 107-8. See further below under "Dickens in
Russia" and "Dickens and Dostoevsky".)

Harte 1870: p 15 above.
  "He read aloud the book wherein the Master
      Had writ of Little Nell..."
  Cf Pearson 1949 qu below under "Sentiment and Sentimentality"

Wilde, Oscar. c1890. "One must have a heart of stone to read
the death of Little Nell without laughing" (qu Hesketh
Pearson, intn Wilde's Plays, Prose Writings and Poems, EL 19:
p xiii.)

Kitton 1897: p 17 above. Describes (p 66) how Jeffrey and
Macready were overcome with grief at death of Little Nell.
Cf Johnson 1952 vol 1 p 304. But see House 1969 below.

Gissing 1899: p 18 above. One of the best accounts.

Swinburne 1902: p 19 above. "...the first book in which the
background or setting is often as important as the figures
who can hardly be detached from it in our remembered impress
of the whole design. From Quilp's Wharf to Plashwater Wier
Mill Lock, the river belongs to Dickens by right of conquest
or creation" (pp 19-20 1913 edn; see further under "Our
Mutual Friend" and "Dickens's London".)

Wilkins 1911 (see "Dickens in America" below) gives details
of response in USA to Nell's death, qu Boston Advertiser and
other contemporary sources. Cf Harte 1870 above.

The Old Curiosity Shop, cont.

Saintsbury 1916: p 22 above. "On the vexed question of little
Nell, there is no need to say much here... She could be cut
out of the book with little loss... There would remain enough
to make a book of the first class... The Marchioness... is
simply unique - the sentimental note being never forced,
the romantic pleasantly indicated and the humorous
triumphantly maintained" (pp 319-20 1932 edn.)

Dexter 1924: see below under "Dickens's England".

Rutherford, Mark (William Hale White). Little Nell. Pages
from a Journal, Oxford 1930. Written c1910.

Huxley, Aldous. "The case of Dickens is a strange one. The
really monstrous emotional vulgarity, of which he is guilty
now and then in all his books and almost continuously in
The Old Curiosity Shop, is not the emotional vulgarity of one
who simulates feelings which he does not have. It is evident
...that Dickens felt most poignantly for and with his Little
Nell... He had an overflowing heart; but the trouble was
that it overflowed with such curious and even rather repellant
secretions... The overflowing of his heart drowns his head..."
(Vulgarity in Literature. 1930; rp Music at Night 1931.)

Dent 1933: p 4 above. "Little Nell is not a child; she is the
apotheosis of maltreated childhood... It is... our non-
comprehension of how childhood could be, and was, treated in
the 1840s which prevents us today from seeing her clearly"
(p 201 1935 edn; see further below under "Dickens and
Childhood".)

Wilson 1939-41: p 27 above; p 56 UP edn.

Bennett, W.C. The Mystery of the Marchioness. Dickensian 36
1940. Cf Grubb 1953 below.

House 1941: p 27 above; pp 179-80.

Lindsay 1950: p 5 above. Suggests (p 193) that there was
something of Dickens himself in the character of Quilp.
Sybil Thorndike and others have testified to the attraction
of Quilp when first read about in childhood. Cf perhaps
Punch in Punch-and-Judy. See further Johnson 1970 below.

Hill, T.W. Notes on The Old Curiosity Shop. Dickensian 49
1953.

The Old Curiosity Shop, cont.

Grubb, Gerald G. Dickens's Marchioness Identified. Modern
   Language Notes Mar 1953. Shows by study of MS cancellations
   that the Marchioness was originally intended to be the love-
   child of Quilp and Sally Brass. See Johnson 1970 below.

Ford 1955: p 31 above; p 38.

Cockshut 1957: see below under "Sentiment and Sentimentality".

Spilka, M. Little Nell Revisited. Papers of Michigan Academy
   of Sciences & Letters 45 1959.

Pearson, Gabriel. In Gross 1962: p 7 above.

Reid 1962: p 33 above. Cf Lindsay 1950 qv.

Gibson, J.W. The Critical Allegory. Dickensian 60 1964.

Dyson, A.E. Innocence and the Grotesque. CQ 8 1966. See
   further below under "Fantasy and the Grotesque".

Senelick, L. Little Nell and the Prurience of Sentimentality.
   DS 3 1967. Cf Huxley 1930 above.

House 1969: p 6 above. Pref discusses question of public's
   varied response to death of Nell (pp ix-xii).

Holloway, John. In Slater 1970: p 8 above. Relates Oliver
   to Old Curiosity Shop (pp 60-7).

Johnson, Pamela Hansford. In Slater 1970: p 8 above. Quilp
   and Nell, Dick and the Marchioness (pp 176-9). See further
   below under "Sex in Dickens". Wall 1970 (pp 490-2) qu
   comparable passage from Steven Marcus, The Myth of Nell,
   in Marcus 1965: p 34 above. "The raging contrarieties of
   Quilp's sadism and masochism are the counterparts of the
   contradictory, sentimental emotions with which Dickens
   invested Nell..." (p 159; cf Huxley and Senelick above.)

Kincaid, James R. Laughter and Pathos in The Old Curiosity Shop
   DSA 1 1971.

Easson, Angus (ed). PEL edn 1972. Incl passages in MS deleted
   at proof stage, mostly in order to reduce instalments to their
   customary length. See further below under "Serial Novelist".

Barnaby Rudge

Anon (Edgar Allan Poe). Saturday Evening Post Philadelphia
1 May 1841; rp Dickensian 9 1913 pp 174-8.

Lytton, Bulwer. Letter to Forster 9 Jul 1841. "Dickens is
greatly improved in the art of story - but does not seem to
be so good in character - Barnaby is too Scott like. Ditto
the smith and his daughter - Old Chester is a failure - his
son a non entity" (qu House 1969 p 233n.)

Anon. Argus 7 Aug 1841. Criticizes sketch of "the country
gentleman" in ch 47 of Barnaby Rudge "which some irreverently
call Barnaby Rubbish" (qu House 1969 p 369n.)

Poe, Edgar Allan. Graham's Mag Philadelphia Feb 1842; rp
The Book of Poe, New York 1929 pp 97-115. See discussion of
Poe's theories in Leacock 1933 pp 58-62; cf John Buchan,
intn Nelson Classics edn Poe's Tales pp 6-7.)

Gissing 1899: p 18 above.

Swinburne 1902: p 19 above. "...it is difficult...to imagine
a faultless work of creation...but the story of Barnaby Rudge
can hardly, in common justice, be said to fall short of this
crowning praise" (pp21-2 1913 edn.)

Ulrich, A. Studien zu Dickens' Roman Barnaby Rudge. Jena 1931.

Brush, L.M. A Psychological Study of Barnaby Rudge. Dickensian
31 1935.

Orwell 1939: p 26 above. On the Gordon Riots (pp 13-14 1946 edn).
Cf Dent 1933 pp 212-13 1935 edn (qu Forster 1872) and Darwin
1933 qqv.

Edmund Wilson 1939-41: p 27 above; pp 16-21 UP edn.

Lukacs, Georg. The Historical Novel. New York 1950; London 1962.

Tillotson, Kathleen. Intn New Oxford edn 1954.

Hill, T.W. Notes on Barnaby Rudge. Dickensian 50-3 1954-7.

Folland, H.F. The Doer and the Deed: Theme and Pattern in
Barnaby Rudge. PMLA 74 1959.

Lindsay, Jack. In Gross 1962: p 7 above.

Monod, Sylvère. Rebel with a Cause: Hugh of the Maypole.
DS 1 1965.

Barnaby Rudge, cont.

Dyson, A.E. The Genesis of Violence. CQ 9 1967.

Ryan, Katherine. Dickens and Shakespeare: Probable Sources of
   Barnaby Rudge. English Summer 1970.

Angus Wilson 1970: p 35 above. One of the best recent accounts

Angus Wilson in Slater 1970: p 8 above. "...in my opinion
   the turning point in Dickens's growth from an extraordinary
   to a great novelist" (p 199). See further below under
   "Development".

Lucas 1970: p 36 above. Both Lucas and Wilson argue that the
   novel has been rather neglected and will repay more serious
   attention than it has generally received. Point borne out
   by comparative paucity of items on Barnaby in this or earlier
   bibliographies. House 1941 p 34 maintained that "the two of
   Dickens's novels which can least be read for historical
   reasons are Barnaby Rudge and A Tale of Two Cities. Yet
   even they have a special interest, because they show what
   he, in 1841 and 1859, was thinking about the past."

Spence, Gordon W. (ed). PEL edn 1973. Intn discusses whether
   Dickens's treatment of the Gordon Riots was influenced by
   his attitude to the Chartist Movement which was developing
   when the novel was being written. "The relation is
   problematic, because of the difficulty of saying what his
   attitude towards Chartism was at that time." See further
   below under "Radical and Reformer".

American Notes

Anon. New York Herald Oct 1842. "...coarse, vulgar, impudent
   and superficial..." (qu Peter Bracher, The New York Herald
   and American Notes, DS 5 1969.)

Longfellow. Letter to Sumner 16 Oct 1842. "You will read it
   with delight, and for the most part approbation. He has a
   grand chapter on Slavery" (qu House 1974 p 335n.)

Robinson, Crabb. "...in his highest style of humour...also
   serious passages of great worth" (Diary Oct 1842 qu House
   1974 p 411n.)

American Notes, cont.

Macaulay. Letter to Napier 19 Oct 1842 refusing to review
book for Edinburgh Rev. "It is impossible for me to review
it... I cannot praise it; and I will not cut it up... It is
written like the worst parts of Humphrey's Clock. What is
meant to be easy and sprightly is vulgar and flippant..."
(letter attributed to Thackeray in Pope-Hennessy 1945 p 189).

Anon. Times 25 Oct 1842. Praised satirical passages as
having "a moral, not a tainting effect."

Anon. Fraser's Mag Nov 1842. Considered that the author of
"monthly and weekly effusions touching Cockneys and the
peculiar regions...in which they flourish" was quite
unqualified to write a work on the United States. Nothing
really new in the book but "everything is made to wear
Boz's peculiar colours."

Bryant, William Cullen. New York Evening Post 9 Nov 1842.
Protested at Dickens's too sweeping condemnation of the
American press.

Anon. Boston Daily Evening Transcript 12 Nov 1842. "For the
life of us, we cannot discover any 'shocking injustice'...
or any 'unthankful spirit' in the late work, which has called
up such newspaper invective..." (qu House 1974; cf New York
Herald above.)

Emerson, Ralph Waldo. "Truth is not his object for a single
instant... As an account of America...not to be considered..."
(Journal 25 Nov 1842 in Journals 8 p 222.)

Anon. English Notes by Quarles Quickens. Boston 1842; ed
Lewis M.Thompson New York 1920 with critical comment by
J.Jackson and G.H.Sargent. Attributed to Poe in some
booksellers' catalogues but NCBEL 1969 says no. One of
several retorts and parodies. See William Glyde Wilkins,
American Parodies on American Notes, Dickensian 4 1908.

Anon (Samuel Warren). Blackwood's Mag Dec 1842. Approved
some chapters but on the whole thought the book "very flimsy"
and its style "slipshod".

Felton 1843: p 11 above. Says that the book, "scattered all
over the country" - ie USA - "by the penny press", had been
read "with general approbation"; admits some justice in the
attacks on American newspapers but thinks them exaggerated;
in general considers the humorous descriptions of American
life to be the work of a creative artist, not satires on
American civilization. Cf Wilson 1939 below.

American Notes, cont.

Anon (James Spedding). Edinburgh Rev Jan 1843; rv Reviews
and Discussions 1879. Considered that owing to the
author's "desultory education" the book lacked sound
knowledge and showed hurried, superficial observation and
Dickens's "habitual exaggeration".

Anon (J.T.Thompson). New Englander Jan 1843. "...a compound
of egotism, coxcombery, and cockneyism..." (qu House 1974;
cf Boston Transcript 1842 above.)

Anon (Poe?). Southern Literary Messenger Richmond Va Jan 43.
"...one of the most suicidal productions ever deliberately
published by an author who had the least reputation to lose".
(cf Dana, Journal, qu House 1974 p 348n: "The book will make
him unpopular without adding to his reputation. He is not
a gentleman and his genius is in a narrow line... His
journey to America has been a Moscow expedition for his
fame"). See further below under "Dickens in America".

Anon (John Wilson Croker). Quarterly Rev Mar 1843. "Our
readers will...wonder how any man, with a tithe of Mr
Dickens's cleverness and a grain of tact, could publish
such trash..." Tactlessness was the main contemporary
criticism, in both countries. It was reasonably felt that
an honoured visitor, who had received a welcome fit for a
king, could have expressed his honest opinion - both here
and in Chuzzlewit - more circumspectly. On the other hand,
Felton's words about "creative artist" (qu p 59 above) apply
to the novel if not to the Notes and Dickens himself pointed
out that he had not spared British feelings in his creations
of Bumble, Pecksniff and other non-American characters.

Tellkampf, J.L. Remarks on American Notes. Essays on Law
Reform, 1859. Cf pamphlet 1894 - Dickens's Prison Fiction
by W.Tallack - issued by Howard Assoc for Penal Reform.
See further below under "Dickens and Crime".

Whipple, Edwin P. Atlantic Monthly Boston Apr 1877. See
Whipple 1912: p 3 above.

Phelps 1916: p 22 above. "He was the most creative and the
least critical of all our writers of fiction; he attempted
no formal essays; his American Notes ought not to have been
written, and his Child's History of England would have
blighted the reputation of a lesser man" (p 109).

American Notes, cont.

Leacock 1933: p 4 above. "The first of Dickens's American
  notes should have been a note upon himself. It would have
  saved much disillusionment..." (p 65; cf Orwell 1939 below.)
  Leacock's account is very fair, both to Dickens and to
  America, as befitted an English-born Canadian writer partly
  educated in the USA.

Orwell 1939-40: p 26 above. "If Dickens were alive today he
  would make a trip to Soviet Russia and come back with a book
  rather like Gide's Retour de l'URRS" (p 27 1946 edn). Ref is
  to "the American chapters of Martin Chuzzlewit" - "the reaction
  of a generous mind against cant" - but the comparison with
  Gide applies more to American Notes than to the novel. Cf
  Dent 1933 p 237.

Wilson 1939-41: p 27 above. Qu criticism of Jackson 1937
  (p 26 above) but adds: "Yet Dickens's picture of the United
  States in 1842, at a period of brave boastings and often
  squalid or meagre realities, has a unique and permanent
  value" (pp 21-2, 24-5 UP edn.)

Churchill 1937-42: p 26 above; p 372. Cf L.H.Johnson, The
  Source of the Chapter on American Slavery, American Literature
  14 1943.

Fielding, K.J. American Notes and Some English Reviewers.
  MLR 59 1964.

Whitley, John S. and Arnold Goldman (ed). PEL edn 1972.

Martin Chuzzlewit

Smith, Sydney. Letter to Dickens 6 Jan 1843 after reading
  first no. "Pecksniff and his daughters, and Pinch, are
  admirable - quite first-rate painting such as no one but
  yourself can execute". His opinion of the first American
  chapters was similar: "Excellent! Nothing can be better!...
  full of wit, humour, and power of description" - "tremendous
  panegyrics" commented Dickens, "which from such an authority
  are worth having" (House 1974 p 526) ref Smith's status as
  veteran literary critic, co-founder of Edinburgh Rev. But
  Smith's opinion of the later American chapters was less
  favourable: he was "very sorry for the turn Dickens's novel
  has taken". Like Elizabeth Barrett, he thought it showed
  ingratitude to Dickens's former hosts (House p 541n.)

Carlyle. Letter to Forster 3 Jul 1843. "The last Chuzzlewit
on Yankeedoodledodum is capital. We read it with loud
assent..." (qu House 1974 p 541.)

Hone, Philip. Ref same chs. "...an exceedingly foolish
libel... unmitigated trash..." (Diary 29 Jul 1843.)

Anon. Brother Jonathan New York 29 Jul 1843; rp Dickensian
10 1914. Ref chs 16-17 wrote of Dickens's "malignity"
and "infuriated malice", "determination to distort and
misrepresent". Cf Coombes 1953 below.

Dickens to Forster 2 Nov 1843. "I think Chuzzlewit in a
hundred points immeasurably the best of my stories"
(qu Forster 1872 bk 4 ch 2). Cf Gissing on Chuzzlewit:
"Every quality of Dickens is seen at its best".

Belinsky 1844: see below under "Dickens in Russia".

Anon (John Forster). Examiner 26 Oct 1844. "...Mr Dickens's
best work, taken as a whole..." (qu Collins 1971 pp 184-6).
Cf Forster 1872 bk 9 ch 1: "one of his greatest
achievements".

Taine 1856: p 13 above. "...Dickens is admirable in
depicting hallucinations. We see that he feels himself
those of his characters, that he is engrossed by their
ideas, that he enters into their madness... The portrait
of Jonas Chuzzlewit is... terrible..." See further below
under "Dickens and Crime".

Gissing 1898: p 17 above. "...Mrs Gamp...stands unique,
no other novelist can show a piece of work...worthy of a
place beside her; we must go to the very heights of world-
literature, to him who bodied forth Dame Quickly, and
Juliet's nurse, for the suggestion of equivalent power"
(pp 82-3 1926 edn.)

Swinburne 1902: p 19 above. Considered that the language
of Mrs Gamp rivals "the unspeakable perfection of Mrs
Quickly's eloquence at its best" (p 26 1913 edn; cf Gissing
above and see further below under "Dickens and Shakespeare").
Even Samuel Butler admired Mrs Gamp's flow of speech,
drawing on it for his own Mrs Jupp and in 1894 "in
consequence of a challenge" translating a typical
utterance (ch 19) into Greek Homeric hexameters.

Saintsbury 1916: p 22 above. "...one of Dickens's greatest successes...an intensity of verve, a warmth of imagination... never surpassed, and seldom, even in David Copperfield, equalled later" (p 322 1932 edn; cf Cecil 1931-4 below.)

Quiller-Couch 1922-5: p 23 above. "Who will deny that the American chapters of Martin Chuzzlewit are its best and, save for any given chapter upon which Sarah Gamp knocks in, its most memorable?" (pp52-3.)

Osborne 1927: see below under "Characters".

Cecil 1931-4: p 25 above. Chuzzlewit and Copperfield: "the masterpieces of his middle period. I still think these are his greatest works, because they are the most solidly human..." (p 8 FL edn.)

Older, M. The Mysterious Mrs Harris. Dickensian 29 1933.

Leacock 1933: p 4 above. "Many people have liked it best of Dickens's books, and all readers have found it one of the books they liked best" (p 108.)

Churchill 1937-42: p 26 above. Concurs with Gissing and other predecessors on greatness of Chuzzlewit but discusses "the extraordinary difference in intelligence between the mind which produced the best parts of Gamp and Pecksniff, and the American interlude, and the mind which produced the worst parts of Thomas Pinch, the mind being the same man's, writing the same book" (p 360; cf Churchill 1958 p 120 and see Lucas 1970 below.)

Anon. TLS 9 Jan 1943. Dickens in America: the Martin Chuzzlewit Centenary. Cf R.B.Heilman, The New World in Dickens's Writings, Trollopian 1 1947.

Hill, T.W. Notes on Martin Chuzzlewit. Dickensian 42-3 1946-7.

Pound, L. The American Dialect of Dickens. American Speech 22 1947. Cf Churchill 1958 p 130.

Nisbet, Ada. The Mystery of Martin Chuzzlewit. Essays... Dedicated to Lily Campbell, Berkeley 1950.

Van Ghent, Dorothy. The Dickens World: A View from Todgers'. Sewanee Rev 58 1950. Cf Gissing 1901 qv.

Grubb, Gerald G. Dickens's Western Tour and the Cairo Legend. SP 48 1951. Cf Coombes below.

Coombes, H.   Literature and Criticism.   1953.   "When Dickens
gave his feelings a loose rein, the effect on his writing was
harmful and sometimes disastrous; for instance, when he was
unable to control his resentful feelings about America...he
produced...those descriptions of the valley of Eden which are
quite unconvincing because they are grossly exaggerated...
He was not, in this instance, sufficiently an artist" (PB edr.
1963 pp 93-4; cf Grubb 1951 above and see also Van Wyck
Brooks, The World of Washington Irving, 1944 p 293 and H.G.
Baetzhold, The Model for Martin Chuzzlewit's Eden, Dickensian
55 1959.)

Benjamin, E.B.   The Structure of Martin Chuzzlewit.   PQ 34 1955.

Stone, Harry.   Dickens's Use of his American Experiences in
Martin Chuzzlewit.   PMLA 72 1957.

Churchill 1958: p 32 above under Ford.   "...the greatest work
of comic genius in the whole of English literature" (p 120;
qu Blount 1968 below.)

Miller 1958: p 31 above.   "...The novel is full of people who
are wholly enclosed in themselves, wholly secret, wholly
intent on reflexive ends which are altogether mysterious to
those around them..." (pp 104-5).   Argument developed ref
Mrs Gamp, Nadgett, Pips, etc.

Hardy, Barbara.   In Gross 1962: p 7 above.   Cf Lucas 1970 below

Whitley, J.S.   The Two Hells of Martin Chuzzlewit.   Papers of
Michigan Academy of Science & Letters 50 1965.

Dyson, A.E.   Howls the Sublime.   CQ 9 1967.

Blount 1968: p 35 above.   See pp 25-6.   It should be noted
that Blount's insistence that the greatness of Chuzzlewit is
largely one of style and language is not a contradiction of
Churchill, as might be thought, but an agreement with him and
others.   Cf Churchill 1937-42 as well as the Churchill 1958
qu Blount.

Lucas 1970: p 36 above.   "With the exception of Barbara Hardy
I do not know of any contemporary critic honest enough to
admit that Chuzzlewit, marvellous though it undoubtedly is
in parts, is something of a marvellous mess (p 113).   Cf
Churchill 1937-42, 1951, 1958 etc where this point is
repeatedly made.

Martin Chuzzlewit, cont.

Churchill, R.C.   Boz Goes to America.   Contemporary Rev Sep 1974.
  Review of House 1974: p 6 above.   "In regard to Cairo,
  Illinois - the ironically-named 'Eden' of Chuzzlewit...
  Dickens failed to allow for the American rate of progress;
  as he failed to realize that for a boy like Mark Twain, the
  future 'Dickens of America', the 'intolerable' Mississippi
  was to be as nostalgic a stream as the Thames to himself"
  (pp 161-2; cf Leacock 1933 and Brooks 1944 and see further
  below under "Dickens in America" and "Dickens and Mark Twain").
  Churchill, Birmingham Post 24 Aug 74, makes same point:
  "There would have been plenty of work for Chuzzlewit & Co.,
  Architects, if only they had stuck it out."

The SC edn has Afterword by Martin Mudrick; the PEL edn is
  ed P.N.Furbank.

Christmas Books

See also below under "Christmas Carol", "Chimes", etc.

Howells, William Dean.   Dickens's Christmas Books.   In Howells
  1891: p 17 above.

Cazamian 1904: see below under "Dickens and Christmas".

Swinburne 1902: p 19 above.   "...the best of them are far
  surpassed in excellence by his contributions to the Christmas
  numbers of his successive magazines... The Wreck of the
  Golden Mary is the work of a genius till then unimaginable -
  a Defoe with a human heart" (pp 67-8 1913 edn.)

Shorter, Clement.   Intn 1912 edn.   Cf Swinburne above.

Quiller-Couch 1922-5: p 23 above.   "...I dislike them; I find
  them...grossly sentimental...I greatly prefer several of his
  later Christmas stories in Household Words and All the Year
  Round...to this classic five" (p 16; cf Swinburne above.)

House 1941: p 27 above; pp 16, 41, 53.

The New Oxford edn has intn Eleanor Farjeon; the PEL edn is
  ed Michael Slater. See also Collins 1971 pp 144-6.

A Christmas Carol

Anon. Morning Chronicle 19 Dec 1843. Enthusiastic review,
perhaps by assistant ed Charles Mackay, father of Marie
Corelli.

Jeffrey to Dickens Xmas 1843. "...you have done more good
by this little publication...than can be traced to all the
pulpits and confessionals in Christendom since Christmas
1842" (letter qu Forster 1872 bk 4 ch 2).

Michael Angelo Titmarsh (W.M.Thackeray). Fraser's Mag Feb 1844.
"...the work of the master of all the English humourists now
alive; the young man who came and took his place calmly at
the head of the whole tribe, and who has kept it. Think of
all we owe Mr Dickens since those half-dozen years... Every
month...has brought us some kind token from this delightful
genius... As for the Christmas Carol...I am not sure that
the allegory is a very complete one, and protest...against
the use of blank verse in prose; but here all objections
stop. Who can listen to objections regarding such a book as
this? It seems to me a national benefit, and to every man
or woman who reads it a personal kindness..."

Sammons, William Layton. Sam Sly's African Journal Cape Town
15 Aug 1844. Favourable review of new book "by our friend
and correspondent Charles Dickens". But only letter to
Sammons from Dickens extant (House 1965 pp 501-2) begins
"Sir" and ends "Your very obedient Servant".

Barnett, C.Z. A Christmas Carol: or the Miser's Warning.
1844; rp 1872, 1886. One of several stage versions. See
Malcolm Morley, Curtain Up on A Christmas Carol, Dickensian
47 1951, and further below under "Stage and Platform".

Kitton, Frederic G. Intn 1890 edn; rp 1906.

Chesterton 1906: p 20 above. "...the tale is everywhere
irregular and in some places weak. It has the same kind of
artistic unity that belongs to a dream... Scrooge is not
really inhuman at the beginning any more than he is at the
end. There is a heartiness in his inhospitable sentiments
that is akin to humour and therefore to humanity... The
beauty and the real blessing of the story do not lie in
the mechanical plot...the repentance of Scrooge, probable
or improbable; they lie in the great furnace of real
happiness that glows through Scrooge and everything around
him; that great furnace, the heart of Dickens. Wther the
Christmas visions would or would not convert Scrooge, they
convert us. Whether or no the visions were evoked by real
Spirits of the Past, Present and Future, they were evoked by
that truly exalted order of angels who are correctly called
High Spirits..." (pp 174-5.)

A Christmas Carol, cont.

Chesterton 1913: p 21 above. "When we think...of the uncountable riches of religious art, imagery, ritual, and popular legend that has clustered round Christmas through all the Christian ages, it is a truly extraordinary thing to reflect that Dickens (wishing to have in A Christmas Carol a little happy supernaturalism by way of a change) actually had to make up a mythology for himself. Here was one of the rare cases where Dickens, in a real and human sense, did suffer from the lack of culture" (p 57 OPUS edn; cf Santayana 1921 and see further below under "Dickens and Religion".)

Saintsbury 1916: p 22 above. "...the Carol is delightful. We must, of course, grant - as...in the case of The Ancient Mariner - that its story is 'improbable'; there is scarcely another objection that can be sustained against it except in the eyes of those to whom all sentiment and all fairy tales are red rags" (p 324 1932 edn.)

Fiedler, F. Dickens' Gebrauch der rhythmischen Prosa im Christmas Carol. Archiv 139 1919.

Fiedler, F. Wie Dickens das Christmas Carol feite. Archiv 144 1922.

Newton, A.E. The Greatest Book in the World and Other Papers. Boston 1925.

Leacock 1933: p 4 above. "Literature has no finer picture than the redeemed Scrooge at his window in the frosty Christmas morning... It is of no consequence whether A Christmas Carol is true to life. It is better than life" (pp 110-11.)

Darwin 1933: p 4 above. "In some ways there is nothing strikingly original about the Carol. Superficially, at any rate, it has a strong Pickwickian flavour..."

Dent 1933: p 4 above. See ppp 276-86 in 1935 edn.

Wilson 1939-41: p 27 above.

Butt, John. A Christmas Carol: Its Origin and Design. Dickensian 51 1955.

Morris, W.E. The Conversion of Scrooge. Studies in Short Fiction 3 1965.

Slater, Michael. In Slater 1970: p 8 above. Relation to The Chimes (p 102). See further below.

A Christmas Carol, cont.

Lane, Margaret. In Slater 1970: p 8 above. "...the simple
moral, that the world would be a better place...if rich
employers were both generous and kind, was congenial...to
readers who would have shied away from more basic or more
organized social reforms" (p 156; cf Orwell 1939.)

Wilson, Angus. Ibid. "Autobiographical paradox" in the
Carol (pp 206-7). See further below under "Dickens and
Childhood".

Lucas 1970: p 36 above. "...persuasive as neither J.S.Mill
nor Carlyle could hope to be, just because Dickens's fable
has the sort of compressed intensity that in the literature
of the past two hundred years is rivalled only perhaps by
the Songs of Experience". See further below under "Dickens
and Blake".

The Chimes

Jeffrey to Dickens 1844. "All the tribe of selfishness and
cowardice and cant...will accuse you of wicked exaggeration
and incitement to discontent... But never mind. The good
and the brave are with you, and the truth also" (letter qu
Forster 1872 bk 4 ch 5.)

Anon. Globe Dec 31 1844. Noted that the story was being
"attacked and defended with...ardour..." (qu Michael Slater,
The Christmas Books, Dickensian 65 1969).

Anon (John Forster). Edinburgh Rev Jan 1845. Compares it
with the Carol: "What was there the individual lapse is here
the social wrong... the impression of sadness predominates
... Name this little tale what we will, it is a tragedy in
effect..." Cf Forster 1872: "...not one of his greater
successes, and it raised him up some objectors; but...in
his own heart it had a cherished corner to the last. The
intensity of it seemed always best to represent to himself
what he hoped to be longest remembered for" (bk 4 ch 5.)
The "objectors" incl the Times reviewer (25 Dec 44) and
Brookfield 1845 below. There were imitations by Planche
and others.

Brookfield, W.H. "...as utter trash as was ever trodden
under foot" (letter 12 Mar 1845 qu Pope-Hennessy 1945 p 232).
Lady Blessington, however, like Lord Jeffrey, "wept over the
story", as did Harness and Dyce during Dickens's own reading
of it to Carlyle and other friends 2 Dec 1844. See
Maclise's famous sketch of the occasion and reports in
Forster and other biographies.

The Chimes, cont.

Lemon, Mark and Gilbert à Beckett. The Chimes: A Goblin Drama
in Four Quarters. One of several stage versions. See Malcolm
Morley, Ring Up the Chimes, Dickensian 47 1951, and further
below under "Stage and Platform".

Chesterton 1913: p 21 above. "...he wrote against Mr Gradgrind
long before he created him. In The Chimes, conceived in quite
his casual and charitable season...he hit hard at the
economists..." (p 34 OPUS edn; cf Chesterton on Oliver Twist
1907 qu p 46 above.)

Dent 1933: p 4 above. "...the reformer triumphed over the
humorist in The Chimes...quite decisively and sufficiently
to place it far below the Carol" (p 309 1935 edn.)

House 1941: p 27 above. "There is a difference of atmosphere
between A Christmas Carol (1843), which is a story of vague
undated benevolence, and The Chimes (1844), which is a
topical satire" (p 136; cf pp 72-3 qu W.R.Greg, Westminster
Rev Jun 1845, and further below under Slater.)

Wagenknecht 1965: p 5 above.

Slater, Michael. In NCF centenary no 1970. See also below.

Slater, Michael. Dickens's Tract for the Times. In Slater
1970: p 8 above. "...Filer stood for all the Malthusians
and political economists, all the utilitarians and
statisticians - the 'philosophers' of Oliver Twist - whom
Dickens had always detested and on whom he was eventually to
launch a full-scale attack in Hard Times..." (p 114; cf
Chesterton 1913 above.) Dr Slater emphasizes topicality of
The Chimes eg by pointing out (pp 105-6) that "the corrected
proofs...show that Dickens changed Fern's native county from
Hertfordshire to Dorsetshire..." This topicality observed
by some contemporary reviwers (p 115) eg in Northern Star
Dec 21 1844. Even some thought to the detriment of the
story (p 122) like the reviewer who questioned whether
Dickens had not "injured the general interest of his story
by making so much of it unintelligible save to the 'constant
readers' of the police reports in The Times" (Slater pp 122-3;
cf Dent above.) See further below under "Radical and
Reformer".

Wilson, Angus. In Slater 1970: p 8 above. "...The Chimes,
that fictionalized political tract, dwells on the social
problem which is the third strand in his approach to the
subject of children..." (p 206).

The Cricket on the Hearth

Anon (John Forster). Examiner 27 Dec 1845. Cf Forster 1872
bk 5 ch 1 where he explains that The Cricket was the
proposed title of a weekly paper Dickens considered starting
in 1845 and that the story arose "in connection" with it.
"Its sale at the outset doubled that of both its
predecessors" but some of the reviewers - in The Times
(27 Dec 45) and elsewhere - were less enthusiastic. See
below.

Anon. Mephystopheles Dec45-Jan46. The Critic on the Art
(of Humbug) v. The Cricket on the Hearth. Satirized
Dickens's sentimentality in this story, which however the
public admired as much as he did. They "read it
rapturously... Dramatised for the Keeleys at the Lyceum
for Christmas 1845, a fortnight later versions of it were
being played at twelve London theatres" (Pope-Hennessy 1945
pp 245-6; see further Malcolm Morley, Dickensian 48 1952,
and under Orwell below.)

Anon. Chambers's Edinburgh Journal 17 Jan 1846. "...a picture
of humble life, contemplated in its poetic aspects... shows
its author...ambitious of becoming the Wordsworth of prose
fiction. Deficient in the profundity and stern power of
that great master, the novelist yet has some requisites
which the poet wants - a certain wit and humour and...an
experience of civic life that the bard of Rydal has failed
to cultivate..." (qu Collins 1971 pp 174-5).

Anon. Macphail's Edinburgh Ecclesiastical Journal Feb 1846.
"...not much ingenuity and no nature in the plot of The
Cricket... Its merit lies in its sentiment, which is yet
extremely liable to the charge of being mawkish and maudlin.
The attempts at wit...are exceedingly forced and affected..."
(qu Collins 1971 pp 175-6.)

Morley, Henry. Intn 1887 edn; rp 1904.

De la Mare, Walter. Intn 1933 edn illustr Hugh Thomson.

Orwell 1939: p 26 above. "...Nadezhda Krupskaya...relates
that towards the end of his life Lenin went to see a
dramatized version of The Cricket on the Hearth and found
Dickens's 'middle-class sentimentality' so intolerable
that he walked out in the middle of a scene" (p 7 1946 edn).

Lane, Margaret. Dickens on the Hearth. In Slater 1970: p 8
above; pp 156-8.

The Battle of Life

Jeffrey to Dickens Dec 1846.   "I like and admire the Battle
extremely.   It is better than any other man alive could have
written... The dance of the sisters in that autumn orchard is
of itself worth a dozen inferior tales..." (qu Forster 1872
bk 5 ch 6.)

Anon.   Morning Chronicle 24 Dec 1846.   "If this climate of ours
had only been sunny and dry, instead of cold and rainy, we very
much doubt whether Mr Dickens would ever have achieved the
high position in literature which he now enjoys.   He is so
peculiarly a writer of home life...a painter of domestic
scenes, that we feel convinced, had Italy or Spain...
produced him...he would have migrated to our more northern
shores for the sake of firesides, purring cats, boiling
kettles...and chirping crickets..." (qu Lane 1970: p 70 above;
p 154).

Anon.   The Times 2 Jan 1847.   Repeated severe criticism - first
levelled at The Cricket - this time writing of "the unheard-of
effrontery" of the new story.   "I see the good old Times is
again at issue with the inimitable B." commented Dickens.
"Another touch of a blunt razor on B.'s nervous system...
Dreamed of 'Timeses' all night.   Disposed to go to New
Zealand and start a magazine" (qu Forster 1872 bk 6 ch 2.)

Dickens to Lytton 1849.   "What you said of the Battle of Life
gave me great pleasure.   I was thoroughly wretched at having
to use the idea for so short a story... I have always felt
that I might have done a great deal with it, if I had taken
it for the groundwork of a more extended book" (qu Forster
bk 5 ch 6.)

Forster 1872: p 2 above.   "I read it lately with a sense that
its general tone of quiet beauty deserved well the praise
which Jeffrey...had given it... The story would not be
Dickens's if we could not discover in it the power peculiar
to him of presenting the commonest objects with freshness and
beauty, of detecting in the homeliest forms of life much of
its rarest loveliness, and of springing easily upward from
everyday realities into regions of imaginative thought"
(bk 5 ch 6.)

Saintsbury 1916: p 22 above.   "...probably the worst thing
Dickens...ever did in fiction except George Silverman's
Explanation" (p 323 1932 edn.)

Gibson, F.A.   A Reconsideration of The Battle of Life.
Dickensian 58 1962.

The Haunted Man

Anon (John Forster). Examiner 23 Dec 1848. Cf Forster 1872
bk 6 ch 4: "...the supernatural takes a shape which is not
forced or violent; and the dialogue...is a piece of ghostly
imagination better than Mrs Radcliffe... The juxtaposition
of two people whom such opposite means have put in the same
moral position is a stroke of excellent art. There are
plenty of incredibilities and inconsistencies, just as in
the...Cricket...which we...enjoy rather than otherwise..."

Dickens to Forster 1848 answering certain objections to the
"machinery" of the tale. "...my point is that bad and good
are inextricably linked in remembrance..." See Pope-
Hennessy below.

Forster 1872: p 2 above. "...sold largely...and had a great
success on the Adelphi stage, to which it was rather cleverly
adapted by Lemon..." See Malcolm Morley, Dickensian 1952,
for details of this and other stage versions. Leacock 1933
mentions fact that "young John Tenniel", future illustrator
of Alice in Wonderland, was among the illustraots for The
Haunted Man. Mark Lemon's daughter was the original of
Tenniel's Alice.

Among the parodies were those in The Man in the Moon (Jan 1849)
and in Bret Harte's Condensed Novels (New York 1870).

Saintsbury 1916: p 22 above. "...the Tetterbys are of the firs
water; they are, indeed, better than the Cratchits... the goo
angel Milly is managed with an unusual freedom from
exaggeration or mawkishness; and, in the serious parts...
there are touches...of a true romantic quality which Dickens
often attempted but less often attained" (p 324 1932 edn.)

House 1941: p 27 above. Relation to Dombey (pp 192-3).

Pope-Hennessy 1945: p 4 above. "...the moral of this story...
is that it is better not to seek forgetfulness... The Haunted
Man may be taken as a pointer to the way Dickens's mind had
been working... he could promise himself no comfort in a
ghost's bargain..." (pp 294-5). The story, in other words,
leads on to Copperfield, begun the following spring. Dombey
was published 1846-8: after The Cricket but before The Haunte
Man. The Battle of Life was the Christmas Book published
while Dombey was appearing in monthly parts.

Stone, Harry. Dickens's Artistry and The Haunted Man. South
Atlantic Quarterly 61 1962.

Wilson, Angus. In Slater 1970: p 8 above; pp 222-3.

Pictures from Italy

Anon. The Times 1 Jun 1846 qu TLS 23 Nov 1973 (see below).
"...drowsy volume...the most vapid and dullest" of his works.
"We did not expect learning, but we did look for fun... We are
sadly disappointed. "

Savonarolo, Don Jeremy (F.S.Mahony, Father Prout). Facts and
Figures from Italy: addressed to Charles Dickens. 1847.
See also P.A.Murray, Dublin Rev 21 1846, and below under
House.

Cannavo, F. Nuova Antologia 1 Aug 1918. See further below
under "Dickens in Italy".

Massoul 1924: see below under "Dickens in Italy".

Cecil 1931-4: p 25 above. "Scott...can write on France with
the educated appreciation of a man of the world, while Dickens
writes on Italy with the disapproving self-complacency of a
provincial schoolmaster" (p 26 FL edn).

Leacock 1933: p 4 above. "...a few passages worthy of note
in a study of the art and mind of Dickens... his gruesome
account of the torture chamber at Avignon... the account of
the execution of an Italian murderer under the guillotine...
as a De Maupassant or a Zola would have written it... Students
of the literature of the nineteenth century who contrast the
'romanticism' of 1840 with the 'realism' of 1890 may mark
these passages with interest" (pp 119-20).

House 1941: p 27 above. "In nothing was Dickens so much of an
elementary John Bull as in his hatred of Roman Catholicism.
The Pope is the real villain of his Child's History of
England, and Pictures from Italy is full of the most stagey
descriptions of visits to the scenes of inquisitional torture.
Monks in the streets are pitied or smiled at, and the whole
system of the Catholic Church is treated as a cunning
imposture..." (pp 128-9).

Brunner 1959: see below under "Dickens in Italy".

Anon. Drowsy Dickens. TLS 23 Nov 1973. Review of 1973 edn
ed David Paroissien. See above under Anon 1846.

The New Oxford edn has intn Sacheverell Sitwell. Vol incl
American Notes (pp 58-61 above.)

Dombey and Son

Dickens's "outline" for Dombey. In letter to Forster 25 Jul
1846 qu in full in Forster 1872 bk 6 ch 2 and almost in full
in Leacock 1933 pp 137-9, Wall 1970 pp 78-9, and elsewhere.
See Churchill 1974 below.

Anon. Economist 10 Oct 1846. Welcomes return of "this great
painter of English manners" to the "walk of literature in
which he is unrivalled", adding: "There was urgent need to
paint such a man as Dombey". Cf Economist 7 Nov 46 when
2nd no was applauded: "supports the high hopes...which the
first number inspired."

Chambers's Journal 24 Oct 1846. "An excellent first number."

Anon. Athenaeum 31 Oct 1846. Praised particularly chs 5 and
6, latter containing description of Staggs's Gardens as
devastated by "the yet unfinished and unopened Railroad",
symbol of "civilization and improvement". See further below
under "Dickens and the Railway Age".

Jeffrey to Dickens Jan 1847. "Oh, my dear, dear Dickens!
what a No 5 you have now given us. I have so cried and sobb*
over it last night, and again this morning, and felt my hear*
purified by those tears, and blessed and loved you for making
me shed them; and I never can bless and love you enough.
Since the divine Nelly was found dead on her humble couch,
beneath the snow and the ivy, there has been nothing like the
actual dying of that sweet Paul, in the summer sunshine of
that lofty room..."

Thackeray to Lemon Jan 1847. "Thackeray strode into the
Punch office and flinging down his number on Mark Lemon's
desk said 'There's no writing against this, one hasn't an
atom of a chance; it's stupendous.'" (qu Pope-Hennessy 1945
p 272 from Lemon's reminiscences; cf Quiller-Couch p 130.)

Dickens to Forster 10 Feb 1847. "...Paul's death has amazed
Paris. All sorts of people are open-mouthed with admiration
..." (qu Forster 1872 loc cit; see further below under
"Dickens in France".)

Patmore 1847 and Hallam 1847: see below under "Sentiment and
Sentimentality". Reaction to Paul's death in No 5 was not
all approving. The Man in the Moon (Mar 47) publ An Inquest
on the late Master Paul Dombey which expressed a different
opinion from Jeffrey's and Thackeray's.

* more accurately in Collins 1971 p 219.

Dombey and Son, cont.

Nicholson, Renton. Dombey and Daughter: A Moral Fiction. 1847. One of several imitations.

Anon (William Kent). Sun 3 Aug 1847. Expresses attitude remarked on by Forster (below) in regard to the more melodramatic parts of the novel. But Jeffrey thought these parts contained "all the lofty and terrible elements of tragedy... bringing before us the appalling struggles of a proud, scornful and repentant spirit" (cf Wilkie Collins qu above p 46). It was Jeffrey who persuaded Dickens to alter his original intention to make Edith Carker's mistress (cf Bulwer Lytton below under "Great Expectations").

Belinsky 1848: see below under "Dickens in Russia".

Taine 1856: qu Forster below.

Forster 1872-4: p 2 above. "Obvious causes have led to grave under-estimates of this novel. Its first five numbers forced up interest and expectation so high that the rest of necessity fell short; but it is not therefore true of the general conception that thus the wine of it had been drawn and only the lees left... the so-called 'violent change' in the hero has more lately been revived in the notices of Mr Taine, who says that 'it spoils a fine novel'; but... in the apparent alteration no unnaturalness of change was involved and certainly the adoption of it was not a sacrifice to 'public morality'" (bk 6 ch 2). "Of Edith from the first Jeffrey judged more rightly; and when the story was nearly half done expressed his opinion about her, and about the book itself, in language that pleased Dickens for the special reason that at the time this part of the book had seemed to many to have fallen greatly short of the splendour of its opening" (ch 2 further on; cf Jeffrey and Kent above.)

Brougham, John. Captain Cuttle. 1884. Produced New York 1850. One of several stage versions. See Malcolm Morley, Dickensian 1952. Even more popular was the famous ballad (c1850) by Glover and Carpenter, What are the Wild Waves Saying? Cf Leavis 1970 below.

Gissing 1898: p 17 above. Ref Alice Marlow and her part in the story: "...a story sufficiently theatrical; but the dialogue. One fails to understand how Dickens brought himself to pen the language - at great length - he puts into this puppet's mouth. It is doubtful whether one could pick out a single sentence, a single phrase, such as the real Alice Marlow could conceivably have used... The words... would be appropriate to the most stagey of wronged heroines... A figure less life-like will not be found in any novel ever written" (ch 5.)

Dombey and Son, cont.

Swinburne 1902: p 19 above.   "...the story of Dombey has no
plot... The struttingly offensive father and his gushingly
submissive daughter are failures of the first magnitude"
(p 31 1913 edn.)

Chesterton 1907-11: p 20 above.   Noticed a change in artistic
structure compared with the earlier novels (p 114 1933 edn;
see further below under "Bleak House".)

Saintsbury 1916: p 22 above.   "...marks a very important
transition in the handling of scene and personage...his first
attempt at painting actual modern society..." (pp 324-5 1932
edn; cf Chesterton 1907 and Economist 1846 above.)

Santayana 1921: p 23 above.   "He needed to feel, in his writing
that he was carrying the sympathies of every man with him...
He denounced scandals without exposing shams, and conformed
willingly and scrupulously to the proprieties... Mrs Dombey
is not allowed to deceive her husband except by pretending t
deceive him... Dickens could not bear to let Walter Gay turn
out badly, as he had been meant to do, and to break his
uncle's heart as well as the heroine's; he was accordingly
transformed into a stage hero miraculously saved from
shipwreck, and Florence was not allowed to reward the
admirable Toots, as she should have done, with her trembling
hand..." (pp 540-1; cf Sun 1847 above: it was Jeffrey who
persuaded Dickens to change his mind over Edith and probably
Forster was partly responsible for the change over Walter.
In the fictional world of Dickens Toots could no more marry
Florence than Kit Nell, Tom Mary, Smike Kate or John Chivery
Little Dorrit.   Such characters are destined to come off
second-best, like their originals in pantomime and comic
opera.)

Quiller-Couch 1922-5: p 23 above.   Compares Dombey with Bleak
House (p 10).

Leacock 1933: p 4 above.   "...marks...a landmark in Dickens's
life...shows the contrast with the unconscious and planless
composition of Pickwick...leading on to the overplanned and
uninspired work of much of the later books" (pp 137-9; cf
Chesterton and Saintsbury above.) Leacock 1916 (p 22 above)
has Dr Blimber as one of its main Dickensian characters who
come in to explain or exemplify Dickens's artistic methods.

Dombey and Son, cont.

Dent 1933: p 4 above. "The theme of the book was to have been
Pride. It had a moral purpose, as had Martin Chuzzlewit.
Whereas, however, Dickens succeeded magnificently with Mr
Pecksniff, he failed signally with Mr Dombey and still more
so with Edith" (p 338 1935 edn.)

House 1941: p 27 above. "It is dangerous to be too exact, but
it is clear that in the Forties a different style of person
comes on the Dickens scene, and that the scene itself changes...
it is safe to say that in Dombey and Son the new style is so
far developed as to be unmistakable. The people, places and
things become 'modern'..." (pp 136-7; see further below under
"Dickens and the Railway Age"). The "modern" parts of Dombey,
however, are bound up - literally - with a good deal of old-
fashioned melodrama, as Gissing and others have remarked.
It was "old-fashioned" in the Forties - in a different sense
from Paul - and seemed ludicrously so to Gissing in the
Nineties and to Swinburne in the early 1900s.

Brumleigh, T.K. (T.W.Hill). Notes on Dombey and Son.
Dickensian 38-9 1942-3; rp with others in PEL edn 1970 qv.

House, Humphry. The Macabre Dickens. BBC Third Programme
3 Jun 1947; pbd House 1955: p 31 above. "Carker has most
often been regarded as a typical villain out of melodrama...
It is nearer the truth to say that in this scene" - ch 55 -
"Carker shakes off the last suggestion of melodrama and
becomes a figure of immense significance... There is much of
Dickens himself in Mr Carker... His own temptations and
imaginings...were the authentic sources of his great criminal
characters..." (pp 186-9; see further below under "Dickens
and Crime").

Butt, John and Kathleen Tillotson. Dickens at Work on Dombey
and Son. Essays & Studies ns 4 1951.

Tillotson 1954: p 30 above. The novel in relation to the
contemporary background.

Allen 1954: p 30 above. See pp 171-2 PB edn.

Leavis, F.R. Dombey and Son. Sewanee Rev 70 1962; rv Leavis
1970 below. Expresses the critic's sense of "the
inexhaustibly wonderful poetic life" in the language of
Dickens. Cf Churchill 1937-42 qv and see further below
under "Style and Language".

Moynahan, Julian. In Gross 1962: p 7 above.

Axton, W.F. Tonal Unity in Dombey and Son. PMLA 78 1963.

Dombey and Son, cont.

Axton, W.F.   Dombey and Son: From Stereotype to Archetype.
ELH 31 1964.

Stone, Harry.   The Novel as Fairytale: Dombey and Son.   English
Studies 47 1966.

Collins, Philip.   Dombey and Son Then and Now.   Dickensian 63
1967.

Donoghue, Denis.   In NCF Centenary No 1970.

Williams, Raymond.   Intn PEL edn 1970 ed Peter Fairclough.
Emphasizes relation of the novel, and of Dickens's literary
development, to the social conditions of the Forties.   Cf
House and Tillotson above and see further below under
"Development" and "Railway Age".

Wilson, Angus.   In Slater 1970: p 8 above.   "...a dexterously
organized novel that is near to a masterpiece" (p 196).

Williams, Raymond.   In Slater 1970: p 8 above.   "His descripti
...of the dislocation and then the reorganization of life
around the railway, in what had been Staggs's Gardens, is a
fine and deeply worked example of this way of seeing the
effects of a system..." (Dickens and Social Ideas, p 93;
cf Athenaeum 1846.)

Holloway, John.   In Slater 1970: p 8 above.   Discusses symbol
of caged bird in ch 45 (Dickens and the Symbol, pp 56-7; see
further below under "Symbolism" and "Sex in Dickens".)

Lane, Margaret.   In Slater 1970: p 8 above.   "...the fire...is
powerful in all the novels, and particularly so in Dombey,
which concerns a home and a parent-child relationship
notoriously lacking in love.   It is no accident that the
rooms, the meals, the atmosphere of Mr Dombey's house are
cold..." (Dickens on the Hearth, pp 161-2.)

Johnson, Pamela Hansford.   In Slater 1970: p 8 above.   "It is
curious how much at home Dickens is with the wildly passion
nature and how poor at giving it human speech.   There is an
echo of 'Unhand me, sir.'' every time Edith Dombey opens her
mouth.   She is stilted and histrionic in her utterance, a
creature of the stage: a fact which has prevented her from
being fully appreciated.   Yet in herself she is fascinating
not at all an a-sexual creature, such as the Ruth Pinches,
the Rose Maylies, seem to be..." (The Sexual Life in
Dickens's Novels, pp 186-7; see further below under "Sex in
Dickens" and "Dickens and Trollope".)

Leavis 1970: p 36 above.   "The first major novel" (p 1);
observation qualified almost immediately when the authors
speak of "the strong parts" of Dombey (p 12).   There are
"strong parts" of course in Oliver and Chuzzlewit but the
"weak parts" of Dombey are even more obvious and were noticed
by the contemporary reviewers Forster quoted above.   Cf
Churchill 1937-42 or Churchill 1958 for a more balanced view.

Gomme 1971: p 36 above.   Incl studies of "four major novels"
beginning with Dombey.   Cf Leavis 1970 above.

Horsman, Alan (ed).   Clarendon edn Oxford 1974.   Appx B incl
Dickens's notes and plans for the monthly numbers; Appx D
describes the public reading versions which began with The
Story of Little Dombey (1858).   Horsman suggests (intn p xv)
that contrast insisted upon by Forster, Chesterton and others,
in regard to "constructive care at the outset" (Forster bk 6
ch 2) "can easily be exaggerated".

Churchill, R.C.   The Monthly Dickens and the Weekly Dickens.
Written 1974.   Questions Mrs Leavis's observation on "the
first batch of impromptu fiction-writing before Dombey"
(Leavis 1970 p 48) showing how all the novels first pbd in
monthly numbers - incl Dombey - were partly planned, partly
improvised, and that it was only in the comparatively few
novels first pbd in weekly instalments that Dickens kept to
his original intentions without much alteration as he went
along.   Only exceptions to this general rule are the monthly
Pickwick (for obvious reasons) and the weekly Curiosity Shop
which was originally intended to be a short story.

The SC edn has Afterword by Alan Pryce-Jones; the New Oxford
edn has intn H.W.Garrod; for PEL edn see under Williams p 78.

David Copperfield

Dickens to Bulwer Lytton 1849.   "You gratify me more than I can
tell you by what you say about Copperfield, because I hope
myself that some heretofore deficient qualities are there"
(letter qu Forster 1872 bk 6 ch 7).

Mr Brown (W.M.Thackeray).   Recommends Copperfield in his
Letters to a Young Man about Town in Punch 1849.   "How
beautiful it is!"   Cf Thackeray below.

Dickens to Forster 10 Jul 49 ref autobiographical part.   "I
really think I have done it ingeniously, and with a very
complicated interweaving of truth and fiction."

David Copperfield, cont.

Thackeray c1849-50. "Get David Copperfield: by jingo, it's
beautiful; it beats the yellow chap of this month hollow" –
meaning his own Pendennis, then being issued in monthly
parts in a yellow wrapper – "...those inimitable Dickens
touches which make such a great man of him..." (letter qu
Quiller-Couch 1922-5 qv.) See further below under "Dickens
and Thackeray".

Brougham, John. David Copperfield: A Drama. New York Jan 185.
Pbd 1885. One of several stage versions, another being call
Little Emily. See Malcolm Morley, Dickensian 1953, and
further below under "Stage and Platform".

Thackeray 1851: see below under "Dickens and Sterne".

Dickens. Pref 1867 edn. "...like many fond parents, I have
in my heart of hearts a favourite child. And his name is
David Copperfield." Cf letter to Forster 1855: "I can never
open that book as I open any other book"; and letter to
Forster 1860: "I read David Copperfield again the other day,
and was affected by it to a degree you would hardly believe.

Forster 1872-4: p 2 above. "...it can hardly have had a
reader, man or lad, whodid not discover that he was somethin
of a Copperfield himself. Childhood and youth live again fo
all of us in its marvellous boy-experiences" (bk 6 ch 7.)

Collins, Wilkie. "The latter half of Dombey no intelligent
person can have read without astonishment at the badness of
it, and the disappointment that followed lowered the sale
of the next book Copperfield, incomparably superior to Dombe
as it certainly is" (marginal note to Forster 1872-4 qu
Kenneth Robinson, Wilkie Collins, 1974 edn p 235; cf Collins
p 46 above.)

Arnold, Matthew. Nineteenth Century Apr 1881. "What a pleasu
to have the opportunity of praising a work so sound, a work
so rich in merit, as David Copperfield.'... What treasures of
gaiety, invention, life, are in that book.' what alertness
and resource.' what a soul of good nature and kindness
governing the whole.'..." (rp Irish Essays 1882 p 709-10;
see further below under "Dickens and Education".)

Bluhm, R. Autobiographisches in David Copperfield.
Reichenbach 1891.

Swinburne 1902: p 19 above. "...perhaps the greatest gift
bestowed on us by this magnificent and immortal benefactor..
one of the masterpieces to which time can only add a new
charm..." (pp 33-5 1913 edn.)

David Copperfield, cont.

Saintsbury 1916: p 22 above. "...hardly any possibility of
denying that David Copperfield is Dickens's most varied and,
at the same time, most serious and best sustained effort"
(p 327 1932 edn.)

Kafka, Franz. "...Dickens's opulence and great, careless
prodigality, but in consequence passages of awful insipidity
in which he wearily works over effects he has already
achieved. Gives one a barbaric impression because the whole
does not make sense... There is a heartlessness behind his
sentimentally overflowing style..." (Diary 8 Oct 1917 tr Max
Brod qu Wall 1970 pp 257-8; see further below under "Sentiment
and Sentimentality".)

Priestley 1925: see below under "Comedy and Satire".

Woolf, Virginia. David Copperfield. Nation 22 Aug 1925.
"...His sympathies...have strict limitations... They fail him
when he has to treat of the mature emotions - the seduction
of Emily, for example, or the death of Dora; whenever it is
no longer possible to keep moving and creating, but it is
necessary to stand still and search into things and penetrate
to the depths of what is there. Then, indeed, he fails
grotesquely, and the pages in which he describes what in our
convention are the peaks and pinnacles of human life, the
explanation of Mrs Strong, the despair of Mrs Steerforth,
or the anguish of Ham, are of an indescribable unreality..."
(rp The Moment and Other Essays 1947 pp 65-7.)

Cecil 1931-4: qu above p 63.

Dent 1933: p 4 above. "...the climax of his powers..." (p 340
1935 edn; cf Monod 1953 below.)

Graves, Robert (ed). The Real David Copperfield. 1933.
A version with the more sentimental, melodramatic and
"Victorian" passages omitted or abridged. Intn claims to
"sort what is true from what is false". Cf Saintsbury 1916
qu above p 55 and Leavis 1948 qv where a version of Daniel
Deronda was contemplated under title "Gwendolen Harleth"
with the Deronda chs omitted or abridged. There is a case,
too, for a version of Hamlet without the intrusive, rather
"Elizabethan" presence of the Prince of Denmark. But see
Maugham 1948 below.

Leacock 1933: p 4 above. "...the greatest achievement of his
mature life" (p 140). "Of the works of imagination written
in the English language David Copperfield to many people
stands first" (p 151.)

David Copperfield, cont.

Orwell 1939-40: p 26 above; pp 17-18, 20, 30, 32-3, 50 1946 edr

Wilson 1939-41: p 27 above. "...a departure from the series of
his social novels... not one of Dickens's deepest books: it :
something in the nature of a holiday" (pp 38-9 UP edn; cf
Angus Wilson 1970 and Leavis 1970 below.)

House 1941: p 27 above. Class problem in the novel (pp 160-1;
cf Orwell above.)

Hill, T.W. Notes on David Copperfield. Dickensian 39-40 1943-

Mason 1944: see below under "Dickens and the Brontës".

Brown, E.K. David Copperfield. Yale Rev 37 1948.

Maugham, W.Somerset (ed). Abr edn Philadelphia 1948. Pref rp
Ten Novels and Their Authors 1954; PB edn 1969. "Some stude:
of literature...will exclaim that it is a shocking thing to
mutilate a masterpiece, and that it should be read as the
author wrote it. That depends on the masterpiece. I cannot
think that a single page could be omitted from so enchanting
a novel as Pride and Prejudice, or from one so tightly
constructed as Madame Bovary; but that very sensible critic
George Saintsbury wrote that 'there is very little fiction
that will stand concentration and condensation as well as th
of Dickens'. There is nothing reprehensible in cutting. Fe'
plays have ever been produced that were not to their advanta
more or less drastically cut in rehearsal..." (pp 9-10 PB ed
cf Graves 1933 above.)

Dickensian 45 1949. Copperfield Centenary No.

Adrian, Arthur. David Copperfield: A Century of Critical and
Popular Acclaim. MLQ 11 1950.

Oppel, H. Interpretation des David Copperfield. Die Kunst de
Erzählens im Englischen Roman des 19 Jahrhunderts, Bielefeld
1950.

Fielding, K.J. The Making of David Copperfield. Listener 19
Jul 1951.

Monod 1953: p 30 above. "...le sommet de l'oeuvre..." (cf Dent
1933 above.)

Maugham 1954: see Maugham 1948 above. "He was a very great
novelist. He had enormous gifts. He thought David Copperfi
the best of all his books... Dickens's judgment seems to me
correct" (p 147 PB edn; cf Shaw 1939 qu below under Little
Dorrit.)

David Copperfield, cont.

Needham, G.B.   The Undisciplined Heart of David Copperfield.
   NCF 9 1955.

Spilka, M.   David Copperfield as Psychological Fiction.   CQ 1
   1959.

Quirk 1959: see below under "Style and Language".

Priestley 1960: p 33 above.   "...its earlier chapters use a
   highly subjective technique that anticipates much
   characteristic modern fiction" (p 239 PB edn; cf Leavis 1962:
   "I now think that, if any one writer can be said to have
   created the modern novel, it is Dickens" - corrective fn PB
   edn The Great Tradition.)

Marshall, W.H.   The Image of Steerforth and the Structure of
   David Copperfield.   Tennessee Studies in Literature 5 1960.

Kettle, Arnold.   David Copperfield.   REL 2 1961.

Beebe, M.   Ivory Towers and Sacred Founts: The Artist as Hero
   in Fiction.   New York 1964.

Gard, R.   David Copperfield.   EC 15 1965.

Garis 1965: p 34 above.   "When self-knowledge came to Dickens,
   it took a form which has little to do with what we ordinarily
   understand by the term... The fact that Dickens never really
   developed a fictional mode suitable for self-examination
   suggests that what took place within him was not really self-
   examination at all..." (pp 94-5.)

Schilling, B.N.   The Comic Spirit.   Detroit 1965.   Incl chs
   on Mr Micawber.   See further below under "Comedy and Satire".

Kincaid, J.R.   The Structure of David Copperfield.   DS 2 1966.

Oddie, William.   Mr Micawber and the Redefinition of Experience.
   Dickensian 63 1967.

Dabney 1967: p 34 above.

Wilson 1970: p 35 above.   "...this most inner of Dickens's
   novels is the most shallow, the most smoothly running, the
   most complacent - indeed, in the pejorative sense of that
   word, the most Victorian" (cf Graves 1933 and Edmund Wilson
   1939 above and Angus Wilson below.)

David Copperfield, cont.

Wilson, Angus. In Slater 1970: p 8 above. "...surely, for all
its extraordinary, almost revolutionary analysis of childhood
thoughts, the most false of all his major books" (p 209).

Q.D.Leavis in Leavis 1970: p 36 above. Considers the novel as
a serious study of marriage and of "the experience of growing
up in the first half of the nineteenth century" and discusses
its influence upon Tolstoy. See further below under "Dickens
in Russia" and "Dickens and Tolstoy".

The Paris edn 1956 is ed and tr Sylvère Monod; Bateson (p 1
above) recommends Boston 1958 edn ed G.H.Ford; the SC edn has
Afterword by Edgar Johnson; the PEL edn 1966 is ed Trevor
Blount.

Household Words

Dickens. A Preliminary Word. Household Words no 1 30 Mar 1850
"...We aspire to live in the Household affections...of our
readers..." Cf Forster 1872 bk 6 ch 4.

FitzGerald, Percy. Two English Essayists: Lamb and Dickens.
Afternoon Lectures, 1864.

Saintsbury 1916: p 22 above. "...enriched popular literature
with a great deal of good work besides his own... There are
few luckier 'finds' on a wet day in a country house or...a
country inn than a volume of Household Words or All the Year
Round" (p 326 1932 edn; cf TLS 1974 below.)

House 1941: p 27 above.

Grubb, Gerald G. The Editorial Policies of Dickens. PMLA 58
1943.

Buckler, W.E. Dickens's Success with Household Words.
Dickensian 46 1950.

Collins 1961: see below under "Dickens the Journalist".

Stone, Harry. Dickens and the Idea of a Periodical. Western
Humanities Rev 21 1967.

Stone, Harry. Dickens and Composite Writing. DS 3 1967.

Stone, Harry. New Writings by Dickens. Dalhousie Rev 47 1967

84

Lohrli, Anne.   Household Words...List of Contributors...etc.
Toronto 1974.

Anon. TLS 19 Apr 1974. Review of above. "Anyone who has
attempted to read Household Words extensively may well have
echoed the Duke of Wellington's stentorian comment, during the
interval at Dickens's production of Every Man in his Humour:
'I knew this play would be dull, but that it would be so
damnably dull as this I did not suppose.'" (cf Saintsbury
1916 above.)

See further below under "Christmas Stories", "A Child's History
of England", "Hard Times" and "Dickens the Journalist".

Christmas Stories

Forster 1872-4: p 2 above. Bk 9 ch 4 mentions "three sketches
in his happiest vein at which everyone laughed and cried in
the Christmas times of 1862, '3 and '4..." Of the story
Somebody's Luggage Forster writes: "Call it exaggeration,
grotesqueness, or by what hard name you will, laughter will
always intercept any graver criticism."

Swinburne 1902: qu above p 65. On The Wreck of the Golden Mary
(Household Words Xmas 1856). Cf House below.

Quiller-Couch 1922-5: qu above p 65. Agrees with Swinburne
over superiority of Christmas Stories to the Christmas Books.

House 1941: p 27 above. Ch 5 p 131 mentions the hymn — "a pale
and spiritless affair" — in The Wreck of the Golden Mary and
Dickens's subsequent correspondence with a clergyman who had
written to him about it. See Forster bk 11 ch 3 and further
below under "Dickens and Religion".

Wilson, Angus.   In Slater 1970: p 8 above.   See pp 196-7.

The New Oxford Illustrated edn has intn Margaret Lane whose
Dickens on the Hearth (Slater 1970 pp 153-71) is also
generally relevant. Kenneth Robinson, Wilkie Collins (1974
edn p 99) gives details as to Collins's collaboration with
Dickens on Christmas stories like The Wreck of the Golden
Mary to which he contributed two chapters (see also pp 103-18).

A Child's History of England

Chesterton 1913: p 21 above. "It was no disgrace to Homer
   that he had not discovered Britain... or to Dryden that he
   had not discovered the steam-engine... We feel that it <u>is</u>
   a disgrace to a man like Dickens when he makes a blind
   brute and savage out of a man like St Dunstan; it sounds as
   if it were not Dickens talking but Dombey" (OPUS edn pp 69-70

Saintsbury 1916: p 22 above. "...the capital instance of a
   man of genius... going far out of his way to write something
   for which he was... absolutely disqualified" (p 329 1932 edn).

Phelps 1916: qu above p 60.

Leacock 1933: p 4 above. "In some senses... the most notable
   history of England that was ever written... No history book
   ever carried a nobler inspiration" (pp 166-9.)

Shaw 1937: p 26 above. "To educate his children religiously
   and historically he wrote A Child's History... which has not
   even the excuse of being childish, and a paraphrase of the
   gospel biography... He had much better have left the history
   to... Mrs Markham and Goldsmith, and taken into account the
   extraordinary educational value of the Authorized Version
   as a work of literary art... Dickens thought his Little Nell
   style better for his children than the English of King
   James's inspired scribes..." (latter work Shaw refers to was
   The Life of Our Lord: Written Expressly for his Children by
   Charles Dickens, 1849; not intended for pbn but pbd 1934 -
   perhaps from example of The Personal History... of David
   Copperfield... which he never meant to be published on any
   account...)

House 1941: qu above p 73.

Pope-Hennessy 1945: p 4 above. "...this rather deplorable
   production... In its shallow, vituperative judgments it is
   a little reminiscent of Hawthorne's contribution to English
   history for schools (1836)..." (pp 338-9).

Birch, D. A Forgotten Book. Dickensian 51 1955.

The New Oxford Illustrated edn has intn Derek Hudson. See
   p 52 above.

Bleak House

Denman, Lord. Articles in Standard 1853, rp 1853, qu Dickens
1892: p 17 above. The former Chief Justice, who was "an old
friend of Charles Dickens", thought the novel had some of the
author's "old faults in an aggravated form", with "some that
had not appeared before". The story is "artificial", while
"the author's love of low life appears to grow upon him."
Denman thought Dickens too apt to find "the delicacy of
virtuous sentiment in the lowest depths of human
degradation". But Mayhew sometimes found same in real life,
as Churchill 1958 (pp 345-6) and other critics point out.
See further below under "Dickens and Henry Mayhew".

United States Mag Sep 1853: see below under "Dickens and
Bulwer Lytton".

Anon (Henry F.Chorley). Athenaeum 17 Sep 1853. "There is
progress in art to be praised in this book - and there is
progress in exaggeration to be deprecated..." (qu Collins
1971 pp 276-9).

Anon (George Brimley). Spectator 24 Sep 1853; rp Essays 1858.
"...chargeable with, not simply faults, but absolute want of
construction... we must plead guilty to having found it dull
and wearisome as a serial, though certainly not from its
want of cleverness or point... Dickens has never yet
succeeded in catching a tolerable likeness of man or woman
whose lot is cast among the high-born and wealthy... Sir
Leicester Dedlock...with his wife and family circle, are no
exceptions..." (qu Dickens 1892 intn Bleak House p xxvii and
more fully Collins 1971 pp 283-6.)

Anon (C.F.Riggs). Putnam's Monthly Mag New York Nov 1853.
"...in none of his works are the characters more strongly
marked, or the plot more loosely and inartistically
constructed" (qu Dickens 1892; cf Chesterton below.)

Mill, John Stuart. In letter 20 Mar 1854 qu Wall 1970,
Collins 1971, etc. Refers to "that creature Dickens" and
calls Bleak House "much the worst of his things". Mill
objected to Dickens's "vulgar impudence" in ridiculing
"rights of women" in character of Mrs Jellyby.

James 1865: p 14 above. "...Bleak House was forced..."
See further below under "Our Mutual Friend".

Forster 1872: p 2 above. "Nothing is introduced at random,
everything tends to the catastrophe..." (bk 7 ch 1; cf
Chesterton below.)

Ramsay, Dean. Letter to Forster 1872. "We have been reading
Bleak House aloud. Surely it is one of his most powerful and
successful.' What a triumph is Jo.'... To my mind, nothing in
the field of fiction is to be found in English literature
surpassing the death of Jo.'" (qu Forster 1872-4 bk 7 ch 1;
wording slightly different from the original: see House 1965
p xiii.)

Simpson, J.P. Lady Dedlock's Secret. 1874. One of several
stage versions. See Morley, Dickensian 1953.

Gissing 1898: p 17 above. "As a picture of actual life in a
certain small world, Bleak House is his greatest book; from
office-boy to judge, here are all who walk in 'the valley of
the Shadow of the law'... No strain of improbable intrigue ca
threaten the vitality of these dusty figures..." (ch 5.)

Gissing 1899: p 18 above. "Does there, I wonder, exist in all
literature a scene less correspondent with any possibility of
life than that description of Jo's last moments? Dickens
believed in it... Not a line, not a word, is insincere...
we can only mark with regret how the philanthropist in him
so often overcame the artist... His true pathos comes when
he does not particularly try for it and is invariably an
aspect of his humour..." (pp 235-6 1925 edn.) Cf Ramsay abov

Swinburne 1902: p 19 above. "'Esther's Narrative' is as good
as her creator's; and no enthusiasm of praise could overrate
the excellence of them both. For wealth and variety of
character none of the master's works can be said to surpass
and few...to equal it" (pp 35-6 1913 edn.)

Chesterton 1907-11: p 20 above. "...not certainly Dickens's
best book..." - Chesterton had given that honour to David
Copperfield - "...but perhaps it is his best novel",
representing "the highest point of his intellectual
maturity" (p 148 1933 edn). "When we come to Bleak House,
we come to a change in artistic structure" compared to the
early novels, though Chesterton had noticed (p 114) an
earlier change with Dombey. "...no longer a string of
incidents; it is a cycle of incidents. It returns upon
itself; it has recurrent melody and poetic justice; it has
artistic constancy" (p 150). "The artistic unity of the
book, compared to all the author's previous novels, is
satisfying, almost suffocating... The fog of the first
chapter never lifts" (pp 152-3; see further below under
"Moral Artist" and "Symbolism".)

Munro 1908: p 20 above. Theme of childhood in Bleak House.
Cf Gissing above.

Bleak House, cont.

Conrad, Joseph. "...a work of the master for which I have such
an admiration, or rather such an intense and unreasoning
affection, dating from the days of my childhood, that its
very weaknesses are more precious to me than the strength of
other men's work. I have read it innumerable times, both in
Polish and in English" (A Personal Record, 1912; see further
below under "Dickens and Conrad").

Saintsbury 1916: p 22 above. "...there is so much that is
good in the book that one is loth to speak anything but good
of it. But it certainly does show a 'black drop'...of
quarrelling excessively with the world and of over-
emphasizing scenes and characters" (p 329 1932 edn.)

Lubbock 1921: p 23 above. "Stevenson noted how Dickens's way
of dealing with his romantic intrigues was to lead gradually
into them, through well-populated scenes of character and
humour; so that his world is actual, its air familiar, by the
time that his plot begins to thicken. He gives himself an
ample margin in which to make the impression of the kind of
truth he needs, before beginning to concentrate upon the
fabulous action of the climax. Bleak House is a very good
case; the highly coloured climax in that book is approached
with great skill and caution, all in his most masterly style..."
(pp 213-14; see further below under "Dickens and Balzac" and
"Dickens and Thackeray".)

Shaw, Bernard. "Like Esther Summerson, she (Mark Twain's Joan)
makes her creator ridiculous..." (Pref Saint Joan dated May
1924: Standard edn 1932 p 26; cf Swinburne 1902 above.)

Forster 1927: p 24 above. "Logically, Bleak House is all to
pieces, but Dickens bounces us, sothat we do not mind the
shiftings of the view-point" (pp 86-7 PB edn). Forster goes
on to compare it in this way with Gide's Faux Monnayeurs.
See too Lubbock 1921 above, qu Forster p 85.

Eliot 1927: p 24 above. "Dickens's 'best novel' is probably
Bleak House: that is Mr Chesterton's opinion, and there is
no better critic of Dickens living than Mr Chesterton...
Bleak House is Dickens's finest piece of construction..."
(pp 423-4 1934 edn; cf Chesterton 1907 above and see further
below under "Dickens and Wilkie Collins".)

Darwin 1933: p 4 above. "From the moment that we begin with
the Court of Chancery in a fog, Chancery gets its grip on
the story and never relaxes it" (cf Chesterton above.)

Wickhardt 1933: p 25 above. Cf Lubbock 1921 and Forster 1927.

Leacock 1933: p 4 above. In "no other book" by Dickens
  "is there such majestic treatment of a theme, such a complete
  fusion of the story of the book with its theme and purpose...
  The theme has all the majesty and inevitability of Greek
  tragedy... It is a great book" (pp 158-9.)

Churchill 1937-42: "... Bleak House, praised by Chesterton and
  undoubtedly one of Dickens's best, gives us the excellent
  comedy of Chadband and Guppy and the Snagsbys, the skilful
  melodrama of Chesney Wold, the satire on Chancery, the
  impressive delineation of London; but there is also the
  sillier side of the Dedlock story and the pathetic figure
  of the consumptive crossing-sweeper, who might have been
  presented with success had not so many tears fallen on the
  writer's manuscript ('Jo, is it thou?')..." (p 361; cf
  Gissing above and Churchill 1958 below.)

Wilson 1939-41: p 27 above. "...the masterpiece of this
  middle period..." (pp 32-8 UP edn; cf Leacock above.)

House 1941: p 27 above. See pp 30-3, 87-90, 193-4. "The
  Jellyby episode in Bleak House is an excellent example of the
  strength and the weakness of Dickens's use of fiction as a
  medium of social criticism..." (p 87; see further below
  under "Radical and Reformer".)

Hill, T.W. Notes on Bleak House. Dickensian 40 1944.

Liddell 1947: p 28 above. "If, in Bleak House, it rains in
  Lincolnshire, it is because it rains in the heart of Lady
  Dedlock..." (pp 115-16; see further below under "Symbolism".)

Allen 1954: p 30 above. "...all the Chancery parts of the book
  seem to be shrouded in fog. The first chapter...establishes
  the mood of the whole..." (p 172 PB edn; cf Chesterton and
  Darwin above.)

Craig 1956: see below under "Dickens and the Brontës".

Grenander, M.E. The Mystery and the Moral: Point of View
  in Bleak House. NCF 10 1956. Cf Forster 1927 above.

Butt and Tillotson 1957: p 31 above.

Zabel 1957: p 31 above. See also his intn Boston edn 1956.

Crompton, L. Satire and Symbolism in Bleak House. NCF 12
  1958. Cf Chesterton and Liddell above and see further below
  under "Symbolism" and "Comedy and Satire".

Bleak House, cont.

Ford, George H. Self-Help and the Helpless in Bleak House.
In symposium From Jane Austen to Joseph Conrad ed R.C.
Rathburn and M.Steinmann, Minneapolis 1958.

Churchill 1958: p 32 above under Boris Ford. "Never before
had Dickens commanded so surely such a wide range..." (p 134).
"The portrait of Skimpole is one of the best things in
Dickens..." (pp 134-6). Cf Churchill 1937 above.

Butt, John. Bleak House Once More. CQ 1 1959.

Cox, C.B. A Dickens Landscape. CQ 2 1960.

Krieger, M. The Tragic Vision. Chicago 1960.

Deen, L.W. Style and Unity in Bleak House. Criticism 3 1961.

Donovan, R.A. Structure and Idea in Bleak House. ELH 29 1962.

Harvey, W.J. Chance and Design in Bleak House. In Gross
1962: p 7 above. See Harvey 1965 below.

Harvey, W.J. Character and the Novel. 1965. Incl rv above.
"Bleak House is for Dickens a unique and elaborate experiment
in narration and plot composition... Indeed, the narrative
method seems to me to be part of the very substance of
Bleak House, expressive of what, in the widest and deepest
sense, the novelis about..." (pp 90-92.)

Garis 1965: p 34 above. "... Dickens's purpose in Bleak House
is to demonstrate that the whole world is penetrated, stifled
and terrorized by a huge network of interconnecting systems:
the structure of the novel embodies this vision by offering
a satisfyingly large number of examples of systematized
characters, and by contriving many and pointed interrelations
between them..." (pp 98-9).

Blount, Trevor. Dickens's Slum Satire in Bleak House. MLR 60
1965.

Blount, Trevor. The Importance of Place in Bleak House.
Dickensian 61 1965

Blount, Trevor. Chancery as Evil and Challenge. DS 1 1965.

Fradin, J.I. Will and Society in Bleak House. PMLA 81 1966.

Wilkinson, A.Y. Bleak House: From Faraday to Judgment Day.
ELH 34 1967.

Bleak House, cont.

Dyson, A.E.(ed). Dickens: Bleak House. Casebook series 1969.
  Incl extracts from Engels on the London poor and article from
  Household Words on The Martyrs of Chancery, besides selections
  from contemporary reviews and some modern comments by Edgar
  Johnson, J.Hillis Miller, W.J.Harvey ao.

Dyson 1970: p 35 above. Considers Esther Summerson "perhaps
  Dickens's greatest study of virtue".

Q.D.Leavis 1970: p 36 above. Defends Bleak House which "has
  been so generally accepted as a characteristically muddled
  piece of indignation" (p 123). But when Mrs Leavis was
  disparaging most of Dickens's novels, including Bleak House
  (qu above p 25), Leacock (qu above p 90) was giving it the
  greatest possible praise. See too praise by Swinburne,
  Chesterton, Eliot, Wilson ao qu above pp 88-91.

Hardy, Barbara. In Slater 1970: p 8 above. See pp 33-7, 44-7.

Fielding, K.J. and A.W.Brice. Bleak House and the Graveyard.
  DSA 1 1971.

Gomme 1971: p 36 above. Discusses Dickens's "forced symbolism"
  "...the whole symbolic apparatus of Bleak House is attached
  to the narrative by factitious contrivance..." See further
  below under "Symbolism".

Koichi Miyazaki. A Study of Two of Dickens's Later Novels.
  Seijo English Monographs 7, Tokyo 1971. Bleak House and
  Hard Times briefly discussed for Japanese students.

Quirk, Eugene F. Tulkinghorn's Buried Life: A Study of
  Character in Bleak House. JEGP Oct 1973.

Rabkin, Eric S. The Comedy and the Melodrama. Narrative
  Suspense, Ann Arbor Mich 1973.

Reinhold, Heinz. Charles Dickens: Bleak House. In Der
  englische Roman im 19 Jahrhundert: Interpretationen, ed
  Paul Goetsch ao, Berlin 1973.

Churchill, R.C. Chesterton on Dickens: The Legend and the
  Reality. DSN 5 Jun 1974. Discusses Chesterton's pioneer
  criticism of Bleak House in relation to later critical
  opinion (pp 34-6). Cf Sylvère Monod, Confessions of an
  Unrepentant Chestertonian, DSA 3 1974.

The New Oxford edn has intn Osbert Sitwell; the SC edn has
  afterword Geoffrey Tillotson; the PEL edn, ed Norman Page,
  has intn J.Hillis Miller.

Hard Times

Anon (John Forster). Examiner 9 Sep 1854. Cf Forster 1872
bk 7 ch 1: "It was the first story written by him for his
weekly periodical; and in the course of it the old troubles
of the Clock came back, with the difference that the greater
brevity of the weekly portions made it easier to write them
up to time, but much more difficult to get sufficient interest
into each... He went on, however, and of the two designs he
started with, accomplished one very perfectly and the other
at least partially. He more than doubled the circulation of
his journal; and he wrote a story which, though not among his
best, contains things as characteristic as any he has written"
(cf later criticism below, which in general agrees with
Forster that Dickens succeeded in his moral design - see
letter to Knight below - but comparatively failed in his
social or political.)

Cooper, F.F. Hard Times: A Domestic Drama. 1854; rp 1886.
One of several stage versions. See Malcolm Morley, Hard Times
on the Stage, Dickensian 50 1954.

Macaulay 1854. See below under Orwell 1939 and House 1941.

Dickens to Charles Knight 30 Jan 1855. "My satire is against
those who see figures and averages and nothing else - the
representatives of the wickedest and most enormous vice of
this time..." (letter qu Wall 1970 p 96.)

Hodgson, W.B. On the Importance of the Study of Economic
Science. Lectures on Education, 1855. Cf Ruskin below.

Anon (Mrs Oliphant). Blackwood's Mag Apr 1855. Complained of
"the petulant theory of a man in a world of his own making,
where he has no fear of being contradicted and is absolutely
certain of having his own way..." But the novel was dedicated
to Carlyle and is obviously written very much under his
influence. See Oddie 1973 below.

Taine 1856: p 13 above. "...He contrasts the souls which
nature creates with those which society deforms. One of his
last novels, Hard Times, is an abstract of all the rest. He
there exalts instinct above reason, intuition of heart above
positive knowledge; he attacks education built on statistics,
figures and facts... He seeks out poor artisans, mountebanks,
a foundling, and crushes beneath their common sense,
generosity, delicacy, courage and gentleness, the false
science, false happiness and false virtue of the rich and
powerful who despise them..."

Yates, E.H. and R.B.Brough. Hard Times (refinished) by Charles
Diggins. Parody incl in Our Miscellany, 1857.

Ruskin 1860-2: p 13 above.   "...to my mind, in several respects
   the greatest he has written..." but its "usefulness...
   seriously diminished because Mr Bounderby is a dramatic
   monster, instead of a characteristic example of a worldly
   master; and Stephen Blackpool a dramatic perfection, instead
   of a characteristic example of an honest workman.   But let us
   not lose the use of Dickens's wit and insight, because he
   chooses to speak in a circle of stage fire.   He is entirely
   right in his main drift and purpose in every book he has
   written..." (p 26n WC edn 1911; see further below under
   "Drama and Melodrama" and "Radical and Reformer".)

Ludwig, Otto.   "Dickens is truly a poet, and a great one.
   Always action and feeling, never abstract reflection.   Fantasy
   is the basis of his poetry as of all true poetry, the other
   faculties that serve fantasy are completely transformed into
   it... One of his principal arts is that of dialogue... It mus[t]
   be said of Boz as of Shakespeare that he entertains the reade[r]
   not merely by his works, but also in them..." (note on Hard
   Times, c1860, qu Wall 1970 p 153; see further below under
   "Style and Language".)

Ruskin 1870: see below under "Dickens and the Railway Age".

Forster 1872-4: see above under Forster 1854.

Martineau, Harriet.   "...his vigorous erroneousness about
   matters of science as shown in Oliver Twist about the new
   poor-law (which he confounds with the abrogated old one) and
   in Hard Times, about the controversies of employers.   Nobody
   wants to make Mr Dickens a political economist; but there are
   many who wish that he would abstain from a set of difficult
   subjects, on which all true sentiment must be underlain by a
   sort of knowledge which he has not.   The more fervent and
   inexhaustible his kindliness... the more important it is that
   it should be well-informed and well-directed..." (Autobiogra[phy]
   1877 qu Wall 1970 pp 209-10; cf House 1941.)

Swinburne 1902: p 19 above.   Incl Hard Times among "the author['s]
   very ripest and thoughtfulest work" (p 9 1913 edn) and remar[ks]
   (p 42) that "Mrs Sparsit is as typical and immortal as any
   figure of Molière's."

Anon (John Buchan?).   "The story of Sissy Jupe, the Gradgrinds
   and Mr Bounderby was one of the most popular of Dickens's
   later works.   That popularity shows no sign of waning"
   (advert for Nelson Classics edn c1907; Leacock p 173 and
   Pearson p 211 confirm Forster above that Hard Times doubled
   circulation of Household Words – a fact Buchan may have been
   thinking of – but any Dickens serial might have had similar
   effect.)

Hard Times, cont.

Chesterton 1907-11: p 20 above. Points out that there was one
  Englishman in the nineteenth century who kept his head among
  all the social changes of early Victorian times, while "the
  men who lost their heads" - Spencer, Bentham, Bright, Mill -
  "lost highly scientific and philosophical heads" (p 174 1933
  edn.) Dickens in Hard Times "did this work" of the
  sociologist "much more genuinely than...Carlyle or Ruskin."
  Dickens "protested against the commercial oppression...
  because it was not only an oppression but a depression...
  Hard Times may be bitter, but it was a protest against
  bitterness. It may be dark, but it is the darkness of the
  subject and not of the author. He is...dealing with hard
  times, but not with a hard eternity, not with a hard
  philosophy of the universe..." (p 176; cf Chesterton on
  Oliver Twist qu above p 46.)

Stumpf, W. Der Dickensche Roman Hard Times: seine Entstehung
  und seine Tendenzen. Freienwalde 1910.

Shaw, Bernard. "...such masterpieces as Hard Times, Little
  Dorrit, Our Mutual Friend...their mercilessly faithful and
  penetrating exposures of English social, industrial and
  political life... The Old Curiosity Shop was written to amuse
  you, entertain you, touch you; and it succeeded. Hard Times
  was written to make you uncomfortable...." (intn 1912 edn.)

Saintsbury 1916: p 22 above. "The book has had its admirers...
  There is certainly genuine pathos...in the Stephen and Rachel
  part, while...Louisa...is more of a real live girl of the
  nineteenth century than Dickens ever achieved, except in the
  more shadowy sketch of Estella... But these good things....
  are buried in such a mass of exaggeration and false drawing
  that one struggles with the book as with a bad dream... It is
  difficult...not to put it lowest among Dickens's finished
  novels" (pp 329-30 1932 edn.)

Dent 1933: p 4 above. "This story was published in Household
  Words to stimulate the circulation. It succeeded: it more
  than doubled it. It is difficult to know why... Mr Gradgrind
  ...and Mr Bounderby...are...third-rate stagy villains... The
  only really Dickensian part...is the account of Sleary's
  circus" (p 393 1935 edn.)

Leacock 1933: p 4 above. "...half story, half sermon... A large
  part of the book is mere trash...the humour is forced...the
  pathos verges on the maudlin" (pp 169-71.)

Jackson 1937: p 26 above. Criticizes Dickens's attitude towards
  Slackbridge and the trade unions. Cf Orwell below.

Hard Times, cont.

Shaw 1937: p 26 above. "...that immensely broadened outlook and knowledge of the world which began with Hard Times and Little Dorrit, and left all his earlier works behind..."

Churchill 1937-42: p 26 above. "...of perhaps almost equal interest to the historian and the literary critic...that impressive production Hard Times" (p 372) "...his most impressive statement of the problems of poverty..." (p 374.)

Orwell 1939-40: p 26 above. "It is said that Macaulay refused to review Hard Times because he disapproved of its 'sullen Socialism'*... There is not a line in the book that can properly be called Socialistic; indeed, its tendency if anything is pro-capitalist... Bounderby is a bullying windbag and Gradgrind has been morally blinded, but if they were better men, the system would work well enough - that, al through, is the implication..." (p 10 1946 edn.) "...he displays no consciousness that the **structure** of society can be changed. He despises politics...and he is slightly hostile to the most hopeful movement of his day, trade unionism. In Hard Times trade unionism is represented as something not much better than a racket... Stephen Blackpool' refusal to join the union is rather a virtue in Dickens's eyes..." (pp 12-13.) See further below under "Radical and Reformer."

House 1941: p 27 above. "Discussion of the book has often centred too much on Macaulay's condemnation of it as 'sullen socialism', and the almost exaggerated praise that Ruskin gav it in Unto This Last; for it is the least read of the novels and probably also the least enjoyed by those who read it. Even Mr Edwin Pugh called it 'dry', 'hard' and 'the least alluring' of them all..." (pp 203-11). Ref is to Pugh, Dickens: The Apostle of the People, 1908; but House ignored Swinburne 1902, Chesterton 1907, Shaw 1912.

Leavis, F.R. The Novel as Drmatic Poem: (1) Hard Times. Scrutiny 14 1947; rp as appx Leavis 1948; rv Leavis 1970. The best modern criticism of Hard Times, only marred by inaccuracy of opening para. "If there exists anywhere an appreciation, or even an acclaiming reference, I have missed it" (p 249 PB edn 1962; p 187 Leavis 1970). "Missed" in fac (or ignored?) Churchill 1937-42 qu above, as well as Ruskin, Swinburne, Chesterton, Shaw qu above pp 94-5. See Churchill 1974 - p 92 above - for further discussion of Leavis on Hard Times in relation to earlier criticism particularly Chestert in the Everyman prefaces (pp 36-8) and connection of Hard Times with Oliver Twist. See also below under Leavis 1948 and Waldock 1948.

* Macaulay's actual words are qu Collins 1971 p 300.

Hard Times, cont.

Leavis 1948: p 29 above. "I can think of only one of his books
in which his distinctive creative genius is controlled
throughout to a unifying and organizing signifance, and that
is Hard Times" (p 29 in PB edn). "...there is only one
Hard Times in the Dickensian oeuvre" (p 30). "...the
greatness of Hard Times passed unnoticed..." (p 30). See
comment under Leavis 1947 above.

Waldock, A.J.A. The Status of Hard Times. Southerly 9 1948.
Criticizes view of Leavis above. See also D.H.Hirsch,
Criticism 6 1964.

Hill, T.W. Notes on Hard Times. Dickensian 48 1952.

Fielding, K.J. Dickens and the Department of Practical Art.
MLR 18 1953.

Boulton, J.T. Charles Knight and Hard Times. Dickensian 50
1954. Cf Dickens 1855 above.

Fielding, K.J. Mill and Gradgrind. NCF 11 1957. Relation
between Mill's education, as testified in his Autobiography,
and education of Gradgrind children. Cf G.D.Klingopulos,
PGEL 6 pp 35-6, and further under "Dickens and Education"
below.

Churchill 1958: p 32 above under Ford. "...a masterpiece of a
minor order - a novel of the stature of Silas Marner rather
than of Middlemarch... A Dickens who had written only Hard
Times would not be the great novelist he so evidently is"
(p 123; cf Churchill 1937-42 qu above and Churchill 1953
p xviii.)

Williams, Raymond. "...more a symptom of the confusion of
industrial society than understanding of it, but...a symptom
...significant and continuing" (Culture and Society, 1958;
pp 104-8 in PB edn.)

Crockett, J. Theme and Metaphor in Hard Times. Spectrum 6 1962.

Holloway, John. In Gross 1962: p 7 above. Atkinson below is
useful comparison.

Atkinson, F.G. Hard Times: Themes and Motifs. Use of English
14 1963. Cf Crockett and Holloway above.

Carnall, G.D. Dickens, Mrs Gaskell and the Preston Strike.
Victorian Studies 8 1964. Cf House 1941 and see further
below under "Dickens and Mrs Gaskell".

Garis 1965: p 34 above. "Hard Times is a logical refutation of the Utilitarian definition of human nature and of the Utilitarian mechanics for the production of human happiness: the structure of this novel is accordingly that of a 'moral fable' (to use Dr Leavis's term), a pointed cautionary tale.. In neither" Bleak House nor Hard Times "is the success of the whole structure damaged by the generally recognized failure o individual elements: an experienced habitué of the Dickens theatre can casually reject the sentimentalities connected with Esther Summerson and Stephen Blackpool without believing that this rejection in the least endangers the success of the books as wholes" (pp 97-8; cf Leavis 1947 above.)

Lodge, David. The Rhetoric of Hard Times. The Language of Fiction, 1966. See further below under "Style and Language".

Ford, George H. and Sylvère Monod (ed). Hard Times: An Authoritative Text; Backgrounds, Sources, etc. New York 1966 Incl selections from contemporary reviews and later comments by Shaw, Leavis, Holloway ao.

Slater 1970: p 8 above. Comments by Walter Allen (pp 4-5), Barbara Hardy (pp 47-51), Raymond Williams (pp 83-92) and Michael Slater (pp 114-15).

Koichi Miyazaki 1971: p 92 above. Ch on Hard Times is sub-titled "A Fairy Tale Interspersed with Realistic Elements". See review by Maurice McCullen DSN Jun 1974 pp 44-5.

Meckier, Jerome. Dickens and the Dystopian Novel. In The Nov and its Changing Form, ed R.G.Collins, Winnipeg 1972. "What Dickens wrote, one can see in retrospect, was not an allegor fable, or fairy tale, but a seminal dystopia in which he expressed his fear that the Industrial Revolution was having adverse effects on the national character and on human natur generally. With its title as a value judgement on its own era and the years to come, Hard Times was Dickens's Brave Ne World..." The novel anticipates not only Huxley but Wells and Lawrence, allowing them to "state the values" of their societies "in dramatic form". See review by McCullen DSN 5 pp 47-8 and further below under "Dickens and Wells" and "Dickens and Lawrence".

Oddie, William. Dickens and Carlyle: The Question of Influenc 1973.

Craig, David. Hard Times and the Condition of England. The Real Foundations: Literature and Social Change, Oxford 1974.

Sloane, David E.   Phrenology in Hard Times: A Source for Bitzer.
DSN Mar 1974.

Bateson (p 1 above) recommends New York edn 1958 ed W.W.Watt;
the New Oxford edn has intn Dingle Foot; the SC edn has
afterword by Charles Shapiro; the PEL edn is ed David Craig.

Little Dorrit

Dickens to Forster 19 Aug 1855.   "As to the story, I am in the
second number, and last night and this morning had half a
mind to begin again, and work in what I have done, afterwards"
(letter qu Forster 1872 bk 8 ch 1.)

Dickens to Forster 16 Sep 1855.   "I am just now getting to work
on number three... There is an enormous outlay in the Father
of the Marshalsea chapter, in the way of getting a great lot
of matter into a small space.   I am not quite resolved, but
I have a great idea of overwhelming that family with wealth.
Their condition would be very curious.   I can make Dorrit very
strong in the story, I hope" (letter qu Forster as above.)

Dickens to Forster 30 Jan 1856.   "...Society, the Circumlocution
Office, and Mr Gowan, are of course three parts of one idea or
design..." (ibid).

Dickens to Forster 7 Apr 1856.   "...I approach number ten,
where I have finally resolved to make Dorrit rich.   It should
be a very fine point in the story..." (ibid.   Accordingly the
book-version 1857 was divided into "Book the First – Poverty"
and "Book the Second – Riches", the second main alteration,
the first having been the change of title from Nobody's Fault
to Little Dorrit, the change being delayed "to the eve of its
publication".)

Cooper, F.F.   Little Dorrit.   Nov 1856.   One of several stage
versions.   See Morley, Dickensian 1954.

Andersen, Hans.   Letter to Dickens 1857.   "I would and must
admire you for the sake of this one book alone even if you had
not previously bestowed upon the world those splendid
compositions David Copperfield, Little Nelly, and the rest..."
(qu Pope-Hennessy 1945 pp 382-3.)

Anon (E.B.Hamley).   Blackwood's Mag Apr 1857.   One of several
extremely critical reviews.   Cf Stephen below.

Stephen 1857: p 13 above. "...not one of the most pleasing
or interesting of Mr Dickens's novels. The plot is
singularly cumbrous and confused...the style often strained
to excess. We are not however tempted, by the comparative
inferiority of this production of a great novelist, to
forget the indisputable merits of Mr Dickens... a spirit of
tenderness and humanity which does honour to his heart.
We wish he had dealt as fairly and kindly with the upper
classes of society as he has with the lower... it is to be
regretted that he should have mistaken a Lord Decimus for
the type of an English statesman or Mr Tite Barnacle for a
fair specimen of a public servant... His injustice to the
institutions of English society is...even more flagrant..."
(qu Dickens 1892, House 1941, Snow 1970, Wall 1970, Collins
1971, etc. See further below.)

Dickens 1857: p 13 above under Stephen. Dickens's reply qu
Dickens 1892, House 1941, Snow 1970, Wall 1970.

Hollingshead 1857: p 13 above. An imaginary dialogue between
Hylas and Philonous about "the reception of Little Dorrit".
Hylas observes that some critics "attempt to pull down the
idol more for political than for literary reasons". He
concludes with a picture of Dickens "far from the din of
the critical Babel, surrounded by...the children of his pen
...a fit companion for that low player of the olden time
who wrote King Lear and acted at the Globe" (qu Collins
1971 pp 375-7.)

Ludwig, Otto. "Like many of Dickens's other novels, Little
Dorrit is a comic-horrific fairytale, in the manner of the
Thousand and One Nights... Boz's poetry is popular
romanticism, a synthesis of Tieck, Jean Paul, Hoffmann...
Shakespeare's grimacing mask returned to the land of its
fair original..." (note on Little Dorrit c1860 qu Wall 1970
pp 153-4.)

James 1865: p 14 above. "...Little Dorrit was laboured..."

Anon (G.Fraser). Saturday Rev 11 Jun 1870. "With the
single exception of Little Dorrit, there is not one of his
numerous stories that has not touches of the master-hand
and strokes of indisputable genius" (qu Dickens 1892).

Anon. Two English Novelists: Dickens and Thackeray. Dublin
Rev Apr 1871. "Little Dorrit and Our Mutual Friend are the
only two books which leave no impression of humour upon the
reader's mind, which present him with nothing but
caricature" (qu Dickens 1892.)

Little Dorrit, cont.

Dickens 1892: p 17 above. Intn Little Dorrit discusses
Stephen 1857, Dickens 1857 and other criticisms and replies.

Shaw, Bernard. "Mrs Dudgeon is a variation on Dickens's Mrs
Clennam" (discussing The Devil's Disciple 1897; qu Hesketh
Pearson, Bernard Shaw, p 208; see further below under
"Dickens and Shaw".)

Gissing 1898: p 17 above. "...some of Dickens's finest work,
some passages in which he attains an artistic finish hardly
found elsewhere" (p 52 1924 edn). "...a competent judge...
will find in it some of the best work Dickens ever did; and
especially in this matter of characterization; pictures so
wholly admirable...that he is tempted to call Little Dorrit
the best book of all..." (pp 80-1; see further below under
"Characters".)

Swinburne 1902: p 19 above. "...the unsurpassable excellence
of the finest passages and chapters...comparable only with the
kindred work of such creators as the authors of Les Misérables
and King Lear" (pp 45-6 1913 edn.)

Chesterton 1906: p 20 above. "The best of his work can be
found in the worst of his works. The Tale of Two Cities is a
good novel; Little Dorrit is not a good novel. But the
description of The Circumlocution Office in Little Dorrit is
quite as good as the description of Tellson's Bank in The
Tale of Two Cities" (pp 169-70).

Shaw, Bernard. Dickens and Little Dorrit. Dickensian 4 1908.

Shaw, Bernard. "...remains the most accurate and penetrating
study of the genteel littleness of our class governments in
the English language" (pref The Shewing-Up of Blanco Posnet
dated 14 Jul 1910; Standard edn 1932 p 356.)

Shaw 1912: qu above p 95. "...such masterpieces as...Little
Dorrit..."

Quiller-Couch 1922-5: p 23 above. "...his most undeservedly
misprized book..." (p 31). Ref close of ch 35: "the true
novelist's stroke; rightly divined..." (pp 88-9.)

Leacock 1933: p 4 above. "... Nor is there any more
marvellous depiction of character in all fiction than that
of Edward Dorrit" (p 191.)

Powys, John Cowper. "I can recall sitting on a bench in the
autumn, in some public park at Southampton, absolutely
absorbed in a trance of delight in Little Dorrit..."
(Autobiography 1934 p 308.)

Little Dorrit, cont.

Shaw 1937: p 26 above. "...Even in Little Dorrit, Dickens's masterpiece among many masterpieces... Dickens's sense of fun ran away with him... If we have absolutely no fun in us we may even state gravely that there has been a lapse from the artistic integrity of the tragic picture of English society which is the subject of the book... Little Dorrit is a more seditious book than Das Kapital... And yet Dickens never saw himself as a revolutionist..." (cf Orwell 1939).

Churchill 1937-42: p 26 above. "...Oliver Twist, Martin Chuzzlewit, Bleak House, Little Dorrit, give us a Dickens whose criticism of society is part and parcel of his skill and virtue as a novelist..." (p 372; same point was made in Churchill's review of House 1941, Scrutiny 10 pp 304-7.)

Shaw, Bernard. Letter to Hesketh Pearson 4 Sep 1939. "Dickens had a birthday book preference for David Copperfield because he had put certain experiences of his own into it; but he knew quite well that Great Expectations was a better book and Little Dorrit a bigger one" (qu Pearson op cit p 439.)

Orwell 1939-40: p 26 above; pp 39-40 1946 edn.

Wilson 1939-41: p 27 above; pp 46-53 UP edn.

House 1941: p 27 above. "It was, of course, the Crimean campaign that made the Circumlocution Office parts of Little Dorrit peculiarly topical, and they were substantially fair.. (pp 187-90; cf Stephen 1857, Shaw 1937, Snow 1970 qqv.)

Hill, T.W. Notes on Little Dorrit. Dickensian 41-2 1945-6.

Burn, W.L. The Neo-Barnacles. Nineteenth Century Feb 1948.

Pearson 1949: p 4 above. Mr Dorrit "the most subtly conceived character in Dickens's work, and the one leading figure in all his novels which was not only sustained with brilliance of execution but developed throughout with absolute fidelity to nature" (cf Leacock above.)

Lindsay 1950: p 5 above. Discusses Circumlocution Office as exposure of Victorian capitalist administration. Cf Shaw and Snow qqv.

Trilling, Lionel. Little Dorrit. Kenyon Rev 15 1953. See Trilling below.

Trilling, Lionel. "With a body of works as large and as
enduring as that of Dickens, taste and opinion will never
be done. They will shift and veer as they have...with...
Shakespeare, and each generation will have its special
favourites... Little Dorrit, one of the most profound of
Dickens's novels and one of the most significant works of
the nineteenth century, will not fail to be thought of as
speaking with a peculiar and passionate intimacy to our own
time..." (intn New Oxford edn 1953).

Churchill 1958: p 32 above under Ford; pp 137-40.

Butt, John. The Topicality of Little Dorrit. UTQ 29 1959.
Cf Trilling above.

Sherif, N. The Victorian Sunday in Little Dorrit and Thyrza.
Cairo Studies in English 1960. Cf Churchill 1958 pp 123-4
and see further below under "Dickens and Gissing".

McMaster, R.D. Little Dorrit: Experience and Design.
Queen's Quarterly 1961.

Wain, John. In Gross 1962: p 7 above.

Jump, J.D. Clennam at the Circumlocution Office. Critical
Survey 1 1963.

Wilde, A. Mr F's Aunt and the Analogical Structure of
Little Dorrit. NCF 19 1965.

Bell, V.M. Mrs General as Victorian England. NCF 20 1966.

Hewitt, D. An Embarrassment of Symbolic Riches. London Rev
1 1966.

Reid, J.C. Dickens: Little Dorrit. 1967.

Meckier, Jerome. Sundry Curious Variations on the Same Tune.
DS 3 1967.

Holloway, John. Intn PEL edn 1968.

Hodgart, Matthew. Satire. World University Library, 1969.
In Little Dorrit Dickens "uses the device of reduction
with extreme force..." (p 230.)

Little Dorrit, cont.

Fielding, K.J. and Anne Smith.   In NCF centenary no.   1970.

Snow, C.P.   Dickens and the Public Service.   In Slater 1970:
p 8 above.   Discusses Circumlocution Office with detailed ref
contemporary Civil Service practice.   Critical view of aspect
of "one of the best novels in the language" (p 127).   Cf
Stephen above.

Lucas 1970: p 36 above.   "Dickens's greatest novel" (p 287).
Cf Gissing, Swinburne, Shaw above.

Leavis 1970: p 36 above.   "...the art in general of Little
Dorrit is more complex in its subtlety than that of Hard
Times" (p 247; cf Leavis 1948 qu above p 97.)

Hobsbaum 1972: p 8 above.   Little Dorrit seen as the culminatic
of the "infantile syndrome of Dickens's humble origins,
childhood illness, detention in the blacking factory,
irresponsible parents..." (cf Wilson 1939 above) "...the
great poet of claustrophobia has refined the tradition in
which he works until all that is recognisably left of it is
the passive hero enclosed by a situation he is unable to
alter..."

Roopnaraine, R.Rupert.   Time and the Circle in Little Dorrit.
DSA 3 1974.

Easson, Angus.   Marshalsea Prisoners: Mr Dorrit and Mr Hemens.
DSA 3 1974.

Tick, Stanley.   The Sad End of Mr Meagles.   DSA 3 1974.

All the Year Round

Forster 1872: p 2 above.   Bk 8 ch 5.   Discusses relation to
and difference from Household Words.

Tinsley, William.   Random Recollections of an Old Publisher.
Qu Robinson, Wilkie Collins, pp 197-8.   "The Moonstone and
The Woman in White were two of the very few exceptions of the
many serials in All the Year Round which increased the
circulation to any great extent.   The Moonstone perhaps did
more for it than any other novel, not excepting Great
Expectations..."   See further below under "Dickens and
Wilkie Collins".

Saintsbury 1916: qu above p 84.

House 1941: p 27 above.

Grubb 1943: qu above p 84.

Collins 1961: see below under "Dickens the Journalist".

Stone 1967: p 84 above.

Thomas, Deborah A. In Dickensian Jan 1974.

See further under "Christmas Stories", "A Tale of Two Cities",
  "Great Expectations", "The Uncommercial Traveller" and
  "George Silverman's Explanation".

A Tale of Two Cities

Dickens to Forster 25 Aug 1859. "...I set myself the little
task of making a picturesque story, rising in every chapter,
with characters true to nature, but whom the story should
express more than they should express themselves by dialogue..."
(letter qu Forster 1872 bk 9 ch 2. Cf letter 9 Jul 59 in which
Dickens writes that the short instalments "drive me frantic;
but I think the tale must have taken a strong hold...A note I
have had from Carlyle about it has given me especial pleasure").

Dickens. "When I was acting, with my children and friends, in
Mr Wilkie Collins's drama of The Frozen Deep, I first conceived
the main idea of this story... It has been one of my hopes to
add something to the popular and picturesque means of
understanding that terrible time, though no one can hope to
add anything to the philosophy of Mr Carlyle's wonderful book"
(pref first edn 1859; cf Orwell 1939 below.)

Anon (J.F.Stephen). Saturday Rev 17 Dec 1859. Accuses Dickens
of distorting the facts of history through "working upon the
feelings by the coarsest stimulants"

Taylor, Tom and Charles Dickens. A Tale of Two Cities: A Drama.
1860. One of several stage versions. See Malcolm Morley,
Dickensian 51 1955, and further below under Martin-Harvey.

Dickens to Bulwer Lytton 5 Jun 1860. Letter discussing the
feudal privileges of noblemen under the old order in France.
Qu Wall 1970 pp 154-5; cf Stephen 1859 above.

Ward, A.W. "...one of the very few of Mr Dickens's works
which require an effort in the perusal..." (Charles Dickens:
A Lecture, 30 Nov 1870, pbd Manchester 1870; qu Collins 1971
pp 537-41.)

"An American critic" (Edwin P.Whipple?) qu Forster 1872 bk 9
ch 2. "There is not a grander, lovelier figure than the
self-wrecked, self-devoted Sydney Carton in literature or
history; and the story itself is so noble in its spirit,
so grand and graphic in its style...that it deserves and
will surely take a place among the great serious works of
imagination".

Swinburne 1902: p 19 above. "This faultless work of tragic
and creative art" which "has the classic and poetic symmetry
of perfect execution and of perfect design" (p 50 1913 edn.)

Chesterton 1906: qu above p 101.

Anon (John Buchan?). "...must be ranked very high among the
great tragedies in literature" (advt for Nelson's Classics
edn c1907.)

Bottger, C. Dickens' historischer Roman...und seine Quellen.
Konigsberg 1913.

Phelps 1916: p 22 above. "Dickens lacked everything but
imagination in this field, and to me A Tale of Two Cities
is the poorest of all his stories, with the one exception of
Little Dorrit" (p 110.)

Falconer, J.A. The Sources of A Tale of Two Cities. MLN 36
1921.

Martin-Harvey, Sir John. The Story of The Only Way.
Dickensian 23 1927. By the actor who played Carton in this,
the most famous of all stage versions of Dickens, first
produced 1899. See further below under "Stage and Platform"

Dent 1933: p 4 above; pp 437-41 1935 edn.

Leacock 1933: p 4 above. "...not historical in the stricter
sense... In Dickens's youth the French Revolution was a
vivid memory of yesterday to all people of middle age"
(p 55). Fanny Burney, whose husband had been a refugee
from the Terror, lived to 1840; Carlyle was 20 at the time
of Waterloo. "...a great book..." (p 232.)

A Tale of Two Cities, cont.

Shaw 1937: p 26 above. "...pure sentimental melodrama from
   beginning to end, and shockingly wanting in any philosophy of
   history in its view of the French Revolution" (cf Stephen 1859
   above.)

Milley 1939: see below under "Dickens and Wilkie Collins".

Orwell 1939-40: p 26 above. Dickens and revolution (pp 14-17
   1946 edn; cf House below.)

House 1941: p 27 above. "...its place in the scheme of
   Dickens's work is with the mob in The Old Curiosity Shop and
   the Gordon Riots. But in spite of the obvious hatred that
   Dickens has for the mad and uncontrollable fury of the mob,
   he uses the description of it to express, or to work off,
   something of his own neurotic impatience and anger. He
   danced and slaughtered with the crowd" (p 214).

Hill, T.W. Notes on A Tale of Two Cities. Dickensian 41 1945.

Lukacs, Georg. "Even with a writer of Dickens's rank, the
   weaknesses of his petty bourgeois humanism and idealism are
   more obvious and obtrusive in his historical novel on the
   French Revolution...than in his social novels... Dickens, by
   giving pre-eminence to the purely moral aspects of causes and
   effects, weakens the connection between the problems of the
   characters' lives and the events of the French Revolution.
   The latter becomes a romantic background..." (The Historical
   Novel, 1950; qu Wall 1970 pp 432-3; see also under Barnaby
   Rudge and cf Shaw, Orwell, House above.)

Reinhold, H. A Tale of Two Cities und das Publikum. Germanisch-
   romansche Monatsschrift 36 1955.

Stange, G.R. Dickens and the Fiery Past. Englisj Journal 46
   1957.

Zabel 1957: p 31 above. The Revolutionary Fate. Cf Orwell and
   House above.

Blair 1958: see below under "Dickens and Mark Twain".

Manheim, L. A Tale of Two Cities: A Study in Psycho-analytic
   Criticism. English Rev Spring 1959.

Gross, John. In Gross 1962: p 7 above.

Davis 1963: p 33 above.

Elliott, R.W.V. Dickens: A Tale of Two Cities. 1966.

A Tale of Two Cities, cont.

Monod, Sylvère. In NCF centenary no. 1970.

Monod, Sylvère. A French View of A Tale of Two Cities.
Dickens Memorial Lecture 1970.

Snow, C.P. In Slater 1970: p 8 above. Compares opening of
ch 10 of Little Dorrit with "the passages on revolution" in
A Tale of Two Cities: "...in that opening, Dickens was writin
in one of those moods of manic incantatory rhetoric which car
upon him when he had something simple to say upon a public
issue..." (pp 131-2).

Monod, Sylvère. In DSA 1971.

Oddie 1973: see below under "Dickens and Carlyle".

Bateson 1965 (p 1 above) recommends New York 1958 edn ed M.D.
Zabel; New York 1950 edn is ed Edward Wagenknecht; the PEL
edn is ed George Woodcock.

Great Expectations

Dickens to Forster Oct 1960. "The book will be written in the
first person throughout, and during these first three weekly
numbers you will find the hero to be a boy-child, like David
You will not have to complain of the want of humour as in th
Tale of Two Cities... To be quite sure I had fallen into no
unconscious repetitions, I read David Copperfield again the
other day, and was affected by it to a degree you would hard
believe" (letter qu Forster 1872 bk 9 ch 3 who adds: "It may
be doubted if Dickens could better have established his righ
to the front rank among novelists claimed for him, than by t
ease and mastery with which in these two books...he kept
perfectly distinct the two stories of a boy's childhood, bot
told in the form of autobiography.")

Dickens to Forster 1 Jul 1861. "You will be surprised to hear
that I have changed the end of Great Expectations... Bulwer
(who has been...extraordinarily taken by the book) so stron
urged it upon me, after reading the proofs, and supported hi
views with such good reasons, that I resolved to make the
change... I have put in a very pretty piece of writing, and
I have no doubt the story will be more acceptable through t
alteration" (qu Forster above who adds: "This turned out to
the case; but the first ending nevertheless seems to be mor
consistent with the drift, as well as natural working out,
the tale".)

108

Great Expectations, cont.

Anon. Saturday Rev 20 Jul 1861. "Mr Dickens may be reasonably
proud of these volumes. After a long series of his varied
works - after passing under the cloud of Little Dorrit and
Bleak House - he has written a story that is new, original,
powerful, and very entertaining... It is in his best vein...
worthy to stand beside Martin Chuzzlewit and David
Copperfield" (qu Collins 1971 p 427.)

Anon (Edwin P.Whipple). Atlantic Monthly Sep 1861. "...we
take great joy in recording our conviction that Great
Expectations is a masterpiece..." (qu Collins 1971 p 430.)

Anon (Mrs Oliphant). Blackwood's Mag May 1862. "...feeble,
fatigued, and colourless. One feels that he must have got
tired of it as the work went on..." (qu Wall 1970, Collins
1971, etc.)

Gilbert, W.S. Great Expectations: A Drama. 1871. One of
several stage versions. See Morley, Dickensian 1955.

Gissing 1898: p 17 above. Compares with Copperfield (pp 96-7).

Swinburne 1902: p 19 above. "Among the highest landmarks of
success ever reared for immortality by the triumphant genius
of Dickens... The tragedy and the comedy...are fused...with
little less than Shakespearean strength and skill" (pp 51-3).

Phelps 1916: p 22 above. "...one of the best novels in English
literature..." (p 110.)

Saintsbury 1916: p 22 above. "...he had never done anything,
not even in Copperfield itself, so real as 'Pip', with his
fears, his hopes, his human weaknesses and meannesses, his
love, his bearing up against misfortune. Never did he
combine analysis and synthesis so thoroughly as here" (pp
333-4 1932 edn.)

Shaw 1937: p 26 above. "...his most compactly perfect book...
consistently truthful as none of the other books are...
the conventional happy ending is an outrage on it."

Jackson 1937: p 26 above. "Self-satisfied, mid-Victorian,
British society buoyed itself up with as great 'expectations'..
as did poor, deluded Pip... respectable society...was as
little aware...as was Pip of the source of (their)
advantages" (qu House 1941 below.)

Shaw 1939: qu above p 102.

Orwell 1939: p 26 above; p 29 1946 edn.

Great Expectations, cont.

Wilson 1939-41: p 27 above; pp 53-5 UP edn.

House 1941: p 27 above.   "...a remarkable achievement to have
kept the reader's sympathy throughout a snob's progress.
The book is the clearest artistic triumph of the Victorian
bourgeoisie on its own special ground..." (pp 156-61; cf
Jackson and Orwell above.)

Butt, John.   Dickens's Plan for the Conclusion of Great
Expectations.   Dickensian 45 1949.

Van Ghent 1953: p 30 above.   See pp 128-31 qu Wall 1970 pp
375-9.

Hagan, J.H.   Structural Patterns in Great Expectations.
ELH 21 1954.

Connolly, T.E.   Technique in Great Expectations.   PQ 34 1955.

Jones, Howard Mumford.   On Re-reading Great Expectations.
South-West Rev Dallas Tex Autumn 1954 pp 328-35.

Stange, G.R.   Expectations Well Lost: Dickens's Fable for
his Time.   College English Chicago Oct 1954.

Hagan, J.H.   The Poor Labyrinth: The Theme of Social Injustice
in Great Expectations.   NCF 9 1955.

House 1955: p 31 above.   G.B.S. on Great Expectations.
Cf Shaw 1937 and 1939 above.

Drew, A.P.   A Structure in Great Expectations.   Dickensian
Jun 1956 pp 123-7.   Cf Hagan 1954 above.

Hill, T.W.   Notes to Great Expectations.   Dickensian 53-6
1957-60.

Nisbet, Ada.   The Autobiographical Matrix of Great
Expectations.   Victorian Newsletter no 15 1959.

Monod, Sylvère.   Great Expectations a Hundred Years After.
Dickensian 56 1960.

Moynahan, Julian.   The Hero's Guilt: The Case of Great
Expectations.   EC 10 1960 pp 60-97.   One of the most
influential of modern accounts.   Cf Van Ghent 1953,
Ricks 1962, and George Levine, Communication in Great
Expectations, NCF Sep 1963 pp 175-81.

Fielding, K.J. The Critical Autonomy of Great Expectations.
REL 2 1961.

Partlow, Robert B. jr. The Moving "I": Point of View in Great
Expectations. College English Nov 1961.

Ricks, Christopher. In Gross 1962: p 7 above.

Bayley 1962: p 48 above. "...reality depends on the convention.
Dickens was the first to protest against the new French
'realism', because he felt it might discredit his mystery.
He has often been blamed for giving the happy ending to
Great Expectations, in deference to Bulwer Lytton, but he has
there a sure sense, as in Oliver Twist, not of what the
donnée demanded, but of upholding the kinds of agreement he
had made with the reader. The artistic rigour of a Flaubert
alienates, and Dickens is faithful only to what he and his
audience can make of the thing together" (qu Wall 1970 p 450;
cf Dickens, Forster, Shaw above.)

Stone, Harry. Fire, Hand and Gate. Kenyon Rev 24 1962.
Symbolism in Great Expectations. Cf Hardy below and see
further under "Symbolism" below.

Hardy, Barbara. Food and Ceremony in Great Expectations.
EC 13 1963. "...Food in Great Expectations, as in Macbeth,
is part of the pulic order, and the meals testify to human
need and dependence, and distinguish false ceremony from the
ceremony of love. They are not symbols but natural
demonstrations" (pp 362-3; cf Stone above.)

Hynes, J.A. Image and Symbol in Great Expectations. ELH 30
1963. Cf Stone and Hardy above.

Killy, W. Der Roman als Märchen. Wirklichkeit und
Kunstcharakter, Munich 1963.

Lettis, R. and W.E.Morris (ed). Assessing Great Expectations.
San Francisco 1963. Critical anthology, with bibliog.

Rostvig, M.S. ao. The Hidden Sense and Other Essays. Oslo
1963. Incl D.Roll-Hansen, Characters and Contrasts in
Great Expectations.

Thomas, R.G. Dickens: Great Expectations. 1964.

Bell, V.M. Parents and Children in Great Expectations.
Victorian Newsletter no 27 1965.

Great Expectations, cont.

Meisel, M.   The Ending of Great Expectations.   EC 15 1965.
  Cf Dickens, Forster, Shaw, Bayley above.

Peyrouton, Noel C.   John Wemmick: Enigma?   DS 1 1965.

Garis 1965: p 34 above.   "...an altogether unique literary
  phenomenon... a beautiful and successful work of art" (p 100
  Cf Swinburne above.

Harvey 1965: p 91 above.   "...Sometimes he achieves an economy
  firmness and clean-cut clarity of control that can only be
  called classical.   This is surely true of Great Expectations
  (qu Wall 1970 p 500.)

Barnes, J.   Dickens: Great Expectations.   1966.

Marcus, P.L.   Theme and Suspense in Great Expectations.
  DS 2 1966.

Ridland 1966: see below under "Dickens and Mark Twain".

Wentersdorf, K.P.   Mirror-Images in Great Expectations.   NCF
  21 1967.

Smith 1969: p 35 above.   Considers Wemmick "the perfect
  representative of the alienated modern man".   Cf Peyrouton
  above.

Stone, Harry.   The Genesis of a Novel.   In Tomlin 1970: p 8
  above.

Leavis, Q.D.   How We Must Read Great Expectations.   In Leavis
  1970: p 36 above.   Supports Dickens's revised ending; cf
  Dickens, Forster, Shaw, Bayley, Meisel above.

Wilson, Angus.   In Slater 1970: p 8 above.   "...a perfect
  novel..." (p 227).   See also Walter Allen (pp 18–19);
  Raymond Williams (pp 84–5); Pamela Hansford Johnson (pp
  185–6.)

Martin, Graham.   A Study Guide to Great Expectations.   Open
  University 1973.

Winner, Anthony.   Character and Knowledge in Dickens: The
  Enigma of Jaggers.   DSA 3 1974.   Cf Peyrouton 1965 above.

Talon, Henri.   Space, Time and Memory in Great Expectations.
  DSA 3 1974.

Great Expectations, cont.

Thomsen, Christian W.   Charles Dickens: Great Expectations.
   In Der Englische Roman im 19. Jahrhundert, Berlin 1974.

DeVries, Duane.   Paperback Editions.   DSN Jun 1974.

Bateson 1965 (p 1 above) recommends 1948 New York edn
   ed Earle Davis; the New Oxford edn 1953 is ed F. Sage;
   the SC edn 1963 has afterword Angus Wilson; Sylvère Monod
   ed and tr Paris edn 1959; the PEL edn 1965 is ed Angus
   Calder; Toronto edn 1965 is ed R. D. McMaster; Collier edn
   New York 1962 has intn Frank Chapman; HC edn New York 1965
   has intn Walter Allen; Riverside edn Boston 1962 has intn
   Monroe Engel.

The Uncommercial Traveller

Anon (J. F. Stephen?).   Saturday Rev 23 Feb 1861.   "... in Mr
   Dickens's good manner... pleasant, witty, shrewd, and
   unhackneyed... a book that does Mr Dickens justice...
   There is no possibility of pretending that Bleak House,
   Little Dorrit and The Two Cities were not surprisingly
   bad – melodramatic, pretentious... deadly dull... We are
   delighted to say that the Little Dorrit days seem over..."
   (qu Collins 1971 pp 408-12.)

Forster 1872-4: p 2 above.   Bk 8 ch 5.   Ch 6 adds that
   "the civil war having closed America" Dickens was tempted
   by an offer of more than £10,000 to go to Australia to
   undertake a series of public readings there.   "He tried
   to familiarize himself with the fancy that he should thus
   also get new material for observation, and he went so far
   as to plan an Uncommercial Traveller Upside Down."

Swinburne 1902: p 19 above.   "Of his lesser works, the best
   and most precious... beyond all question or comparison"
   (p 72 1913 edn.)

Saintsbury 1916: p 22 above.   "... exercises in his own
   earliest kind but of much greater power, variety,
   originality and artistic value..." (p 332 1932 edn.)

Dent 1933: p 4 above.   Compares with Sketches by Boz:
   "Some sentences, a few paragraphs, could be interchanged.
   The rest could not; there is thirty years of age, and three
   hundred years of subtle difference, between them" (p 442
   1935 edn.)

The Uncommercial Traveller, cont.

Churchill 1937-42: p 26 above. "Oliver Twist takes the same
    precedence over The Uncommercial Traveller and American Note
    as Fielding's Joseph Andrews must over his Proposal for the
    Poor" (p 372.)

House 1941: p 27 above; pp 19, 26.

Snow, C.P. In Slater 1970: p 8 above. Little Dorrit and
    Uncommercial Traveller (p 131). See also Pamela Hansford
    Johnson (ibid p 194) and Angus Wilson (pp 218-22).

The New Oxford Illustrated edn 1958 has intn Leslie C.Staples.
    Vol incl Reprinted Pieces.

See further below under "Dickens the Journalist".

Our Mutual Friend

Anon (John Forster). Examiner 28 Oct 1865. Cf Forster 1872
    qu below.

Anon (Henry James) 1865: p 14 above. "...the poorest of Mr
    Dickens's works...poor with the poverty...of permanent
    exhaustion..." (p 31 1968 edn.)

Forster 1872-4: p 2 above. "...will never rank with his high
    efforts... on the whole...it wants freshness and natural
    development... It has not the creative power which crowded
    his earlier page and transformed into popular realities the
    shadows of his fancy; but the observation and humour he
    excelled in are not wanting to it, nor had there been, in h
    first completed work, more eloquent or generous pleading fo
    the poor and neglected, than this last completed work
    contains. Betty Higden finishes what Oliver Twist began"
    (bk 9 ch 5.)

Ward 1882: p 3 above. Critical view of Lizzie Hexam who
    "has to discard the colour of her surroundings and talk the
    conventional dialect as well as express the conventional
    sentiments of the heroic world" (qu Churchill 1937-42; but
    cf Orwell 1939 below.)

Swinburne 1902: p 19 above. "...the real protagonist...is th
    river... the genius of the author ebbs and flows with...the
    Thames" (p 60 1913 edn; cf Wilson 1939-41 and other modern
    critics.)

Shaw 1912: qu above p 95.   "...such masterpieces as...Our
Mutual Friend..."

Chesterton 1932: p 25 above.   "...he gathered up into his last
complete book...all his growing knowledge of the realities of
society, of the growth of plutocracy, and the peril now
threatening the national tradition" (cf Shaw 1912 and Wilson
1939 and see further Chesterton 1907-11.)

Leacock 1933: p 4 above.   "Like...Hard Times...interesting only
as illustrating the failures of genius. It seems amazing that
even the prestige of Charles Dickens in 1865 could have
sustained so poor a book" (p 239.)

Orwell 1939-40: p 26 above.   "...a return to the earlier manner,
and not an unsuccessful return either" (p 11 1946 edn).
"Dickens treats the episode of Eugene Wrayburn and Lizzie
Hexam very realistically and with no appearance of class bias"
(pp 32-3; cf Ward 1882 above.)

Wilson 1939-41: p 27 above.   "...the book compensates for its
shortcomings by the display of an intellectual force which...
here appears in a phase of high tension and a condition of
fine muscular training... Dickens has here distilled the mood
of his later years...delivered his final judgment on the whole
Victorian exploit, in a fashion so impressive that we realize
how little the distractions of this period had the power to
direct him from the prime purpose of his life: the serious
exercise of his art" (pp 66-7 UP edn.)

House 1941: p 27 above.   Compares world of Pickwick with world
of Our Mutual Friend: "the two books are the products of
different climates... The very air seems to have changed in
quality... In Pickwick a bad smell was a bad smell; in Our
Mutual Friend it is a problem" (pp 134-5; cf pp 104-5 on
Betty Higden and contemporary Poor Law severity and see
further below under "Radical and Reformer").

Boll, E. The Plotting of Our Mutual Friend. MP 42 1944.
Prints number-plans. See further below under "Serial
Novelist".

Hill, T.W. Notes on Our Mutual Friend. Dickensian 43 1947.

Morse, R. Our Mutual Friend. Partisan Rev 16 1949.

Quennell, Peter. The Singular Preference. 1952.

Johnson 1952: p 5 above.

Our Mutual Friend, cont.

Allen 1954: p 30 above; p 173 PB edn.

Morley, Malcolm. Enter Our Mutual Friend. Dickensian 52 1956.
Discusses stage versions.

Monod, Sylvère. L'Expression dans Our Mutual Friend: manière
ou maniérisme? Etudes Anglaises 10 1957.

Rerat, A. Le romanesque dans L'Ami Commun. Langues Modernes
52 1958.

Stone 1959: see below under "Dickens and Religion".

McMaster, R.D. Birds of Prey. Dalhousie Rev 40 1960.

Bernard, R. The Choral Symphony in Our Mutual Friend. REL 2
1961.

Kettle, Arnold. In Gross 1962: p 7 above. "One of the
greatest works of prose ever written, a work which finally
vindicates Dickens's right to stand, as no other English wri
can stand, at the side of Shakespeare" (p 225; see further
below under "Dickens and Shakespeare".)

Oppel, H. Our Mutual Friend. Neueren Sprachen Oct 1962; rp
Der moderne englische Roman ed Oppel, Berlin 1965.

Hobsbaum, Philip. The Critics and Our Mutual Friend. EC 13
1963.

Lanham, R.A. The Birds of Prey. Victorian Newsletter no 26.
1963. Cf McMaster 1960 above.

Muir, Kenneth. Image and Structure in Our Mutual Friend.
Essays & Studies 19 1966.

Nelson 1966: see below under "Dickens and Henry Mayhew".

Shea, Francis Xavier. No Change of Intention in Our Mutual
Friend. Dickensian 63 1967.

Dyson 1970: p 35 above. "A real recovery of Dickens's great
comic form.." (cf Orwell above.)

Lucas 1970: p 36 above.

Daleski 1970: p 36 above.

Hardy, Barbara.   In Slater 1970: p 8 above.   "...a dramatic
    expansion and synthesis of comedy and serious action..."
    (pp 32-3).   See also Pamela Hansford Johnson (ibid pp 189-90.)

Hobsbaum 1973: p 8 above.

Robson, John M.   Our Mutual Friend: A Rhetorical Approach to
    the First Number.   DSA 3 1974.

Basch 1974: see below under "Sex in Dickens".

The New Oxford Illustrated edn 1952 has intn E.Salter Davies;
    the SC edn has afterword J.Hillis Miller; the PEL edn is ed
    Stephen Gill.

George Silverman's Explanation

Saintsbury 1916: qu above p 71.

Bradby, M.K.   The Explanation of George Silverman's Explanation.
    Dickensian 36 1940.

Stone, Harry.   Dickens's Tragic Universe.   SP 55 1958.

Wilson, Angus.   In Slater 1970: p 8 above.   "...In the strange,
    ambiguous story...we find a final more sinister account of
    the destructive effects of a neglected and exploited childhood.
    The child gives place to the man..." (p 212; see further below
    under "Dickens and Childhood".)

Thomas, Deborah Allen.   The Equivocal Explanation of Dickens's
    George Silverman.   DSA 3 1974.

Edwin Drood

Dickens to Forster 6 Aug 1869.   "...a very curious and new idea
    for my new story..." (qu Forster 1872 bk 11 ch 2; Forster adds
    further details as to Dickens's probable intentions.)

Anon (F.N.Broome).   Times 2 Apr 1870.   "As he delighted the
    fathers, so he delights the children, and this his latest
    effort promises to be received with interest and pleasure as
    widespread as that which greeted those glorious Papers which
    built at once the whole edifice of his fame."

Longfellow Jun 1870 on learning of Dickens's death. "I hope
his book is finished. It is certainly one of his most
beautiful works, if not the most beautiful of all. It would
be too sad to think the pen had fallen from his hand and left
it incomplete" (qu Forster 1872 bk 11 ch 2.)

Kerr, Orpheus C. The Cloven Foot. New York 1870; rv in
Piccadilly Annual 1870. Adapation to American scenes and
characters, with conclusion and critical intn.

Morford, Henry. John Jasper's Secret: A Sequel to Dickens's
Unfinished Novel. Philadelphia 1871-2, London 1872; rp New
York 1901. Attributed falsely to Wilkie Collins and Charles
Dickens jr. See Kenneth Robinson, Wilkie Collins, 1951, p
223 1974 edn.

Stephens, W. Lost: A Drama. 1871. One of several stage
versions. See Malcolm Morley, Stage Solutions to the Myster
Dickensian 53 1957.

Forster 1872-4: p 2 above. Bk 11 ch 2. Incl fragment on Mr
Sapsea and the Eight Club discovered by Forster among
Dickens's MSS.

Collins, Wilkie. "...Dickens's last laboured effort, the
melancholy work of a worn out brain" (margin note in copy of
Forster 1872-4 qu Robinson op cit p 236.)

Vase, Gillan (Mrs Richard Newton). A Great Mystery Solved.
3 vols 1878; rp 1 vol 1914.

Anon (H.S.Edwards). The Mystery of Edwin Drood: Suggestions
for a Conclusion. Cornhill Mag Mar 1884.

Proctor, Richard A. Watched by the Dead: A Loving Study of
Dickens's Half-Told Tale. 1887.

Dickens 1892: p 17 above. Intn Drood discusses his father's
probable intentions and criticizes sequels by Morford, Vase
and Proctor mentioned above as having "the disadvantage of
being...utterly wrong" (p xiv.)

Gissing 1898: p 17 above. "...Neither at a black-hearted
villain was he really good, though he prided himself on his
achievements in this kind... Whether...John Jasper would ha
shown a great advance, must remain doubtful. The first hal
of Edwin Drood shows him picturesquely, and little more. W
discover no hint of real tragedy. The man seems to us a ve
vulgar assassin, and we care not at all what becomes of him
(ch 5.)

Edwin Drood, cont.

Swinburne 1902: p 19 above. "...has things in it worthy of
Dickens at his best" (p 65 1913 edn.) Cf Spencer 1972 below.

Lang, Andrew. The Puzzle of Dickens's Last Plot. 1905.

Walters, J.Cuming. Clues to Dickens's Mystery of Edwin Drood.
1905. Cf Fildes below.

Fildes, Sir Luke. The Mysteries of Edwin Drood. Times 3 Nov 05.
By Dickens's illustrator. Replies by Lang 10 Nov and J.W.T.Ley
21 Nov 1905.

Dickens, Kate, Mrs Perugini. Edwin Drood and Dickens's Last
Days. Pall Mall Mag Jun 1906. By Dickens's daughter.

Charles, E. Keys to the Drood Mystery. 1908; rp 1915.

Jackson, Henry. About Edwin Drood. Cambridge 1911; rp Folcroft
Pa 1973.

Nicoll, Sir William Robertson. The Problem of Edwin Drood. 1912.
With bibliog by B.W.Matz. Cf Walters below.

Walters, J.Cuming (ed). The Complete Edwin Drood: The Full Text
with the History, Continuations and Solutions 1870-1912. 1912.

Fennell, C.A.M. The Opium-Woman and Datchery in the Mystery of
Edwin Drood. Cambridge 1913.

Grant, M.L.C.(ed). The Mystery of Edwin Drood: Completed by
W.E.C.(W.E.Crisp). 1914.

Trial of John Jasper for the Murder of Edwin Drood. At the
National Sporting Club, Covent Garden London, 7 Jan 1914.
Before Mr Justice G.K.Chesterton. Counsel for the Defence:
Cecil Chesterton. Counsel for the Prosecution: J.Cuming
Walters and B.W.Matz. Foreman of the Jury: Bernard Shaw.
Organized by Dickens Fellowship, reported Dickensian 1914 by
J.W.T.Ley. See Pearson, Bernard Shaw, pp 328-30.

Saunders, Margaret (Mrs Baillie-Saunders). The Mystery in the
Drood Family. Cambridge 1914.

Kavanagh, M. A New Solution of the Mystery of Edwin Drood. 1919.

Dickensian Mar 1919. Special Edwin Drood no.

Carden, P.T. The Murder of Edwin Drood: An Attempted Solution.
1920.

Squire, Sir John. The Great Unfinished. Life and Letters, 1920.

Edwin Drood, cont.

Matz, B.W. A Bibliography of Edwin Drood: 1911-1928.
  Dickensian 24-5 1928-9. Cf Nicoll 1912 above.

Dexter, Walter. New Light on Edwin Drood. Sphere 9 Feb 1929.
  Cf Fildes 1905 above.

Lehmann-Haupt, C.F. New Facts Concerning Edwin Drood.
  Dickensian 25 1929. See also his Studies on Edwin Drood,
  Dickensian 31-3 1935-7.

Duffield, Howard. John Jasper, Strangler. American Bookman
  Feb 1930. Jasper as a Thug (cf Collins's Moonstone 1868).
  See further Duffield 1934 and Wilson 1940 below.

Leacock 1933: p 4 above. Ch 13 gives summary of various
  "solutions" and Leacock's own verdict. Notes 8 books on the
  subject, 80 articles and 5 dramas.

Duffield, Howard. The Macbeth Motif in Edwin Drood.
  Dickensian 30 1934.

Shaw 1937: p 26 above. "...only a gesture by a man three-
  quarters dead" (qu Wall 1970 pp 285-6.)

Wilson, Edmund. The Mystery of Edwin Drood. New Republic
  8 Apr 1940; rv Wilson 1941: p 27 above. Cf Duffield 1930
  above and comment in Wall 1970 p 319 and see further below
  under "Dickens and Crime".

Hill, T.W. Notes on Edwin Drood. Dickensian 40 1941.

Pritchett 1946: p 28 above. "...In every kind of way Dickens
  was isolated. Isolation was the foundation not only of his
  fantasy and his hysteria, but also - I am sure Mr Edmund
  Wilson is correct here - of the twin strains of rebel and
  criminal in his nature... the kind of realism employed in
  Edwin Drood reads like an attempt to reconstruct and co-
  ordinate his world, like a preparation for a final confessio
  of guilt" (pp 78-9; cf Wilson 1941.)

MacVicar, H.M. The Datchery Assumption. NCF 4 1950.

Baker, R.M. The Drood Murder Case. Berkeley 1951. Cf
  MacVicar above.

Symons 1951: p 5 above.

Robinson 1951: see below under "Dickens and Wilkie Collins".

Edwin Drood, cont.

Ford, George H. Dickens's Notebook and Edwin Drood.   NCF 6 1952.

Bleifuss, W.W.   A Re-Examination of Edwin Drood.   Dickensian 50-1 1954-5.

Stelzmann, R.   Ein neuer Lösungsversuch.   Archiv 193 1957.

Stone, Harry.   "...in the time since he had created Jingle, he had grown immeasurably in his ability to understand and depict the intricate ways of the mind.   In this respect, rather than follow Wyndham Lewis and compare Jingle to Bloom, it would be more instructive to juxtapose Jasper and Bloom..." (Dickens and Interior Monologue, PQ 38 1959; qu Wall 1970 pp 422-32. See further below under "Dickens and Joyce".)

Cockshut, A.O.J.   In Gross 1962: p 7 above.

Cox, A.J.   The Morals of Edwin Drood.   Dickensian 58 1962.

Aylmer, Felix.   The Drood Case.   1964.

Collins, Philip.   Inspector Bucket visits the Princess Puffer. Dickensian 60 1964.   Cf Wells, Chesterton etc qu above p 52.

Mitchell, C.   The Mystery of Edwin Drood: The Interior and the Exterior of Self.   ELH 33 1966.

Cohen, J.B.   Artists and Artistry in Edwin Drood.   DS 3 1967.

Hardy, Barbara.   In Slater 1970: p 8 above.   Dickens's "verbal brilliance" relaxed "towards the end..." (p 35.)

Cardwell, Margaret (ed).   Clarendon edn.   Oxford 1972.   Corrects misprints in earlier edns incl the one in first sentence ("tower" for "town") which Dickens failed to notice and which has always puzzled readers.

Spencer, T.J.B.   Review of above in Birmingham Post 28 Oct 72. "Its unfinished state is one of the calamities of literature, for Drood shows many signs of being a masterpiece, with a vigour of imagination and organization equal to Dickens's best work."

Mehl, Dieter.   Review of Cardwell above.   Archiv 210 1973.

Wing, George.   Edwin Drood and Desperate Remedies: Prototypes of Detective Fiction in 1870.   SEL Autumn 1973.

Edwin Drood, cont.

Robson 1974: see below under "Dickens and Chesterton".

Cardwell, Margaret. In Dickensian Jan 1974.

The New Oxford Illustrated edn 1956 has intn S.C.Roberts;
the PEL edn ed A.Cox has intn Angus Wilson; 1952 edn is ed
Michael Innes (J.I.M.Stewart); 1957 edn is ed Cecil Day-
Lewis.

Minor Works

Anon. Metropolitan Mag Mar 1836. "We do not know the
author, but we should apprehend that he has, from the
peculiar turn of his genius, been already successful as a
dramatist; if he has not yet, we can safely opine that he
may be if he will" (review of Sketches by Boz qu Collins
1971 p 30; cf Horne below.)

Horne 1844: p 12 above. "Few are perhaps aware that Mr
Dickens once wrote an opera; not very many perhaps know
that he wrote a farce for the theatre, which was acted;
and the great majority of his readers do not at all care
to remember that he wrote a Life of Grimaldi, in two
volumes" (p 46). See further below under "Stage and
Platform".

Forster 1872-4: p 2 above; bk 2 ch 2 opening paras. Life
of Grimaldi. Cf Horne above. More accurately described
as Memoirs of Joseph Grimaldi. For full details see
House 1965 pp 337-82 qu eg review by John Hamilton
Reynolds, Athenaeum 17 Feb 1838.

Shaw 1937: qu above p 86. The Life of Our Lord (1849).

NCBEL 1969: p 1 above. See cols 815-17, 819-28.

See further below under "Stage and Platform", "Dickens the
Journalist", etc.

ASPECTS OF DICKENS

His Popularity

Wilkie 1839: qu above p 10.

Edgeworth, Maria. "...this reality of _feeling_ is...the secret, joined to his great power of humour, of his ascendant popularity" (letter 1843 qu House 1969 p 195n.)

Bagehot 1858: p 13 above. "...popularity...wherever the English language is spoken...read with admiring appreciation by persons of the highest culture at the centre of civilization... amuse...the roughest settler in Vancouver's Island..." (p 165 EL edn 1911.) Cf Jeaffreson 1858 qu Collins 1971 p382.

Anon. Daily News 10 Jun 1870. "...without any exception or any chance of approach the most popular author of the time... emphatically the novelist of the age..." (qu Collins 1971 p 504.)

Trollope 1870: p 15 above. "Of his novels, the first striking circumstance is their unprecedented popularity... no critic is justified in putting aside the consideration of that circumstance... wherever English is read these books are popular from the highest to the lowest..." (qu Wall 1970 pp 179-80.)

Henley 1890: p 17 above. "...the best beloved of modern writers almost from the outset of his career" (qu Quiller-Couch p 8.)

Saintsbury 1916: p 22 above. "No author in our literary history has been both admired and enjoyed for such different reasons; by such different tastes and intellects; by whole classes of readers unlike each other" (p 304 1932 edn).

Quiller-Couch 1922-5: p 23 above. "...this exaltation of Dickens in the popular mind...is an historical fact... singular in our literary history...it reacted singularly upon the man and his work" (pp 6-7.)

Dent 1933: p 4 above; pp 169-70 1935 edn.

Churchill 1937-42: p 26 above; p 369.

Orwell 1939-40: p 26 above; pp 44-5 1946 edn.

Sampson 1941: p 28 above; p 622 1970 edn. Cf Saintsbury 1916 above.

House 1941: p 27 above. "Carlyle's strictures on novel-
reading in the Essay on Scott became finally irrelevant
when Dickens's reputation had been established. He touched
areas of the reading public that scarcely any other non-
religious writer reached... He is still the only one of the
great English novelists who is read at all widely among
simple people..." (p 224; see further below under "Reading
Public".)

Churchill 1958: p 32 above under Ford; p 119.

Wall 1970: p 7 above; pp 25-6.

Collins, Philip. The Popularity of Dickens. Dickensian
Jan 1974.

His Originality

Macaulay 1836: qu above p 41.

Lister 1838: p 9 above. "We think him a very original writer
...the truest and most spirited delineator of English life,
amongst the middle and lower classes, since the days of
Smollett and Fielding".

Horne 1844: p 12 above. Dickens seen as the product of his
age, a genuine emanation of its spirit, an author of
unexhausted originality. Cf Justin McCarthy, Westminster Rev
Oct 64 qu Collins 1971 pp 446-7.

Mair 1911: p 21 above. "...an innovator in more ways than one
... the earliest novelist to practise a conscious artistry
of plot... made a new departure by his frankly admitted
didacticism and by the skill with which...he squared his
purpose with his art... In him for the first time the
English novel produced an author who dug down into the
masses of the people for his subjects...and reproduced them
with a lively and loving artistic skill" (pp 227-8.)

Saintsbury 1916: p 22 above. "...book after book - most of
them utterly unlike anything that had been seen before, and
hardly one of them...showing that fatal groove-and-mould
character which besets the novelist more than any other
literary craftsman" (p 306 1932 edn.)

Wilson 1939-41: p 27 above. "No artist has ever absorbed his
predecessors...more completely... Using them, he has gone
beyond them all" (p 31 UP edn; cf Dent 1933 and Leavis 1970.

His Originality, cont.

Allen 1954: p 30 above. "There is the movement of the plot,
which is mechanical... But there is also the movement of the
symbolism, and this is something entirely different and
something new in our fiction" (p 171 PB edn.)

Holloway, John. Dickens's Vision of Society. Listener 25 Feb
1965; rp The Novelist as Innovator, ed Walter Allen, 1965.

His Reading Public

Wilkie 1839: qu above p 10.

Wordsworth, William. "Pray tell me what you think is the main
cause of the great falling off in the sale of books... Dr
Arnold told me that his lads seemed to care for nothing but
Bozzy's next No., and the Classics suffered accordingly.
Can that man's public and others of the like kind materially
affect the question? I am quite in the dark" (letter to
publisher Edward Moxon Apr 1842 qu Wall 1970 p 61.)

Felton 1843: qu above p 59.

Arnold 1865: qu above p 14.

Trollope 1870: p 15 above. "I remember another novelist saying
to me of Dickens - my friend and his friend, Charles Lever -
that Dickens knew exactly how to tap the ever newly growing
mass of readers as it sprang up among the lower classes. He
could measure the reading public...and knew what the public
wanted of him" (qu Wall 1970 p 179.)

Butler 1875: p 16 above. "... Kingsley's Alton Locke, which
...he had devoured as he had devoured Stanley's Life of
Arnold, Dickens's novels, and whatever other literary garbage
of the day was most likely to do him harm" (p 210 1933 EL edn;
cf House 1941 p 93n qu Dickens to Forster on Stanley's Arnold:
"I respect and reverence his memory beyond all expression.
I must have that book. Every sentence that you quote from it
is the text-book of my faith". See further below under
"Radical and Reformer".)

Whipple 1876-7: p 16 above. Cf Felton 1843 and see further
below under "Dickens in America".

His Reading Public, cont.

Trollope, Anthony. "The good opinion he had of himself was never shaken by adverse criticism; and the criticism on the other side, by which it was exalted, came from the enumeration of the copies sold" (comment on Dickens in Thackeray EML 1879 qu Churchill 1937-42 p 360n.)

Stephen 1888: p 3 above. "...If literary fame could be safely measured by popularity with the half-educated, Dickens must claim the highest position among English novelists... The criticism of more severe critics chiefly consists in the assertion that his merits are such as suit the half-educated..." (cf Leavis 1932 below.)

Harrison 1894-5: p 17 above; pp 28-9.

Chesterton 1906: p 20 above. "Dickens never talked down to the people. He talked up to the people. He approached the people like a deity and poured out his riches and his blood ..."

Quiller-Couch 1922-5: p 23 above; pp 10-12.

Leavis 1932: qu above p 25.

Churchill 1950: p 29 above; pp 111-13.

Allen 1954: p 30 above; pp 159-61.

Ford 1955: p 31 above.

Altick, Richard D. The English Common Reader: A Social History of the Mass Reading Public 1800-1900. Chicago 1957.

Butt and Tillotson 1957: p 31 above.

Dalziel, Margaret. Popular Fiction a Hundred Years Ago. 1957.

Webb, R.K. The Victorian Reading Public. PGEL 1958: p 32 above under Ford.

Williams, Raymond. The Long Revolution. 1961. Pt 2 ch 2: The Growth of the Reading Public.

James 1963: p 41 above under Reynolds. Incl details of contemporary imitations of Dickens.

Brown 1963: p 33 above.

Marcus 1964: p 34 above.

Garis 1965: p 34 above. "Since Dickens's impulse" in his
early career "is completely outgoing, none of the advantages
of self-criticism is available to him, and we encounter
repeatedly a callow unawareness of his limitations. This
leads on occasion to an undignified and nervous dependence
on the goodwill of his public..." (pp 94-5).

Williams 1970: p 78 above. "The popular tradition - in the
theatre, in newspapers, in songs and spoken stories - is
indeed where he starts from, but not as a liability" (p 14.)

Wall 1970: p 7 above; pp 25-31.

Dickens's England

See also below under "Dickens's London".

Langton, Robert. Dickens and Rochester. 1880.

Frost, Thomas. In Kent with Charles Dickens. 1880.

Hassard, J.R.G. A Pickwickian Pilgrimage. Boston 1881.

Rimmer, A. About England with Dickens. 1883.

Watson, H.Burnett. The Story of Dotheboys Hall. Monthly
Chronicle of North Country Lore & Legend vol I 1887.

Hughes, W.R. A Week's Tramp in Dickens-land. 1891.

Dickens, Charles jr. Disappearing Dickensland. North
American Rev Jun 1893.

Fitzgerald, Percy. Bozland: Dickens's Places and People.
1895.

Hall, H. Mr Pickwick's Kent. 1899.

Allbut, R. Rambles in Dickens's Land. 1899; rv 1903.

Kitton, Frederic G. The Dickens Country. Intn Arthur Waugh.
1905.

Gissing, George. Dickens. In Homes & Haunts of English
Authors, 1906.

Bartholomew, J.G.(ed). A Literary and Historical Atlas of
    Europe. Intn Ernest Rhys. EL nd (c1910). Incl map p 134
    showing "places mentioned in Dickens's works". Cf Hopkins
    1923 below and R.C.Churchill, An Atlas of Fictional
    Geography, REL Apr 1966 pp 99-106.

Harris, E. Dickensian Chatham. Rochester 1911.

Pascoe, C.E. Dickens in Yorkshire. 1912.

Cooper, T.P. With Dickens in Yorkshire. York 1913.

Saintsbury 1916: p 22 above. "Dickens had a singular mastery
    of **travel**, in all its phases, tragic, comic and neutral"
    (p 316 1932 edn.) Cf Quiller-Couch below: "Rapid travel...
    is one of his most potent resources" (p 38.)

Quiller-Couch 1922-5: p 23 above. "A world 'full of folk',
    but not, like Piers Plowman's, a '**field** full of folk'.
    His understanding of England is in many ways as deep as
    Shakespeare's; but it is all, or almost all, of the urban
    England which in his day had already begun to kill the
    rural..." (pp 34-5; cf pp 68-72 and see further below under
    "Dickens and Sport" and "Dickens and the Railway Age".)

Matz 1922: p 43 above.

Hopkins, A.A. A Dickens Atlas. New York 1923.

Dexter, Walter. Little Nell's Journey. Dickensian 20 1924.
    Cf Bartholomew 1910 above.

Dexter, Walter. The Kent of Dickens. 1924.
    The England of Dickens. 1925.

Hayward, Arthur Lawrence. The Days of Dickens. 1926.
    Hayward ed The Dickens Encyclopaedia nd (ref Who's Who 1945)

Gadd, W.Laurence. The Great Expectations Country. 1929.

Barnes, A.W. A Dickens Guide. 1929.

Darwin, Bernard. A Dickens Pilgrimage. nd (c1930).
    Articles rp from The Times. Ref Who's Who 1945.

Dean, F.R. Dickens and Manchester. Dickensian 34 1938.

House 1941: p 27 above.

Cruikshank 1949: see below under "Radical and Reformer".

Tillotson 1954: p 30 above. Social and economic scene in 1840s.

Addison, William. In the Steps of Charles Dickens. 1955.

Brown 1970: p 36 above.

Hardwick, Michael and Mollie. Dickens's England. 1970.

Hutchings, Richard J. Dickens on an Island. Bath 1970.
  Dickens's visit to Isle of Wight 1849 where Copperfield was
  partly written. Cf Pope-Hennessy 1945: "...picnics at
  Shanklin... tea-parties in Lady Jane Swinburne's garden where
  his own youngsters played with a red-headed boy called
  Algernon..." (p 299; cf Swinburne 1913 pp xvi, xix.)

Williams, Raymond. The Country and the City. 1973.
  Cf Quiller-Couch 1922 above.

Nelson 1974: see below under "Dickens and the Railway Age".

Dickens's London

Ainsworth, W.Harrison. "Mr Dickens, with his wonderful
  knowledge of London life and character, and unequalled powers
  of delineation, has done more for this metropolis, in the
  Pickwick Papers and in Oliver Twist, than Paul de Kock, in all
  his works, has done for Paris" (pref new edn Rookwood dated
  18 Oct 1837.)

Emerson 1848: p 12 above. "Dickens, with preternatural
  apprehension of the language of manners, and the varieties of
  street life, with pathos and laughter, with patriotic and still
  enlarging generosity, writes London tracts" (see further below
  under "Dickens and Hogarth".)

Bagehot 1858: p 13 above. "Mr Dickens's genius is especially
  suited to the delineation of city life... He describes London
  like a special correspondent for posterity" (p 176 in 1911 EL
  edn.)

Masson 1859: p 13 above. "The novels of Dickens and Thackeray
  are, most of them, novels of London; it is in the multifarious
  circumstances of London life and its peculiar humours that
  they move most frequently and have their most characteristic
  being. A fact not unimportant in the appreciation of both.'"
  (see further below under "Dickens and Thackeray".)

Mayhew, Henry. London Labour and the London Poor. 4 vols 1861-2 (following articles Morning Chronicle 1849-50). Modern selections incl The Street Trader's Lot ed Stanley Rubinstein 1948; Mayhew's London ed Peter Quennell 1949; WC edn 1965 ed J.L.Bradley; and Voices of the Poor ed Anne Humphreys 1972. See also The Unknown Mayhew 1971 ed E.P. Thompson and Eileen Yeo and further below under "Dickens and Henry Mayhew".

Sala 1870: p 2 above. Describes encountering Dickens in out-of-the-way places in London. "... A hansom whirled you by the Bell & Horns at Brompton, and there he was striding, as with seven-league boots, seemingly in the direction of North-end, Fulham..." (qu Forster 1872 bk 11 ch 3.)

Pemberton, T.E. Dickens's London. Guildford 1870.

Anon. Dickens's Dictionary of London. 1879. Incl 2 maps.

Harrison 1894-5: p 17 above. "...It is quite true: London is a microcosm, an endless and bottomless Babylon; which, perhaps, no man has ever known so well as did Charles Dickens. This was his library: here he gathered that vast encyclopaedia of human nature which some are inclined to call 'cockney', but if it be, 'Cockayne' must be a very large country indeed" (pp 139-40 2nd edn.)

Gissing 1898: p 17 above. "...amid the streets of London... seeking for the places which had been made known to me by Dickens..." (cf Shaw 1876 under Pearson 1942 below.)

Chesterton 1906: p 20 above. Cf Orwell 1939 below.

Smith, F.H. In Dickens's London. New York 1914.

Santayana 1921: p 23 above. "...Dickens is the poet of those acres of yellow brick streets which the traveller sees from the railway viaducts as he approaches London; they need a poet, and they deserve one..."

Chancellor, E.Beresford. The London of Charles Dickens. 1924 TLS reviewer 5 Jun 24 commented that "no ancient city is a particularly lovable place to a keen reformer with a strong taste for police work. But the truth is probably that London got less and less lovable to him as he grew older, for it was continually losing the features he cared for most ... The London of Our Mutual Friend is grimmer and drabber than the London of Pickwick, and Dickens clearly enjoys it less" (qu House 1941 p 147; cf Dickens 1893: p 127 above.)

Dickens's London, cont.

Kent, William. With Dickens in the Borough. 1927.

Dexter, Walter. The London of David Copperfield. Dickensian 27 1931.

Moreland, Arthur. Dickens Landmarks in London. Fwd Sir Henry Dickens. 1931.

Dent 1933: p 4 above. "He was a Londoner to the core...as firmly attached to the grimy, foggy, grey old city...as a homing pigeon to its loft" (p 313 1935 edn.)

Kent, William. London for Dickens Lovers. 1936.

Orwell 1939-40: p 26 above. "...from the age of nine onwards he was brought up in London in commercial surroundings, and generally in an atmosphere of struggling poverty. Mentally he belongs to the small urban bourgeoisie..." (p 22 1946 edn.) "It is interesting to see how Chesterton, another Cockney, always presents Dickens as the spokesman of 'the poor', without showing much awareness of who 'the poor' really are ..." (pp 28-9; see further below under "Radical and Reformer").

House 1941: p 27 above. Ch 6.

Pearson, Hesketh. "Dickens had been dead for six years; but to Shaw London was the novelist's creation and the names of the streets through which he drove seemed to come straight from the pages of Dickens" (on Shaw's first visit to London in 1876: Bernard Shaw 1942 p 49; see further below under "Dickens and Shaw".)

Churchill, R.C. "We see the immense importance of Dickens. He was the first novelist to combine the influence of Fielding with the urban feeling, the receptiveness to the charm and power of the big city. His intensely original genius was set against the background of London..." (Spectator 22 Oct 1943.)

Priestley 1947: p 39 above.

Churchill 1950: p 29 above. Ch 3.

House 1955: p 31 above.

Brown 1963: p 33 above.

Bell, A.D. London in the Age of Dickens. Norman Okla 1967.

Pritchett 1969-70: p 35 above. "The first thing to say about
the comedy of Dickens is that London, the city itself,
becomes the chief character..." (p 20.)

Chesney, Kellow. The Victorian Underworld. 1970. Partly
drawn from Mayhew 1861 above.

Williams 1970: p 78 above. "Dickens was the first English
novelist to explore the modern city - in its form as the
metropolis - as a social fact and as a human landscape"
(p 21; cf Churchill 1943 and Pritchett 1969 above.)

Hibbert, Christopher. Dickens's London. In Tomlin 1970:
p 8 above. Cf Hibbert 1967: p 5 above.

Fletcher, Geoffrey. The London Dickens Knew. 1970.

Greaves, John and Gwen Major (ed). The London of Charles
Dickens. 1970. Centenary pbn by London Transport and
Dickens Fellowship.

Stedman-Jones, Gareth. Outcast London: A Study in the
Relationship between Classes in Victorian Society. Oxford
1971.

Welsh 1971: p 36 above. "Throughout his writings Dickens
comments on the loneliness of the city-dweller..."

Patten 1972: p 45 above. Incl maps of London and England in
Pickwickian times.

Dickens in America

Anon. New York Mirror 13 Oct 1838. "We have seen a letter
from Charles Dickens...in which he expresses his intention
of making an early visit to New York... We know of no
contemporary writer toward whom a more generous welcome
would be extended..." (qu Houtchens 1945 below.)

Clark, Lewis Gaylord. International Copy-right Law: Mr Dickens
Knickerbocker Mag New York Jun 1840. Urges "the necessity
of this measure", qu letter from Dickens "our literary
benefactor" whose "works are perused in every state and
territory...in the whole Union" (qu House 1969 p 6 above
pp 55-6.)

Anon. Boston Notion 22 Jan 1842. Verses in honour of
   Dickens's arrival:
      "Welcome, loved stranger from a distant strand.'
      Welcome, thrice welcome to our happy land..."

Field, Joseph M. Boz.' A Masque Phrenological written in
   Honour of the Arrival of Charles Dickens. Boston 22 Jan 42.
   Characters incl Boz himself, characters from the novels, and
   various phrenological faculties such as Philo-
   progenitiveness in the shape of Queen Victoria.

Longfellow, Henry Wadsworth. "Dickens...is a glorious fellow
   ...a slight dash of the Dick Swiveller about him..."
   (letter Jan 1842 qu House 1969; see further Edward
   Wagenknecht, Dickens in Longfellow's Letters and Journals,
   Dickensian 1955.)

Anon. Extra Boz Herald. Special no New York Herald 15 Feb 42.
   Rowdy Journal in Chuzzlewit probably based chiefly on the
   Herald. See further Paul B.Davis, Dickens and the American
   Press 1842, DS 4 1968.

Anon (probably Horace Greeley). New York Tribune 14 Feb and
   21 Feb 1842. Editorials supporting Dickens in copyright
   issue. Cf Clark 1840 above. National Intelligencer
   Washington DC 19 Mar 42 also supported Dickens, but most
   American commentators were rather resentful at his want of
   tact or courtesy in raising an issue like this at such a
   time.

Clark, Lewis Gaylord. Harper's New Monthly Mag Aug 1862.
   Reminiscences of Dickens's visit in 1842.

Harte 1870: qu above p 15.

Fields, James T. Some Memories of Charles Dickens. Atlantic
   Monthly Boston Aug 1870.

Putnam, George Washington. Four Months with Charles Dickens.
   By his Secretary. Atlantic Monthly Oct & Nov 1870. See
   further Noel C.Peyrouton, Dickensian 1963.

Forster 1872-4: p 2 above. Bk 3 America 1841-2 largely based
   on Dickens's letters home. Bk 10 America Revisited 1867-8
   is less detailed.

Dolby 1885: see below under "Stage and Platform".

Howells 1891, 1895: p 17 above.

Beazell, W.P.(ed). An Account of the Ball given in Honour of
Charles Dickens in New York City... Cedar Rapids Iowa 1908.
Editor argues that Dickens "missed the point" of some of the
parodies. See comment in House 1974 p 73n and cf Churchill
1958 below.

Wilkins, William Glyde (ed). Charles Dickens in America.
New York 1911.

James 1913: qu above p 22.

Phelps 1916: qu above p 60.

Santayana 1921-2: p 23 above.

Payne, Edward F. Dickens Days in Boston: A Record of Daily
Events. Boston 1927.

Leacock 1933: p 4 above. Ch 4 Boz Visits America; ch 11 The
Second Visit to America. Cf Leacock 1939 below.

Dent 1933: p 4 above. Ch 7.

Leacock, Stephen. Dickens and Canada. Queen's Quarterly 46
1939.

American Number. Dickensian 38 1942. Centenary of first
visit. Earlier American nos Aug 1909, Aug 1910, Sep 1916,
Apr 1926, Dec 1941.

Dickens in America. TLS 9 Jan 1943. Chuzzlewit centenary.

Brooks, Van Wyck. The World of Washington Irving. New York
1944; London 1945. See pp 271, 279 and 293 in 1945 edn.

Pacey, W.C.D. Washington Irving and Charles Dickens.
American Literature 16 1945.

Houtchens, L.H.and C.W. Contributions of Early American
Journals to the Study of Dickens. MLQ 6 1945.

Brooks, Van Wyck. The Times of Melville and Whitman. New Yor,
1947; London 1948. See pp 15, 120, 207-8 in 1948 edn.

Adrian, Arthur A. Dickens in Cleveland Ohio. Dickensian
Winter 1947-8.

Hamilton, L. Dickens in Canada. Dalhousie Rev 30 1950.

Dickens in America, cont.

Cunliffe, Marcus. The Literature of the United States. 1954.
Dickens in the West (pp 161-4 in 3rd edn 1967.)

Churchill 1958: p 32 above under Ford; pp 130-1.

Churchill, R.C. The Literature of the United States. Ch 15
Concise CHEL 1970 edn; pp 791, 820-1.

Whitley 1972: p 61 above. Incl some of Dickens's letters home.

See also above under "American Notes" and below under "Dickens
and Mark Twain" etc.

Dickens in France

Dombey and Little Dorrit were partly written in Paris; Bleak
House and Hard Times were partly written at Boulogne.

Chasles, P. Journal des Débats 13 Oct 1838. Review of
Pickwick Papers. French versions eg Le Club des Pickwistes
appeared from 1838 onwards. See also p 41 above under
Reynolds whose imitation Pickwick Abroad was subtitled The
Tour in France. Cf Joseph Nolin, Dickensian 1927 pp 235-9.

Janin 1842: qu above p 50. See Thackeray below.

Thackeray, W.M. Dickens in France. Fraser's Mag Mar 1842.
Reply to Janin's criticisms above, pointing out that Janin
had no English and had taken his account from a melodramatic
stage version of Nickleby at the Ambigu-Comique. See further
p 50 above.

Forgues 1843: p 11 above. See further below under Carlton.

Pichot, Amédée, ed La Revue Britannique, tr Copperfield under
title Le Neveu de ma Tante, Paris 1851. See Sylvère Monod,
Une curiosité dans l'histoire de la traduction, Etudes
Anglaises 14 1962. And further below under Carlton.

Taine 1856: p 13 above; qu above under "Hard Times" and below
under "Sex in Dickens". Cf Arthur Dudley, Revue des Deux
Mondes Mar 1848.

Newspapers in Paris in 1856 greeted him as "l'illustre
Romancier, Sir Dickens". Cf cry of Washington cab-drivers
in 1842: "Lord Boz's carriage!'"

Dickens. Address of the English Author to the French Public.
17 Jan 1857. Prefixed to trn of Nickleby Paris 1857; rp
Collected Papers in Nonesuch edn 1937.

Forster 1872-4: p 2 above. Bk 4 ch 6: Paris and Marseilles
1844. Bk 5 ch 7: Paris 1846-7 where he visited George Sand
and Victor Hugo. Bk 7 ch 4: Boulogne 1853-6. Bk 7 ch 5:
Paris 1855-6.

Flaubert 1872: qu above p 42.

Du Pontavice de Heussey, R.Y.M. Dickens à Paris 1853-6.
Le Livre 10 Apr 1886. See also p 3 above.

Hennequin 1887: p 16 above.

Swinburne 1902: p 19 above. "Dickens was once most unjustly
taxed with injustice to the French..." (pp 47-8 1913 edn).
Goes on to make comparison with Hugo.

Munro 1908: p 20 above.

Maury, Lucien. Figures Littéraires. Paris 1911. Incl review
of French trn of Chesterton 1906 (p 20 above). See comment
by Christiane d'Haussy in G.K.Chesterton 1974 p 211 and
further below under "Dickens and Chesterton".

Wilkins, William Glyde. Early Foreign Translations of Dickens
Dickensian 7 1911. Cf Leacock 1933 below

Chesterton 1913: p 21 above. "...Dickens travelled in a
French railway train, and noticed that this eccentric nation
provided him with wine that he could drink and sandwiches he
could eat, and manners he could tolerate. And remembering t
ghastly sawdust-eating waiting-rooms of the North English
railways, he wrote that rich chapter in Mugby Junction..."
(pp 34-5 OPUS edn; see further below under "Dickens and the
Railway Age".)

Delattre, Floris. Dickens et la France. Paris 1927.

Maurois 1927: p 24 above.

Devonshire, M.G. The English Novel in France 1830-70. 1929.

Garrett, J.(ed). Dickens and Daudet. 1930. Cf Munro above.

Fabre, E. Dickens in France. Dickensian 28 1932.

Leacock 1933: p 4 above. Ch 8 gives details of early French
    translations such as Le marchand d'antiquities (tr A.J.B.
    Defauconpret) and serial translations like Chuzzlewit in Le
    Moniteur 1855. Then "the illustrious house of Hachette
    undertook the publication of all Dickens's works", which
    "brought Dickens widely to the knowledge of the French people.
    The rising generation of the Second Empire heard Dickens's
    books read aloud at home, just as their English cousins of the
    day heard and read Victor Hugo" (pp 178-89.)

Lemonnier 1936: p 26 above.

Shaw 1937: qu above p 107.

Lemonnier 1938: p 26 above.

Orwell 1939-40: p 26 above; pp 25-8 1946 edn.   "...In the whole
    of A Tale of Two Cities there is not a line that could be
    taken as meaning 'Look how these wicked Frenchmen behave.'..."

Wilson, R.A. Translations of Dickens. BMQ 14 1940.

Alain 1945: p 28 above.

Pope-Hennessy 1945: p 4 above; pp 273, 368-9.

Lemonnier 1946: p 4 above.

Monod 1953: p 30 above.

Monod 1958: p 31 above.

Beaumont 1962: p 33 above.

Carlton, W.J. Old Nick at Devonshire Terrace. Dickensian 59
    1963. Describes visit of "Old Nick" (Paul Emile Forgues) and
    Pichot to Dickens's house in 1843. Forgues himself wrote an
    account in L'Illustration 1844 and Pichot in pref 3rd edn Le
    Neveu de ma Tante (p 135 above.)

Fluchère 1969: p 35 above.

Wall 1970: p 7 above; pp 30-1.

Tomlin, E.W.F.(ed). Newly Discovered Dickens Letters. TLS
    22 Feb 1974. Letters in French from Dickens and his wife
    to Ernest Legouvé.

Dickens in France, cont.

Talon 1974: p 112 above.

Monod 1974: p 92 above under Churchill.

See also above under "A Tale of Two Cities" and below under
"Dickens and Balzac", "Dickens and Flaubert" etc.

Dickens in Germany

Kuenzel, J.H.   Article on Dickens and Pickwick Papers.
Leipzig 1838.   Pickwick was tr H.Roberts 5 vols Leipzig
1837-8.   German imitations are mentioned p 41 above under
Reynolds.   Pope-Hennessy 1945 p 260 qu Freytag's Ein Dank
für Charles Dickens, saying that Pickwick "was like a ray of
sunshine in Germany at a time when conditions of life were
dreary in the extreme..."   "...the brave good sense that
shines through the comic treatment" wrote Freytag, "was as
moving to Germans of that day as a melody from home that
strikes unexpectedly on a wanderer's ear."

Dickens to Dr J.A.Diezmann 10 Mar 1840.   Expresses his "delight
and gratification" at learning he was "held in such high
esteem" in Germany (House 1969 p 43).   Diezmann tr Sketches,
Oliver and Nickleby (Brunswick 1838-9).   See article by
Comte de Suzannet in Dickensian 28 1931-2.   Master Humphrey
was tr E.A.Moriarty (Leipzig) and C.von Czarnowski
(Brunswick) 1840-1.   Gummer 1940 below (pp 7-8, 29-31)
points out that Old Curiosity Shop and Barnaby were better
received by German critics than Oliver or Nickleby.

Dickens to Dr Kuenzel 13 Sep 1841.   "Next to my own people
I respect and treasure the Germans" (qu Pope-Hennessy 1945
p 261 who comments that there is "something distinctively
German" about Dickens's "excursions into the world of
phantasy."

Marx, Karl.   Welcomed Dickens's novels, in spite of their
sentimentality, as social documents, confirming reports of
Lord Shaftesbury (Rheinische Zeitung 1841-2 qu Pope-Hennessy
1945 p 262.)   See further under "Radical and Reformer."

Longfellow 1842.   On his visit to the Continent noted that
Dickens had a great vogue in Germany.   By 1844 his books had
all been translated into German and most of them into Dutch
(eg Chuzzlewit 1844).   Ten works by Boz in Tauchnitz edns
1843-6.

Dickens in Germany, cont.

Danzel 1845: p 12 above.

Schmidt 1852: p 12 above.

Ludwig 1860: p 94 above. Comment on Hard Times qu.

Forster 1872-4: p 2 above. Records Dickens's visit to the
  Rhineland in 1846 (bk 5 ch 2). See further Dexter 1938:
  p 6 above.

Dilthey 1877: p 16 above.

Benignus 1895: p 39 above.

Aronstein 1896: p 17 above.

Jugler 1912: see below under "Characters".

Zweig 1920: p 23 above.

Heuer 1927: p 24 above.

Wickhardt 1933: p 25 above.

Dent 1933: p 4 above; p 199 1935 edn.

Gummer, Ellis N. Dickens and Germany. MLR 33 1938.

Gummer, Ellis N. Dickens's Works in Germany 1837-1937. Oxford
  1940. Records 23 critical articles on Dickens in Germany in
  one year, 1839. See further above under Dickens 1840.

Wilson 1940: p 137 above.

Oehlbaum 1944: p 28 above.

Pope-Hennessy 1945: p 4 above. "Moltke and his staff officers
  based their appreciations of the English character on Pickwick
  and Little Dorrit" (p xi; see also pp 259-62, 321.)

Gibson, F. Dickens and Germany. Dickensian 43 1947.

Thalmann 1956: p 31 above.

Seehase 1961: p 33 above.

Oppel 1962-5: p 116 above.

Wall 1970: p 7 above; pp 30-1.

<u>Dickens in Germany, cont.</u>

Reinhold 1973: p 92 above.

Buchloh 1973: see below under "Dickens and Wilkie Collins".

<u>Dickens in Italy</u>

Dickens wrote The Chimes in Genoa.   When he died Genoa
   newspapers carried the headline NOSTRO CARLO DICKENS E MORTO
   Gissing's book on Dickens (1898) was largely written at Sien

Horne 1844: p 12 above.   Notes (p 76) that some of the early
   German and French translations were not very accurate, but
   commends Oliviere Twist (tr Gianbattista Basaggio, Milan)
   and Nicolas Nickleby (tr E.de la Bédollière), Paris 1840.

Savonarolo and Murray 1846-7: p 73 above.

Forster 1872-4: p 2 above.   Bk 4: London and Genoa.   Bk 7 ch 3
   Switzerland and Italy.   See also under "Pictures from Italy"
   and note relation between that book (and Forster) and the
   Italian scenes in Little Dorrit.

Swinburne 1902: p 19 above.   "Italian readers of Little Dorrit
   ought to appreciate and to enjoy the delightful and admirabl
   personality of Cavalletto.   Mr Baptist in Bleeding Heart Yar
   is as attractively memorable a figure as his excellent frier
   Signor Panco" (pp 48-9 1913 edn.)

Welch, D.   Dickens in Genoa.   Harper's Monthly Mag Aug 1906.

Cannavo 1918: p 73 above.

Massoul, H.   Trois voyages d'Italie: Charles de Brosses, Char]
   Dickens, Maurice Maeterlinck.   Mercure de France 1 Jul 1924.

Cecil 1931-4: qu above p 73.

Spaventa-Filippi, S.   Dickens.   Rome 1911; rv 1924; rp
   L'Umorismo e gli Umoristi, Milan 1932.

Leacock 1933: qu above p 73.

House 1941: qu above p 73.

Robinson 1951: p 80 above under Collins.   Italian tour with
   Wilkie Collins 1853 (pp 71-9 1974 edn.)

Praz 1952: p 30 above.

Izzo 1954: p 31 above.

Dickens in Italy: A Letter to Thomas Mitton.   New York 1956.

Brunner, K.   Dickens und Mark Twain in Italien.   Festschrift
    für Walther Fischer, Heidelberg 1959.   See further below
    under "Dickens and Mark Twain".

Carlton, W.J.   Dickens studies Italian.   Dickensian 61 1965.

Fluchère 1969: p 35 above.

Paroissien 1973: p 73 above.

Dickens in Russia

Belinsky 1843: p 54 above.

Belinsky, Vissarion Grigorievitch.   "The most influential
    critic of the period" in Russia who "died in his late
    thirties" (Priestley 1960 p 183).   He praised Chuzzlewit in
    1844 and first chs of Dombey 1848.   "The great critic died
    before the rest of that novel appeared in translation"
    (Anikst 1970 below; see also Katarsky 1966 ref Gifford 1968
    below.)   Article on Dickens and Belinsky by A.M.Brojde is
    mentioned in DSN Jun 1974 p 61.

Dostoevsky 1846-8: p 54 above.

Vvedensky, Irinarkh Ivanovich.   Letter to Dickens from St
    Petersburg 1848 qu Forster 1872-4 bk 6 ch 4.   Name misread
    by Forster (see Anikst below).   Sending Dickens his trn of
    Dombey (cf Belinsky above) Vvedensky assured him that "for
    the last eleven years your name has enjoyed a wide celebrity
    in Russia and from the banks of the Neva to the remotest
    parts of Siberia you are read with avidity".   See further
    Katarsky, Gifford, Anikst below.   "It was Vvedensky's
    versions of Copperfield and Pickwick that Dostoevsky read
    in prison in Siberia in the early 1850s" (Wall 1970 p 31.)

Druzhinin, Alexander.   In 1849 pointed out similarities between
    Dickens and Dostoevsky in their treatment of childhood.
    (Ref Anikst 1970 below; cf Phelps 1916 and see further below
    under "Dickens and Childhood" and "Dickens and Dostoevsky".)

Tolstoy, Count Leo.   Childhood and Youth.   1852.   Boyhood.
   1854.   Trn London 1862, New York 1886; WC edn tr Maude 1921.
   "...could hardly have taken the form it did without the
   example of Copperfield" (Gifford 1968 below).   "Compiling
   the list of books which made a particularly great impression
   upon him between the ages of 14 and 20 Tolstoy included
   Copperfield" (Anikst 1970 below; who goes on to quote from
   Tolstoy's later diaries and journals to effect that he
   regarded Pickwick, Little Dorrit and Bleak House as
   masterpieces "and praised Dickens as a novelist of the
   first rank, a true artist".   See further below.)

Dostoevsky 1868: see below under "Dickens and Cervantes".

Tolstoy 1903: qu above p 19.   Cf Notebook qu Aylmer Maude,
   Life of Tolstoy 1929: "The first condition of an author's
   popularity...is the love with which he treats his
   characters.   That is why Dickens's characters are the
   friends of all mankind; they are a bond of union between
   man in America and man in St Petersburg" (Wall 1970 p 240n.)

Wilkins 1911: p 136 above.

Nabokoff 1912: p 21 above.

Korolenko, V.G.   My First Encounter with Dickens.   1912;
   rp Davie 1965 below.

Phelps 1916: p 22 above.   "Tolstoy and Dostoevsky read Dickens
   with eagerness and profit.   Dickens has been and is today
   more popular in Russia than any other English novelist; the
   common people feel their kinship to him in the touch of
   nature.   In one of the Siberian provincial jails, where
   records are always kept of the prisoners' reading, the
   library minutes for 1914 are interesting.   Of British author
   in Russian translations, Dickens was called for 192 times;
   Scott, 98; Wells, 53; Wilde, 44; Kipling, 41; Shakespeare,
   33" (p 108; see further below under "Dickens and Dostoevsky"

Grossman, Leonid.   Biblioteka Dostoyevskogo.   Odessa 1919.
   "Dostoevsky admired The Old Curiosity Shop for the descript
   of London slums and for the delineation of the psychology o
   all the martyrs and victims of life, the maltreated childre
   and self-styled clowns" (qu Anikst 1970 below; who goes on
   say that "according to Grossman Dickens's influence is
   particularly obvious in The Insulted and Injured as well as
   in Crime and Punishment" (Phelps's opinion also; see furthe
   Gifford below and under "Dickens and Dostoevsky".)

Radlov, Ernest. Critical study of Dickens, 1922; ref Anikst
1970 below.

Dickens 1928: p 4 above. Records he was treated with great
respect in Russia as the son of the novelist.

Chesterton 1929: p 20 above under Chesterton 1906. Russian
trn "met with critical abuse because it extolled Dickens
for his ideals of home and Christmas which were utterly
despised by the then sociologically minded critics" (Anikst
1970 below; cf Orwell 1939-40.)

Yelizarova, Maria. Essay on Dickens, 1934; ref Anikst 1970.

Orwell 1939-40: qu above p 70. Lenin and The Cricket on the
Hearth.

A Russian Correspondent. Dickens in Russia: A Moral Educator.
TLS 7 Sep 1940; rp Davie 1965 below.

Silman, Tamara. Essay on Dickens, Leningrad 1941; expanded
book form 1948, rp 1958, new edn 1970. Ref Anikst 1970.
Her view of Dickens as a "kind of romantic realist"
challenged by Valentina Ivasheva in monograph on Dickens,
Moscow 1954, which stresses his critical realism. Ivan
Katarsy's book of 1960, continues Anikst, takes a stand
"midway between Silman and Ivasheva", emphasizing Dickens's
artistry and his aesthetic views.

Fridlender, Yulia (ed). Charles Dickens 1838-1945. Leningrad
1946; rv 1838-1960 with Ivan Katarsky, Moscow 1962. Bibliog
Russian trns, reviews, books, articles etc and some essays on
Dickens in Russia.

Ivasheva 1954: see above under Silman.

Katarsky 1960: p 5 above. See comment under Silman 1941.

Priestley 1960: p 33 above.

Gilenson, B. Dickens in Russia. Dickensian 57 1961.

Senelick, L. Charl'z Dikkens and the Russian Encyclopaedias.
DS 1 1965.

Davie, D.A.(ed). Russian Literature and Modern English Fiction.
Chicago 1965.

Dickens in Russia, cont.

Katarsky, Ivan. Dickens in Russia: The Middle of the
Nineteenth Century. Moscow 1966. See Gifford 1968 below.

Gifford, Henry. Dickens in Russia: The Initial Phase.
Forum for Modern Language Studies Jan 1968; incl Wall 1970
pp 509-19. See Katarsky 1966 above, from which Gifford
derives his "main argument" and "many of my examples".
Dickens and Gogol pp 510-12 in Wall; Dickens and Tolstoy
pp 513-15; Dickens and Dostoevsky pp 515-19.

Anikst, Alexander, of the Institute of the History of the
Arts, Moscow. Dickens in Russia. TLS 4 Jun 1970. Full-
page summary of his popularity since the 1840s and his
critical reception at various dates before and after the
Revolution. See frequent refs above pp 141-3 and cf
Gifford 1968.

Wall 1970: p 7 above; p 31. And under Gifford 1968.

Brojde 1972: p 141 above under Belinsky.

Cain 1973: see below under "Dickens and Tolstoy".

Lary 1973: see below under "Dickens and Dostoevsky".

See further below under "Dickens and Gogol" etc.

The Serial Novelist

Shakespeare Club (1838-9). One of the subjects discussed at
this club, of which Dickens was a member, was: "Is the
present system of periodical publication calculated to
raise the character of literature?" (qu House 1965 p 392n.)
Cf Dickens 1865 below.

Wilkie 1839: qu above p 10.

Mackenzie, Henry. "The author of a periodical performance
has indeed a claim to the attention and regard of his
readers, more interesting than that of any other writer..."
(qu Dickens pref Nickleby 1839.)

Anon (John Forster). Examiner 4 Dec 1841. "We are not sorry
that Mr Dickens has discontinued the weekly form of
publication..." Goes on to point out the advantages and

disadvantages of these short instalments as against the
longer monthly ones, among the advantages in Dickens's case
being that the opportunities for "self-indulgence" were
rarer and the "tendency to exaggerate" was less (qu House
1969 p ix.)

Dickens. "I have endeavoured in the progress of this tale,
to resist the temptation of the current Monthly Number,
and to keep a steadier eye upon the general purpose and
design" (pref Chuzzlewit 1844; cf Forster above.)

Dickens. Our Mutual Friend. "Postscript in Lieu of Preface"
dated 2 Sep 1865. "...that I hold the advantages of the
mode of publication to outweigh its disadvantages, may be
easily believed of one who revived it in the Pickwick
Papers after long disuse, and has pursued it ever since."

James, Henry. French Poets and Novelists. 1878. Refers to
Dickens as the "great improvisatore".

Harrison 1894-5: p 17 above. "... It is plain that Charles
Dickens had nothing of that epical gift which gave us Tom
Jones and Ivanhoe. Perhaps the persistent use of the serial
form shows that he felt no interest in that supreme art of
an immense drama duly unfolded to a prepared end. In
Pickwick there neither was, nor could there be, any organic
plot. In Oliver Twist, in Barnaby Rudge, in Dombey, in
Bleak House, in the Tale of Two Cities, there are indications
of his possessing this power, and in certain parts of these
tales we seem to be in the presence of a great master of
epical narration. But the power is not sustained... The
serial form, where a leading character wanders about to
various places, and meets a succession of quaint parties,
seems to be that which suited his genius and which he himself
most entirely enjoyed" (pp 141-2.)

Gissing 1898: p 17 above. "...Even Dickens occasionally
suffered from the necessity of filling a certain space.
Think how long his novels are, and marvel that the
difficulty does not more often declare itself" (ch 5.)

Buchan 1907: p 94 above.

Quiller-Couch 1922-5: p 23 above; pp 43-6.

Smith, H.B. How Dickens wrote his Books. Harper's Mag Dec
1924; rp Strand Mag Feb 1925.

The Serial Novelist, cont.

Eckel, J.C. Prime Pickwick in Parts: A Census with Complete
    Collation, Comparison and Comment. Fwd A.E.Newton. New
    York 1928.

Darwin, Bernard (ed). The Dickens Advertiser: A Collection
    of the Avertisements in the Original Parts of Novels by
    Charles Dickens. 1930.

Hatton, Thomas and A.H.Cleaver. A Bibliography of the
    Periodical Works of Charles Dickens. 1933.

Grubb, Gerald G. On the Serial Publication of Oliver Twist.
    MLN 56 1941.
    Dickens's Pattern of Weekly Serialisation. ELH 9 1942.

Boll 1944: p 115 above.

Butt 1948: p 29 above.

Grubb 1953: p 56 above.

Maugham 1954: p 30 above. "The system encouraged them to be
    leisurely and long-winded. We know from their own admission
    how from time to time the authors of these serials, even the
    best of them, Dickens, Thackeray, Trollope, found it a
    hateful burden to be obliged to deliver an instalment by a
    given date. No wonder they padded.' No wonder they burdened
    their stories with irrelevant episodes" (pp 21-2 PB edn.)

Tillotson 1954: p 30 above. "In the serial-writer's relation
    to his public there is indeed something of the stimulating
    contact which an actor or a public speaker receives from an
    audience. Serial publication gave back to story-telling
    its original context of performance..." (p 36; cf Wilkie,
    Mackenzie, Dickens qu above.)

Butt and Tillotson 1957: qu above p 31.

Fielding, K.J. The Monthly Serialisation of Dickens's Novels.
    Dickensian 54 1958.
    The Weekly Serialisation of Dickens's Novels. Ibid.
    Incl tables on chapter distribution etc. Included also
    (from Fielding) in Wall 1970 pp 528-36.

Sucksmith, Harvey Peter. Dickens at Work on Bleak House:
    His Memoranda and Number Plans. Renaissance & Modern
    Studies 9 1965.

The Serial Novelist, cont.

Herring, P.D. Dickens's Monthly Number Plans for Little
    Dorrit. MP 64 1966.

Coolidge, A.C. Charles Dickens as a Serial Novelist. Ames
    Iowa 1967.

Wall 1970: p 7 above; pp 27-30 and under Fielding 1958 above.

Nowell-Smith, Simon. Editing Dickens. TLS 4 Jun 1970.
    Incl detailed information about revisions at the proof stage,
    eg to Chuzzlewit and Great Expectations.

Fader, Daniel. The Periodical Context of English Literature.
    Ann Arbor Mich 1971. See review by Lance Schachterle, DSN 4
    Dec 1973.

Easson 1972: p 56 above.

Anon. Instalment Plans. TLS 22 Jun 1973. Review of Slater
    1973: p 51 above.

Schachterle, Lance. Oliver Twist and its Serial Predecessors.
    DSA 3 1974.

Churchill, R.C. The Monthly Dickens and the Weekly Dickens.
    See p 79 above.

In both the Clarendon and PEL edns the original
    instalment divisions are indicated. Cf Fielding
    and Wall above. Butt and Tillotson (p 31 above)
    remark that Dickens was "never concerned to preserve
    the evidence of where his instalments began and ended.
    Nevertheless, these divisions hold an abiding importance,
    especially for readers interested in Dickens's constructive
    powers..."

Dickens and his Illustrators

Dickens. Letters to George Cruikshank 1835-9; to Robert
    Seymour 1836; to H.K.Browne (Phiz) 1836-9; and to George
    Cattermole 1838-9. In House 1965: p 6 above. Detailed notes.

Browne 1836: p 40 above.

Gibson, Thomas.   Racy Sketches of Expeditions from the
Pickwick Club.   1838; rp Grego 1899 below.

Dickens.   Letters to Cruikshank, Browne, Cattermole 1840-1.
In House 1969: p 6 above.   Detailed notes.

Dickens.   Letters to Cruikshank, Browne, Cattermole 1842-3.
In House 1974: p 6 above.   Detailed notes.
For later letters see Dexter 1938 (p 6 above) or future
vols in House c1977 onward.

Browne, Hablot Knight.   Dombey Characters: from designs by
Phiz.   1848.

Cruikshank, George.   The Artist and the Author.   1872.
Claimed to have originated Oliver Twist.   Cf Forster below
and see further under Miller 1971, Vogler 1970, Patten 1973
and Conrad 1974.

Forster 1872-4: p 2 above.   Gives details of Dickens's
relationship with Cruikshank, Browne and other illustrators.
Refutes Cruikshank 1872.

Jerrold, Blanchard.   The Life of George Cruikshank.   1882.

Kitton, Frederic G.   Phiz: A Memoir.   1882.

Thomson, David Croal.   Life and Labours of Hablot Knight
Browne: Phiz.   1884.

Harrison 1894-5: p 17 above.   "The illustrations of Cruikshank
and Phiz are delightfully droll, and often caricatures of a
high order.   But being caricatures they overload and
exaggerate nature, and indeed are always, in one sense,
impossible in nature... And Dickens's own characters have
the same element of unnatural distortion.   It is possible
that these familiar caricatures have even done harm to his
reputation.   His creations are of a higher order of art
and are more distinctly spontaneous and original..."
(pp 137-8; see further below under "Characters".)

Kitton, Frederic G.   Dickens and his Illustrators.   1899.

Grego, Joseph (ed).   Pictorial Pickwickiana: Dickens and his
Illustrators.   2 vols 1899.

Chesterton 1906: p 20 above.   Compares Boz and Phiz to
Gilbert and Sullivan in their "common creation of a unique
thing."

Dickens and his Illustrators, cont.

Fraser, W.A.   The Illustrators of Dickens.   Dickensian 2 1906.

Stone, Marcus.   Some Recollections of Dickens.   Dickensian
    Aug 1912.   By the illustrator of Great Expectations and
    Our Mutual Friend.

Browne, Edgar A.   Phiz and Dickens.   1913.   By the artist's
    son.

Characters from Dickens.   Series of 50 cigarette cards
    issued by Messrs Player & Sons, Nottingham, c1930.
    No other novelist has had popular recognition of this kind,
    but there was a similar series of Characters from Gilbert
    and Sullivan.   See Orwell 1939 p 52 and Churchill 1958 p 142.

Leacock 1933: qu above p 72 under Forster.

Waugh, Arthur.   Charles Dickens and his Illustrators.   In
    Waugh 1937: p 26 above.   Also incl Thomas Hatton, A
    Bibliographical List of the Original Illustrations.

Churchill 1937-42: p 26 above; p 361n.

House 1941: p 27 above; pp 136, 137, 180.

Cruikshank, R.J.(ed).   The Humour of Dickens.   nd (c1950).
    Anthology illustrated by modern artists incl Ronald Searle
    and Edward Ardizzone.

Pritchett 1953: qu above p 48.

Johannsen, A.(ed).   Phiz: Illustrations from the Novels of
    Charles Dickens.   Chicago 1956.   Detailed discussion.

Hudson, Derek.   Dickens and his Illustrators.   Classics No 1.
    Oxford 1965.   OUP advrt.

Vogler, Richard Allen.   Cruikshank and Dickens: A Review of
    the Role of Artist and Author.   Ann Arbor Mich 1970.

Bentley, Nicolas.   Dickens and his Illustrators.   In Tomlin
    1970: p 8 above.

Harvey, J.R.   Victorian Novelists and their Illustrators.
    1970.   Dickens, Thackeray, Trollope...

Leavis, Q.D.   Appendix to Leavis 1970: p 36 above.

Miller, J.Hillis and David Borowitz. Charles Dickens and
    George Cruikshank. Los Angeles 1971.

Patten, Robert L. (ed). George Cruikshank: A Revaluation.
    Princeton University Library Chronicle 35 1973-4.   Essays
    by Harry Stone, Richard Vogler, Louis James ao.

Conrad, Peter. Wrestling with Demons. TLS 26 Jul 1974.
    Review of Patten above.

The Literary Artist

Hunt 1838: qu above p 9.

Landor 1841: qu above p 10.

Horne 1844: p 12 above. "So far as a single epithet can
    convey an impression of the operation of his genius, it may
    be said that Mr Dickens is an **instinctive** writer. His best
    things are suddenly revealed to him; he does not search for
    them in his mind... This is the peculiar prerogative of a
    true creative genius. "

Thackeray. Letter to David Masson 6 May 1851. "I think Mr
    Dickens has...quite a divine genius... I quarrel with his
    Art in many respects: which I don't think represents
    Nature duly..." (qu Allott 1959 p 7 above p 67; cf below.)

Thackeray. "I may quarrel with Mr Dickens's art a thousand
    and a thousand times; I delight and wonder at his genius;
    I recognize in it - I speak with awe and reverence - a
    commission from that Divine Beneficence, whose blessed task
    we know it will one day be to wipe every tear from every eye
    Thankfully I take my share of the feast of love and kindness
    which this gentle and generous and charitable soul has
    contributed to the happiness of the world. I take and enjoy
    my share, and say a Benediction for the meal" (concluding
    words, lecture on Charity and Humour, New York 1852, rp EL
    edn The English Humorists etc nd c1910 p 286.)

Taine 1856: p 13 above.

Bagehot 1858: p 13 above.

The Literary Artist, cont.

Galloway 1862: p 14 above.

Williams 1863-4: p 14 above.

McCarthy 1864: p 14 above. "We do not at all anticipate
that he will be rescued from oblivion... by his artistic
powers... " (cf James below.)

James 1865: p 14 above. "...it is one of the chief conditions
of his genius not to see beneath the surface of things...
we should, accordingly, call him the greatest of superficial
novelists... It were, in our opinion, an offence against
humanity to place Mr Dickens among the greatest novelists...
He has added nothing to our understanding of human
character" (pp 34-5 1968 edn.)

Whipple 1867: p 14 above.

Friswell 1870: p 15 above.

Hutton 1870: p 15 above.

Flaubert 1872: qu above p 42.

Lewes 1872: p 15 above. "...there probably never was a writer
of so vast a popularity whose genius was so little
appreciated by the critics... How are we to reconcile this
immense popularity with this critical contempt?" (cf James
and McCarthy above but also opposing views of Hutton,
Whipple, Forster, Ruskin, Swinburne, Gissing ao.)

Ward 1882: p 3 above.

James 1884: p 16 above. "...it would take much more courage
than I possess to intimate that the form of the novel, as
Dickens and Thackeray (for instance) saw it, had any taint
of incompleteness. It was, however, naif... " (p 78 1968 edn).

Hennequin 1887: p 16 above.

Stephen 1888: p 3 above. Argument partly qu p 126 above.

Henley 1890: p 17 above. "...he had in him at least as much
of the French artist as of the middle-class Englishman; and
if all his life he never ceased from self-education, but
went unswervingly in pursuit of culture, it was out of love
for his art and because his conscience as an artist would
not let him do otherwise" (qu Quiller-Couch 1922 p 8; cf
James and Lewes above.)

The Literary Artist, cont.

Howells 1891: p 17 above.

Lang 1891: p 17 above. Cf Henley 1890.

Harrison 1894-5: p 17 above. "...We do not criticise one
   whom we love, nor do we suffer others to do so... there
   has been hardly any serious criticism or estimate of
   Dickens as a great artist, apart from some peevish and
   sectional disparagement of his genius, which has been too
   much tinged with academic pedantry and the bias of
   aristocratic temper or political antagonism..." (pp 129-30.)

Saintsbury 1895: p 17 above.

Aronstein 1896: p 17 above.

Kitton 1897: p 17 above.

Gissing 1898: p 17 above. "A literary artist if ever there
   was one..." (cf Henley above.)

Meynell 1899: p 18 above.

Gissing 1899-1901: p 18 above.

Swinburne 1902: p 19 above. "...a great creative genius"
   (p 2 1913 edn). "...the greatest English writer of his day"
   (p 25). "...the very greatest comic poet or creator that
   ever lived" (p 29). "...this great and inexhaustible
   writer" (p 49). "...a genius of such inexhaustible force
   and such indisputable originality" (p 71.)

Meynell 1903: p 19 above.

Tolstoy 1903: qu above p 19. Cf Tolstoy 1852: p 142 above.

Chesterton 1906: p 20 above. "Strictly, there is no such
   novel as Nicholas Nickleby. There is no such novel as
   Our Mutual Friend. They are simply lengths cut from the
   flowing and mixed substance called Dickens - a substance
   any given length of which will be certain to contain a
   given proportion of brilliant and of bad stuff" (cf
   Chesterton 1907-11, particularly on Bleak House.)

Mair 1911: p 21 above. Main argument qu p 124 above.

Powys 1912: p 21 above.

Meynell 1912: p 21 above.

Canning 1912: p 21 above.

Shaw 1912: qu above p 95.

Chesterton 1913: p 21 above. "The art of Dickens was the
    most exquisite of arts: it was the art of enjoying
    everybody... This is the artistic greatness of Dickens,
    before and after which there is really nothing to be said
    ..." (pp 51-2 OPUS edn; see further below under "Characters").

Leacock 1916: qu above p 22.

Saintsbury 1916: p 22 above.

Zweig 1920: p 23 above.

Murry 1920: qu above p 23.

Lubbock 1921: p 23 above. "The method which he finally
    worked out for himself was exactly what he required...
    it surely fulfils its mission very strikingly in the best
    of his work - the best from this point of view - Bleak
    House, Dombey and Son, Our Mutual Friend..." (pp 214-5).

Santayana 1921-2: p 23 above. "...But Dickens was no free
    artist; he had more genius than taste... He worked under
    pressure, for money and applause, and often had to cheapen
    in execution what his inspiration had so vividly conceived"

Quiller-Couch 1922-5: p 23 above. "...an artist of the finest
    literary conscience" (p 7). "...a great novelist - as I
    should contend, the greatest of all English novelists -
    and certainly among the greatest of all the great
    European novelists" (p 46.)

Whibley 1923: p 24 above.

Moore 1924: see comment p 24 above.

Forster 1927: p 24 above. "Those who dislike Dickens have an
    excellent case. He ought to be bad. He is actually one of
    our big writers..." (p 79 PB edn; see further below under
    "Characters".)

Maurois 1927: p 24 above.

The Literary Artist, cont.

Wagenknecht 1929: p 25 above.

Cecil 1931-4: p 25 above. "Creative imagination may not be
the only quality necessary to the novelist, but it is the
first quality. And no English novelist had it quite in the
way Dickens had... His best passages have the immediate
irresistible force of music" (p 54 FL edn.)

Leavis 1932: qu above p 25.

Sitwell 1932: p 25 above. Cf Cecil 1931-4.

Wickhardt 1933: p 25 above.

Leacock 1933: p 4 above. "In due time it will be known that
the works of Charles Dickens represent the highest reach
of the world's imaginative literature... the world's supreme
achievement in art" (p 307.)

Shaw 1937: p 26 above.

Churchill 1937-42: p 26 above; qu below under "Radical and
Reformer". The literary artist and the moral artist are
one. See further below under "Moral Artist" and cf
Quiller-Couch above.

Sitwell 1938: p 26 above.

Ford 1939: p 26 above.

Orwell 1939-40: p 26 above. "Dickens is obviously a writer
whose parts are greater than his wholes. He is all
fragments, all details - rotten architecture, but
wonderful gargoyles" (p 49 1946 edn.)

Wilson 1939-41: p 27 above. "Chesterton asserted that time
would show that Dickens was not merely one of the
Victorians, but incomparably the greatest writer of his
time; and Shaw coupled his name with that of Shakespeare.
It is the conviction of the present writer that both these
judgments were justified" (p 3 UP edn; cf Swinburne,
Quiller-Couch, Leacock qu above.)

Evans 1940: p 27 above. "Like all great artists, he saw the
world as if it was an entirely fresh experience seen for
the first time..." (p 182 1963 edn; see further below under
"Dickens and Childhood" and "Dickens and Shakespeare".)

Silman 1941: p 143 above.

The Literary Artist, cont.

Sampson 1941: p 28 above. "...an exuberant fertility of
device, a daemonic energy of creation and a vast universal
charity to which there is only one parallel in literature"
(p 630 1970 edn; cf Saintsbury 1916 qv.)

Stevenson 1943: p 28 above.

Alain 1945: p 28 above.

Pritchett 1946: p 28 above.

Liddell 1947: p 28 above.

Leavis 1947: qu above p 96.

Leavis 1948: p 29 above. "That Dickens was a great genius
and is permanently among the classics is certain. But the
genius was that of a great entertainer, and he had for the
most part no profounder responsibility as a creative artist
than this description suggests" (p 29 in 1962 PB edn; cf
Leavis 1970 which "challenges sharply and decisively" this
very opinion.)

Lindsay 1950: p 5 above. Puts Dickens next to Shakespeare.
Cf Swinburne, Shaw, Wilson... and see further below under
"Dickens and Shakespeare".

Kettle 1951-3: p 30 above.

Monod 1953: p 30 above. "...un prestigieux et prodigieux
créateur...presque au même degré que Balzac, un créateur
d'univers" (see further below under "Dickens and Balzac".)

Van Ghent 1953: p 30 above.

Allen 1954: p 30 above; ch 4.

Tillotson 1954: p 30 above.

House 1955: p 31 above.

Zabel 1957: p 31 above.

Fielding 1958: p 5 above.

Miller 1958: p 31 above.

Churchill 1958: p 32 above under Ford.

Engel 1959: p 32 above.

Quirk 1959: see below under "Style and Language".

Horsman 1959: p 32 above.

Cockshut 1961: p 33 above.

Leavis 1962: p 77 above.

Davis 1963: p 33 above.

Garis 1965: p 34 above.   "...all the landscapes, all the
    dramatic scenes, come to us in a voice in which we hear an
    infectious delight in what it, itself, is doing" (p 16;
    cf Churchill 1937-42 qv.)

Stoehr 1965: p 34 above.

Brook, G.L.   Dickens as a Literary Craftsman.   BJRL 49 1967.

Blount 1969: p 35 above.

Dyson 1970: p 35 above.

Wilson 1970: p 35 above.

Hardy, Barbara.   The Complexity of Dickens.   In Slater 1970:
    p 8 above.

Lucas 1970: p 36 above.

Leavis 1970: see comment under Leavis 1948 above.

Sucksmith 1970: p 36 above.

Daleski 1970: p 36 above.

Kincaid 1972: p 36 above.

Hobsbaum 1973: p 8 above.

Carey 1974: p 37 above.

Churchill 1974: p 37 above.

The Moral Artist

Ruskin 1860-2: qu above p 94.

Anon. Dickens's Moral Services to Literature. Spectator
17 Apr 1869. (qu Collins 1971 pp 489-91 and attributed to
R.H.Hutton.)

Jowett 1870: p 15 above. "He whom we mourn was the friend of
mankind...the enemy of every form of meanness and oppression
..." (qu Forster 1872 bk 11 ch 3 final para.)

Ham 1870: p 15 above. Cf Stott 1869 qu Collins p 493.

Buchanan 1872: p 15 above.

Ruskin, John. "Is not the entire testimony of Dickens,
traced in its true force, that no position is so good for
men and women, none so likely to bring out their best human
character, as that of a dependant or menial?..." (Fors
Clavigera, Apr 1873, qu Wall 1970 p 204.)

Henley 1890: p 17 above. "...his work...has in full measure
the quality of sincerity. He meant what he did; and he
meant it with his full heart... He regarded his work as a
universal possession; and he determined to do nothing that
...should prove unworthy of his function" (qu Quiller-Couch
1922-5 pp 7-8; cf Henley qu above p 151.)

Gissing 1899-1901: p 18 above. "An instinctive sympathy with
the moral (and therefore the artistic) prejudices of the
everyday man guided Dickens throughout his career" (p 161
1925 edn.)

Chesterton 1907-11: p 20 above. "I repeat: let any one who
thinks that Dickens was a gross and indelicate artist read
that part" of Bleak House concerning Carstone's decline.
"A clumsy journalist would have made Rick Carstone in his
mad career cast off Esther and Ada and the others. The
great artist knew better" (pp 154-5 1933 edn; cf qu above
pp 46, 88 and cf Henley 1890 and Churchill 1937-42.)

Leffmann 1908: p 20 above.

More 1908: p 20 above. Cf Chesterton 1907.

Meynell 1912: p 21 above. Cf Chesterton above.

Dark 1919: p 3 above. There is a recent reprint: Folcroft
Library edn, Folcroft Pa 1973.

The Moral Artist, cont.

Santayana 1921-2: qu below under "Dickens and Religion".

Gide, Andre. "...in Dickens's wonderful novels...I am often
uneasy at the conventionality, childishness even, of his
hierarchy, or to use Nietzsche's phrase, scale of values...
Herein Dickens is true to the opinion of his countrymen and
of his time... All his novels endeavour to show us and make
us realize the shining superiority of qualities of heart
over qualities of head... of all the great novelists...he
uses this classification in its simplest form: which...is
the secret of his popularity" (Dostoevsky, 1923; qu Wall 1970
p 272; cf Taine qu above p 93 and Gissing qu above p 157 and
see further below under "Dickens and Dostoevsky".)

Forster 1927: p 24 above. "Part of the genius of Dickens is
that he does use types and caricatures, people whom we
recognize the instant they re-enter, and yet achieves effects
that are not mechanical and a vision of humanity that is not
shallow" (p 79 PB edn; see further below under "Characters".)

Wagenknecht 1929: p 4 above. Cf Santayana 1921.

Churchill 1937-42: p 26 above. Dickens the literary artist
and Dickens the moral artist at his best one and the same
thing. See further below under "Radical and Reformer" and
cf Chesterton 1907 above and Leavis 1970 below.

Orwell 1939-40: p 26 above. "...Dickens's criticism of society
is almost exclusively moral" (p 9 1946 edn; cf pp 53, 55 and
Dent 1933 qu above p 43 and see further below under "Radical
and Reformer".)

Wilson 1939-41: p 27 above.

Stevenson 1943: p 28 above.

Laird 1946: p 28 above.

Warner 1946: p 28 above. Cf Orwell above.

Leavis 1947: see above under "Hard Times".

Petersen 1949: p 29 above.

Churchill 1950: p 29 above; pp 111-13. Cf Gissing and Gide
qu above.

Angus Wilson 1950: p 30 above. Cf Edmund Wilson 1939-41.

The Moral Artist, cont.

Coveney 1957: see below under "Dickens and Childhood".

A.H.Wilson 1959: p 32 above.

Rees 1960: p 33 above. Cf Orwell 1939.

Hardy 1961: p 33 above.

Leavis 1962: see above under "Dombey".

Smith 1969: p 35 above. Argues that "in all the great novels of his last period, Dickens is bringing the entire nineteenth century to the bar of a rigorous moral and spiritual judgment" (cf Chesterton 1907, Wilson 1939-41 etc.)

Hardy, Barbara. In Slater 1970: p 8 above. "The knowledge of the inner life...is a source of Dickens's complexity...has its roots in his complex awareness of social nature" (pp 43-4; cf Leavis 1970.)

Lucas 1970: p 36 above.

Leavis 1970: p 36 above. Cf Gissing 1899-1901, Chesterton 1907-11, Churchill 1937-42, Orwell 1939-40, Wilson 1939-41.

Hardy 1970: p 36 above.

Gold 1972: p 37 above. See further below under "Dickens and Religion".

Meckier 1972: qu above p 98.

See further below under "Radical and Reformer", "Dickens and Childhood", "Dickens and Religion" etc.

His Development

Hunt 1838: qu above p 9.

Phillips, Samuel. Letter to Alexander Blackwood 4 Dec 1842 predicting that the close of Dickens's literary career would be "as full of useful warning as his rise was sudden and astonishing" (qu House 1974 p 392n; cf Hayward 1837 qu above p 9.)

His Development, cont.

Bagehot 1858: p 13 above. "A man of great genius who has
written great and enduring works must be judged mainly by
them; and not by the inferior productions which...he may
pour forth at moments less favourable to his powers... We
should not like to have to speak in detail of Mr Dickens's
later works, and we have not done so" (p 196 in EL edn 1911;
cf Harrison and Swinburne below.)

Hopkins 1864: p 14 above. "Dickens's literary history is
melancholy to me, yet to take that view of him which is
taken or will be by some people is not just or balanced"
(qu Gardner p 160; cf James 1865.)

Friswell 1870: p 15 above.

Hutton 1874: p 15 above.

Martineau, Harriet. "The finest thing in Mr Dickens's case
is that he, from time to time, proves himself capable of
progress - however vast his preceding achievements had been.
In humour, he will hardly surpass Pickwick...but in several
crises, as it were, of his fame, when everybody was
disappointed, and his faults seemed running his graces down,
there has appeared something so prodigiously fine as to make
us all joyfully exclaim that Dickens can never permanently
fail" (Autobiography, 1877; qu Wall 1970 p 210.)

Dilthey 1877: p 16 above.

Henley 1890: p 17 above; qu p 151. Cf Ward 1882 pp 139-40.

Harrison 1894-5: p 17 above. "...A mature judgment will decide
that the series after David Copperfield...was not equal to tl
series of the thirteen years preceding" (p 130).

Cross 1899: p 17 above.

Swinburne 1902: p 19 above. "...the early works of Dickens
have been made use of to depreciate his later, with the same
enlightened and impartial candour which on the appearance of
Othello must have deplored the steady though gradual decline
of its author's genius from the unfulfilled promise of
excellence held forth by Two Gentlemen of Verona" (p 16 1913
edn.)

Chesterton 1907-11: qu above p 88. These observations should
be borne in mind against those modern critics who see in
Chesterton only such remarks as that quoted on p 152 here.

His Development, cont.

Swinburne 1908: p 20 above. "Nothing could show more
perfectly the progress of creative genius than a comparison
between the admirable chapter of Oliver Twist in which the
Runners play their part and the wonderful chapter of Bleak
House in which Mr Bucket introduces himself to the family
circle of the Bagnets" (p 12 1913 edn.)

Saintsbury 1916: p 22 above. "...that quality of abundance...
of production without reproduction, and variation without
obvious mechanical effort, which only the greatest 'makers'
in verse and prose possess" (p 318 1932 edn.)

Phelps 1916: p 22 above. "...while it is possible to
contemplate the history of the novel minus any other author,
we simply cannot get along without Dickens. The extraordinary
succession of masterpieces that he produced with hardly any
lapses for thirty years put the whole world hopelessly in
his debt" (p 109). The "history of the novel" minus
Dickens was in fact attempted in Leavis 1948 but Dickens
found his way into an appendix and in Leavis 1970 the whole
attempt was conveniently forgotten.

Waugh 1919: p 22 above.

Quiller-Couch 1922-5: p 23 above.

Shaw 1937: qu above p 96. Cf Shaw 1912 on Hard Times and
The Old Curiosity Shop (qu above p 95.)

Jackson 1937: p 26 above. See further below under "Radical
and Reformer".

Churchill 1937-42: p 26 above. Cf Churchill 1958.
Development in some respects, but not in others.

Sitwell 1938: p 26 above. Cf Leavis 1948-70.
Influence of Dickens's own development on the development
of the modern novel.

Ford 1939: p 26 above.

Wilson 1939-41: p 27 above. "Dickens never really repeats
himself: his thought makes a consistent progress, and his
art, through the whole thirty-five years of his career,
keeps going on to new materials and new effects" (p 66
UP edn.)

His Development, cont.

House 1941: qu above p 115 and see the whole of ch 6.

Monod 1953: p 30 above.

Klingopulos 1958: p 32 above under Ford. "...The most impressive Victorian example of such a continuous internal development is that of Dickens, who began with episodic work ...and achieved work, such as Bleak House, Little Dorrit and Hard Times, much more concentrated in its aim and therefore much more intensely imagined and carried out" (p 101; cf Churchill below.)

Churchill 1958: p 32 above under Ford. "Dickens did not progress in his art in quite the straightforward way of Shakespeare and many lesser writers. His great things are scattered throughout his work, and he has no masterpiece without serious weaknesses..." (p 123; cf Churchill 1937-42 and Churchill 1974.)

Allott 1959: p 7 above. "...slow development as a self-conscious artist..." (p 28.)

Priestley 1960: p 33 above. "As a novelist, a serious novelist to be taken seriously, he steadily matured... After David Copperfield...his novels are deeply concerned with society itself, making use of a broad symbolism... some of the deepest and most despairing insights into the structure, pattern, tone, of English society" (p 239 PB edn; cf Shaw 1912, Shaw 1937, Wilson 1939-41 and see further below under "Radical and Reformer".)

Leavis, F.R. Letter to The Spectator 4 Jan 1963. "Dickens in learning how to become a novelist and developing out of a journalist and populac entertainer into a great artist, became more and more conscious of himself as such... he created a highly subtle, penetrating and sophisticated art..." (rp Letters in Criticism, ed John Tasker, 1974, p 96 Cf Leavis 1948: p 29 above.

Hardy, Barbara. In Slater 1970: p 8 above. "It is tempting to see a development in the novels... But as usual with Dickens, generalizations about development are difficult to maintain..." (pp 41-2; cf Churchill above.)

Wilson, Angus. In Slater 1970: p 8 above. "...the increasing stature and growth of maturity in his greatest novels from Bleak House to Great Expectations" (p 210; cf Engel 1959 and Priestley 1960.)

His Development, cont.

Wilson 1970: p 35 above.

Lucas 1970: p 36 above.

Leavis 1970: p 36 above.   Cf Leavis 1963: qu above p 162.

Williams 1970: p 36 above.

Hobsbaum 1973: p 8 above.

His Style and Language

Felton 1843: p 11 above.

Horne 1844: p 12 above; pp 66-8.

North British Rev 1845: p 12 above.   Complains that his style
    is spoilt by "impurities of expression, and even gross
    offences against the English language".

Dickens to Forster 13 Nov 1846.   "If in going over the proofs
    you find the tendency to blank verse...too strong, knock out
    a word's brains here and there" (self-criticism qu Forster
    1872 bk 5 ch 6.   This refers to The Battle of Life, but the
    most striking instances of unconscious blank verse are to be
    found in American Notes, eg ch 15 from "But bring him here,
    upon this crowded deck..." to "...and lay but humble siege
    to heaven at last".   Horne 1844 above gives examples from
    Old Curiosity Shop.   See further below under "Dickens and
    Wordsworth".)

Bagehot 1858: p 13 above.   "There has been much controversy
    about Mr Dickens's taste.   A great many cultivated people
    will scarcely concede that he has any taste at all... The
    truth is that Mr Dickens has what we may call creative
    taste; that is to say, the habit or faculty...which at the
    critical instant of artistic production offers to the mind
    the right word, and the right word only" (p 193 in EL edn
    1911.)   Le mot juste, in fact.   Cf Taine 1856: "this
    minute description...proves its passion by its exactness...
    the boldness of the style renders it visible..." (qu Wall
    1970 p 100 and see further below under "Symbolism",
    "Fantasy and the Grotesque" and "Comedy and Satire".)

Jeaffreson 1858: p 13 above.

Anon. Saturday Rev 8 May 1858. "Mr Dickens's writings are
the apotheosis of what has been called newspaper English... ;
the triumphs which this style has attained in Mr Dickens's
hands...will continue to exercise very considerable influence
on the mould into which people will continue to cast their
thoughts, and indirectly upon their thoughts themselves. We
cannot affect to say that we look upon the growth of this
habit with much satisfaction" (review of Library edn 1858-9.)

Masson 1859: p 13 above. "...In the mere matter of literary
style, there is a very obvious difference" between Dickens
and Thackeray. "Mr Thackeray, according to the general
opinion, is the more terse and idiomatic, and Mr Dickens the
more diffuse and luxuriant writer. There is an Horatian
strictness and strength in Thackeray which satisfies the
most cultivated taste and wins the respect of the severest
critic; but Dickens, if he is the more rapid and careless on
the whole, seems more susceptible to passion, and rises to a
keener and wilder song" (qu Wall 1970 p 148; cf Bagehot
above on "taste" and see further below under "Dickens and
Thackeray".)

Trollope. Autobiography. 1883. "Of Dickens's style it is
impossible to speak in praise. It is jerky, ungrammatical,
and created by himself in defiance of rules - almost as
completely as that created by Carlyle" (qu Quiller-Couch
1925 p 223.)

Ludwig 1891: note on Hard Times c1860 qu above p 94. See Wall
1970 p 153.

Harrison 1894-5: p 17 above. "Side by side with this chastened
English prose, " (of Thackeray, George Eliot, Trollope and
"a dozen living novelists") "we have men of genius who have
fallen into evil habits. Bulwer, who knew better, would quite
revel in a stagey bombast; Dickens, with his pathos and his
humour, was capable of sinking into a theatrical mannerism
and cockney vulgarities of wretched taste; Disraeli...has
printed some rank fustian...and George Meredith at times
can be as jerky and mysterious as a prose Browning..." (pp
18-19.) "...of book-learning of any kind Dickens remained,
to the end of his days, perhaps more utterly innocent than
any other famous English writer since Shakespeare... Not only
do we feel in reading his novels that we have no reason to
assume that he had ever read anything except a few popular
romances, but we note that he can hardly be said to have a
formed literary style of his own. Dickens had mannerisms,
but hardly a style... He often gets verbose...plays with a
fancy out of measure...like a fine comic actor when the house
is in a roar..." (pp 140-1.)

His Style and Language, cont.

Gissing 1898: p 17 above. "In the story of David Copperfield's journey on the Dover road we have as good a piece of narrative prose as can be found in English... Read the chapter entitled 'Our Domestic Life' and try to award adequate praise to the great artist who composed it."

Meynell 1899: p 18 above.

Brownell, W.C.: p 19 above. "...That Brownell even disliked vitality one gathered in his study of the Victorian writers in which he ignored Dickens and depreciated Balzac to throw the value of Thackeray into relief..." (Van Wyck Brooks, The Confident Years, 1952, p 232.)

Meynell 1903: p 19 above.

Swinburne 1913: p 21 above.

Lubbock 1921: p 23 above.

Quiller-Couch 1922-5: p 23 above. "Dickens sometimes wrote execrably: far oftener he penned at a stretch page upon page of comment and conversation that brilliantly effect their purpose and are, therefore, good writing" (pp 94-5.)

Moore 1924: p 24 above.

Eliot 1927: qu below under "Characters".

Huxley 1930: p 55 above. "...whenever he is in the melting mood, Dickens ceases to be able...to see reality. His one and only desire on these occasions is just to overflow, nothing else. Which he does, with a vengeance and in an atrocious blank verse that is meant to be poetical prose and succeeds only in being the worst kind of fustian..." (cf Horne 1844 and Dickens 1846 above and see further below under "Sentiment and Sentimentality".)

Cecil 1931-4: p 25 above.

Sitwell 1932: p 25 above.

O'Faolain 1936: p 26 above. Gives example of "Dickensian" journalese, qu Churchill 1937-42 below. Cf Saturday Rev 1858 qu above.

Straus 1936: p 4 above.

His Style and Language, cont.

Churchill 1937-42: p 26 above.   "One of the strangest
  paradoxes in the artistry of Dickens is that this most
  verbose of novelists, who gloried in his longwindedness
  and never used one word where ten would do, was also a
  master of the pithy, illuminating phrase... It is always
  the language of Dickens that is so important; his genius
  was essentially dramatic" (p 359; cf Eliot 1927; it is
  from Churchill's insistence on the importance of Dickens's
  language that all modern discussion of this question is
  descended; see further below under "Drama and Melodrama".)

Orwell 1939-40: p 26 above.   "When Dickens has once described
  something you see it for the rest of your life.   But...
  wonderfully as he can describe an appearance, Dickens does
  not often describe a process..." (pp 37-8 1946 edn.)
  "The outstanding, unmistakeable mark of Dickens's writing
  is the unnecessary detail..." (pp 45-52.)

Pritchett 1946: p 28 above.   "...His natural genius is for
  human soliloquy not human intercourse..." (Edwin Drood).
  See further below under "Characters".

Leavis 1947: p 28 above.   "The final stress may fall on
  Dickens's command of word, phrase, rhythm and image: in
  ease and range there is surely no greater master of English
  except Shakespeare" (p 272 in PB edn; cf Eliot 1927 and
  Churchill 1937-42 and see further below under "Dickens and
  Shakespeare.")

Yamamoto, T.   Growth and System of the Language of Dickens.
  Osaka 1950; rv 1952.

Churchill 1951: p 30 above.   "He is as central to the early
  Victorian age as Shakespeare to the Elizabethan, and the
  popular verdict on these two writers as being the most
  'English' of geniuses can be justified in detail by their
  use of the language.   With Shakespeare, it was a language
  based on the country, on the rural tradition; with Dickens,
  it is pre-eminently the language of the city and the street"
  (pp 101-2; see further above under "Dickens's London" and
  below under "Dickens and Shakespeare".)

Monod 1953: p 30 above.   "Dickens's most inspired and
  spontaneous, and his most careful and elaborate, novel is
  probably David Copperfield.   It is, therefore, particularly
  well adapted to a study of the author's language and style..
  (cu Wall 1970 pp 519-27.)

Monod 1958: p 31 above.

His Style and Language, cont.

Stone 1958: p 31 above. "Interior monologue" in Dickens:
"attempts to render in written words that semi-structured
and evanescent aspect of private consciousness which is
composed of disorganized and yet meaningfully associated
speech-thought" as Stone defines the term. From Jingle to
Mrs Nickleby, Flora Finching, Jasper... (qu Wall 1970 pp
422-32; see further above under "Edwin Drood" and below
under "Dickens and Joyce".)

Miller 1958: p 31 above; pp 164-5.

Churchill 1958: p 32 above under Ford; pp 122-3, 130-2.

Allott 1959: p 7 above. "...brilliant conversational fantasy
...the verbal inventiveness which is the gift finally
separating his genius from that of almost all other
novelists (Joyce, perhaps, apart)... Dickens's characters
...exist very largely through their speech" (pp 210-11;
cf Churchill 1937-42 above.)

Quirk, Randolph. Charles Dickens and Appropriate Language.
Durham 1959 (qu Wall 1970 pp 409-22.)

Priestley 1960: p 33 above. "Dickens's triumph is not that
of a prose novelist, closely observing man in society: it is
that of a Maker, a dramatic and epic poet of inns and
parlours, fog and street lamps, a mythopoeic genius"
(p 236 PB edn; cf Swinburne and Quiller-Couch above.)

Yamamoto, T. Dickens's Style. Tokyo 1960.

Quirk, Randolph. Some Observations on the Language of Dickens.
REL 2 1961.

Leavis 1962: see above under "Dombey".

Marcus 1964: p 34 above.

Bodelsen 1964: see below under "Symbolism".

Garis 1965: p 34 above.

Lodge 1966: p 98 above.

Gerson, S. Sound and Symbol in the Dialogue of the Works of
Charles Dickens. Stockholm 1967.

Blount 1969: p 35 above; pp 10, 13-14, 26, 36-8.

His Style and Language, cont.

Brook, G.L. The Language of Dickens. Language Library
series, 1970.

Dyson 1970: p 35 above. "...our greatest English prose
writer". Cf Swinburne 1902 above.

Q.D.Leavis. In Leavis 1970: p 36 above. "Dickens shows a
sensitive and intelligent insight into the mysterious
nature of speech as one expression of the unique idiom of
each of us".

F.R.Leavis. In Leavis 1970: p 36 above. "This Dickens,
compelling observer and recorder of life, there is very
obvious point in describing as Shakespearian (consider the
vitality - the surprisingness combined with felicity,
dramatic and poetic - of the speech in which he so
largely renders these characters)..." (p 25; cf Churchill
1937-42 passim.)

Kincaid 1972: p 36 above.

Oddie 1973: see below under "Dickens and Carlyle". Oddie
believes that Carlyle's influence on Dickens's style has
been exaggerated: "nearly always takes effect on a very
much less important level than his ideological influence"
(cf Trollope 1883 above.)

His Symbolism

Swinburne 1902: qu above p 114.

Chesterton 1907-11: p 20 above. The story of Bleak House
"circles round two or three symbolic places... Dickens
begins in the Chancery fog because he means to end in the
Chancery fog... We have the feeling that the author sees
the conclusion and the whole... He means that all the
characters and all the events shall be read through the
smoky colours of that sinister and unnatural vapour...
The whole tale is symbolic and crowded with symbols..."
(pp 151-2 1933 edn; cf above p 88; this is the pioneer
critique of Dickens's symbolism, to which all subsequent
critics, particularly of Bleak House, are consciously or
unconsciously indebted: cf eg Wilson, Liddell, Allen,
Priestley below. See Churchill DSN Jun 1974.)

Powys 1912: p 21 above.

His Symbolism, cont.

Cecil 1931-4: p 25 above. "...his characters are more than
individual creations...they are symbolic figures" (p 56
FL edn.)

Sitwell 1932: p 25 above.

Darwin 1933: qu above p 89.

Sennewald, C. Die Namengebung bei Dickens: eine Studie
uber Lautsymbolik. Leipzig 1936.

Lemonnier 1938: p 26 above.

Wilson 1939-41: p 27 above. "...the people who like to talk
about the symbols of Kafka and Mann and Joyce have been
discouraged from looking for anything of the kind in
Dickens..." (p 34 UP edn; cf Swinburne, Chesterton,
Cecil, Darwin above.)

Stevenson 1943: p 28 above.

Pritchett 1946: p 28 above.

Liddell 1947: qu above p 90.

Allen 1954: qu above p 90.

Trilling 1955: p 103 above. "The subject of Little Dorrit
is borne in upon us by the symbol, or emblem, of the book,
which is the prison..." (cf Wilson above.)

Crompton 1958: p 90 above.

Monod 1958: p 31 above.

Priestley 1960: qu above p 162.

Empson, William. The Symbolism of Dickens. In Gross 1962:
p 7 above. Cf Chesterton 1907 and Wilson 1939.

Reid 1962: p 33 above.

Spilka 1962: see below under "Dickens and Kafka".

Bodelsen, C.A. Symbolism in Dickens. Essays and Papers,
Copenhagen 1964.

Garis 1965: p 34 above. Questions account of Dickens's
symbolic action given by some modern critics.

His Symbolism, cont.

Hewitt, D. An Embarrassment of Symbolic Riches.   London Rev 1
1966. Cf Empson above.

Gerson 1967: p 167 above.

Holloway, John. Dickens and the Symbol.   In Slater 1970:
p 8 above. Cf Empson 1962.

Daleski 1970: p 36 above.

Gomme 1971: qu above p 92.   Dickens's symbolism sometimes
forced. Cf Hewitt 1966.

Hobsbaum 1973: p 8 above.

His Characters

Court Journal 1836: qu above p 38.

Macaulay 1836: qu above p 41.

Southern Literary Messenger 1837: qu above p 41.

Lister 1838: qu above p 45.

Sydney Smith 1839: qu above p 49.

Wilkie 1839: qu above p 10.

Landor 1841: qu above p 10.

Janin 1842: qu above p 50.

Whitman 1842: qu above p 11.

Horne 1844: p 12 above. "It is observable that neither
Hogarth nor Dickens ever portray a mere sentimental
character, nor a morbid one. Perhaps the only exception in
all Mr Dickens's works is his character of Monks which is a
failure - a weak villain, whose pretended power is badly
suggested by black scowlings...and mouths-full of
extravagant curses...and fits of convulsion... In fact,
this Monks is a pretender, and genuine characters only suit
the hand of our author..." (pp 14-15; see further below
under "Drama and Melodrama".)

Working Man's Friend 1852: p 12 above.

Eliot, George (Mary Ann Evans). "We have one great novelist
who is gifted with the utmost power of rendering the
external traits of our town population; and if he could
give us their psychological character - their conceptions
of life and their emotions - with the same truth as their
idiom and manners, his books would be the greatest
contribution Art has ever made to the awakening of social
sympathies. But...he scarcely ever passes from the
humorous and external to the emotional and tragic, without
becoming as transcendent in his unreality as he was a
moment before in his artistic truthfulness. But for the
precious salt of his humour, which compels him to
reproduce external traits that serve, in some degree, as a
corrective to his frequently false psychology, his
preternaturally virtuous poor children and artisans, his
melodramatic boatmen and courtesans, would be as noxious as
Eugene Sue's idealised proletaires in encouraging the
miserable fallacy that high morality and refined sentiment
can grow out of harsh social relations, ignorance and want
..." (Westminster Rev Jul 1856; rp Essays and Leaves from a
Notebook, Edinburgh 1884; Essays of George Eliot, Oxford
1963. See further below under "Radical and Reformer".)

Brimley 1858: qu above p 87.

Bagehot 1858: p 13 above. "When he rises from the toiling
to the luxurious classes, his genius in most cases deserts
him... His delineations of middle-class life have...a
harshness and meanness which do not belong to that life in
reality" (p 173 in EL edn 1911; cf Brimley 1858 and Stephen
1857 qu above p 100.) "He has a very peculiar power of
taking hold of some particular traits, and making a
character out of them... Such delineations become
caricatures" (pp 176-7; cf Lewes, Leacock, Gissing below.)

Masson 1859: p 13 above. "It would be possible for an ill-
natured critic to go through all his works, and to draw out
in one long column a list of their chief characters,
annexing in a parallel column the phrases or labels by which
these characters are distinguished, and of which they are
generalizations... Even this, however, is a mode of art
legitimate, I believe, in principle, as it is certainly
most effective in fact. There never was a Mr Micawber in
nature, exactly as he appears in the pages of Dickens; but
Micawberism pervades nature through and through..." (cf
Leacock 1916 and Forster and Eliot 1927 and see further below
under "Comedy and Satire".)

His Characters, cont.

Gourdault 1865: p 14 above.

James 1865: p 14 above; pp 31-2 in PB edn 1968. Cf Masson 185?

Trollope 1870: p 15 above. "...And no other writer of English
  language except Shakespeare has left so many types of
  character as Dickens has done, characters which are known by
  their names familiarly as household words..." (qu Wall 1970
  p 180). "...his characters, if unnatural, have made a secon
  nature by their own force. It is fatuous to condemn that as
  deficient in art which has been so full of art as to
  captivate all men..." (p 181.)

Lewes 1872: p 15 above. "It is needless to dwell on such
  monstrous failures as Mantalini, Rosa Dartle, Lady Dedlock,
  Esther Summerson, Mr Dick, Arthur Gride, Edith Dombey, Mr
  Carker - needless, because if one studies the successful
  figures one finds even in them only touches of verisimilitud
  ...Micawber always presenting himself in the same situation,
  moved with the same springs...'catchwords' personfied as
  characters..." (cf Leacock 1916 and Churchill 1937 below.)

Hutton 1874: p 15 above. Perhaps the most complete answer to
  Lewes above, anticipating Leacock, Churchill etc. See
  particularly pp 205-7 in Wall 1970.

Collins 1874: qu above p 46.

Harrison 1894-5: p 17 above. "His sphere was wide, but not a?
  all general; it was strictly limited to the range of his own
  indefatigable observations. He hardly ever drew a character
  ...which he had not studied from the life with minute care,
  and whenever he did for a moment wander out of his limits,
  he made an egregious failure... He not only paints a vast
  range of ordinary humanity and suffering or wearied
  humanity, but he speaks for it and lives in it himself,
  and throws a halo of imagination over it, and brings home
  to the great mass of average readers a new sense of sympath;
  and gaiety... It is his great title to honour; and a noveli
  can desire no higher title than this" (pp 132-4.) See also
  pp 136-8 and qu above p 148.

Gissing 1898: p 17 above. "To call Mrs Gamp a caricature is
  an obvious abuse of language; not less so...to apply the wo
  to Mr Pecksniff or to Uriah Heep... Caricature proceeds by
  broad and simple method. It is no more the name for
  Dickens's full fervour of creation than for Shakespeare's..
  Each is a supreme idealist" (p 124 in 1924 edn; see further
  below under "Comedy and Satire" and "Dickens and Shakespear

His Characters, cont.

Gissing 1899: qu above p 42. Cf Gissing 1898.

Swinburne 1902: qu above p 62.

Tolstoy 1903: qu above p 19.

Chesterton 1906: p 20 above. "Dickens's work is to be
    reckoned always by characters, sometimes by groups,
    oftener by episodes, but never by novels..." (p 80; but cf
    Chesterton 1907-11 qu above pp 88, 168.) "Dickens was a
    mythologist rather than a novelist;he was the last of the
    mythologists, and perhaps the greatest. He did not always
    manage to make his characters men, but he always managed...
    to make them gods... They live statically, in a perpetual
    summer of being themselves... whenever he tried to describe
    change in a character, he made a mess of it, as in the
    repentance of Dombey or the apparent deterioration of
    Boffin..." (pp 88-9; but cf Chesterton 1907-11 qu above p
    157.)

Munro 1908: p 20 above.

Mair 1911: qu above p 43.

Wells 1911: qu above p 52.

Pugh, Edwin. The Charles Dickens Originals. 1912.

Jügler, R. Uber die Technik der Charakterisierung in den
    Jugendwerken von Dickens. Halle 1912.

Lightwood, W.R. In Dickens Street. 1912.

Leacock 1916: qu above p 22. Leacock's Dr Blimber (borrowed
    from Dombey) summarizes "the general conclusions of the
    assembly" of Dickens characters by pointing out that "from
    the time of the Romans onward Art had of necessity proceeded
    by the method of selected particulars and conspicuous
    qualities: that this was the nature and meaning of art
    itself: that exaggeration (meaning the heightening of the
    colour to be conveyed) was the very life of it..." (pp
    187-8; cf Hutton above.)

Saintsbury 1916: p 22 above. "...these characters...can hardly
    be said to be in any way developed by the different
    situations. They remain...always 'humours' in the Jonsonian
    sense. Only late in his career, in Hard Times, A Tale of Two

Cities, Great Expectations and, perhaps, Our Mutual Friend, did Dickens attempt anything like a character...prepared to stand analysis and to achieve or suffer development" (pp 313-14 1932 edn; cf Orwell below.)

Phelps 1916: p 22 above. "It is absurd to call his characters mere caricatures: he turned the powerful searchlight of his mind into many dark places, and his persons stand out against the background in a conspicuous glare. But if these people are not true, why is it that all observers since 1840 are continually pointing out persons who 'look like characters from Dickens'?" (p 109; cf Tolstoy 1903 and Leacock 1916.)

Gordon, E.H. The Naming of Characters in the Works of Dickens. Lincoln Neb 1917.

Clark 1918: see below under "Dickens and Religion".

Santayana 1921-2: p 23 above. "When people say Dickens exaggerates, it seems to me they can have no eyes and no ears..." (cf Leacock 1916). "The world is a perpetual caricature of itself..." (see further below under "Comedy and Satire"). Cf Santayana qu above p 76.

Quiller-Couch 1922-5: p 23 above. "...a vivid hurrying world, but the characters in it - until you come to Pip, say, in Great Expectations - are all quite curiously static... Dombey's conversion is a mere stage-trick; and, for Micawber's apotheosis as a prosperous colonist, let him believe it who will" (p 75; cf Saintsbury 1916). "... over and beyond its infertility of thought, Dickens's is a world in which technical or professional skill never comes into play..." (p 76; cf Orwell and House below.)

Priestley, J.B. The English Comic Characters. 1925. Incl "Mr Micawber", rp Essays of Five Decades, New York 1968, London 1969, PB edn 1969 pp 84-106. "...the greatest of alll Dickens's comic figures... With the one exception of Falstaff...the greatest comic figure in the whole range of English literature". See further below under "Comedy and Satire".

Osborne, Charles C. The Genesis of Mrs Gamp. Dickensian 23 1927 pp 27-30. Cf Pugh 1912.

Belloc 1927: p 24 above. Cf Chesterton 1906.

Maurois 1927: p 24 above.

His Characters, cont.

Eliot 1927: p 24 above. "Dickens's figures belong to poetry,
like figures of Dante or Shakespeare, in that a single
phrase, either by them or about them, may be enough to set
them wholly before us... Dickens can with a phrase make a
character as real as flesh and blood... Dickens's
characters are real because there is no one like them"
(p 424 1934 edn; cf Churchill 1937-42.)

Forster 1927: p 24 above. "...Dickens's people are nearly all
flat... Nearly every one can be summed up in a sentence, and
yet there is this wonderful feeling of human depth" (pp 75,
78-9 PB edn; cf Maugham 1954 pp 148-9 PB edn.)

Bennett, Arnold. "Dickens's characters remain in the mind.
They may perhaps be too conventionalized, too simplified...
But they remain in the mind" (Journals, 1931; qu Allott
1959 p 290.)

Cecil 1931-4: qu above p 169.

Dent 1933: p 4 above. "The range and vividness of Dickens's
characters is an extraordinarily impressive fact...a
phenomenon unparalleled in English literary history. The
only other comparable instance is that of Shakespeare"
(p 486 1935 edn.) "His best people are always absolutely
static...'Age cannot wither, nor custom stale' their
infinite sameness" (p 361; but cf Dent qu above p 55.)

Leacock 1933: qu above p 101.

Wells, H.G. "The majority of the Dickens novels were novels
with a purpose, but they never deal with any inner confusion,
any conflicts of opinion within the individual characters,
any subjective essential change" (Digression about Novels;
An Experiment in Autobiography, 1934, pp 487-504.)

O'Faolain 1936: p 26 above. Dickens's characters not drawn
from life. Cf Eliot 1927 and Churchill 1937-42.

Lemonnier 1936: p 26 above.

Shaw 1937: p 26 above.

Jackson 1937: qu below under "Radical and Reformer".
Cf House 1941.

Churchill 1937-42: p 26 above. "...such bright spots in
Dickens nearly always occur when a comic character is

holding forth, occupying the stage, so to speak, addressing
the reader/audience as much as, if not more than, the other
characters in the book. It is this extra-literary life of
his characters which has earned Dickens his greatest applause
and his heartiest abuse" (p 366; cf Eliot 1927 and see
further below under "Comedy and Satire" and "Drama and
Melodrama".)

Orwell 1939-40: p 26 above. See pp 23-5, 27, 28, 31, 34-5
1946 edn. Cf Quiller-Couch 1922 and House 1941.

House 1941: p 27 above. "Nearly everybody in Dickens has a
job: there is a passionate interest in what people do for a
living... Work plays an essential part in the characters'
approach to life..." (pp 55-6; cf completely opposite view
of Quiller-Couch and Orwell above.)

Stoll, E.E. Heroes and Villains: Shakespeare, Middleton,
Byron, Dickens. RES 18 1942; rp From Shakespeare to Joyce,
New York 1944.

Pritchett 1946: p 28 above.

Bowen 1946: p 28 above.

Leavis 1947: see above under "Hard Times". Gradgrind and
Bounderby, Sissy Jupe and Bitzer. Detailed analysis of
ch 2 particularly recommended.

House 1947: qu above p 77.

Hamilton, R. Dickens in his Characters. Nineteenth Century
Jul 1947. Cf Wilson 1939-41 and Lindsay 1950.

Pearson 1949: qu above p 44. Cf p 102.

Lindsay 1950: qu above p 55. Cf Stoll 1942 and Hamilton 1947.

Praz 1952: p 30 above.

Crubb 1953: p 56 above.

Fraser, G.S. "As a psychologist Dickens has not much advanced
on Fielding or Smollett; he presents us with some of the most
vivid figures in all literature, but as Henry James observed
...they are figures, not characters" (The Modern Writer and
His World, 1953, p 26 PB edn. Cf Bennett 1931 above.)

Allen 1954: p 30 above; pp 167-8 PB edn.

Maugham 1954: p 30 above. "If Falstaff is the greatest comic
    character in literature, Mr Micawber is the greatest but one
    ... " (pp 147-8 in PB edn; cf Priestley 1925 and see further
    below under "Comedy and Satire".)

Zabel 1957: p 31 above.

Coveney 1957: see below under "Dickens and Childhood".

Churchill 1958: p 32 above under Ford; pp 122-3, 127-8, 130-2,
    134-6, 138-9. Cf Churchill 1937-42.

Bishop 1959: p 48 above.

Moynahan 1960: p 110 above.

Bayley 1962: qu above p 48.

Harvey, W.J. Character and the Novel. 1965.

Peyrouton 1965: p 112 above.

Jarmuth, 1967: p 34 above.

Pritchett 1969-70: p 35 above. "All Dickens's characters,
    comic or not, issue personal pronouncements that magnify
    their inner life... Our comedy, Dickens seems to say, is not
    in our relations with others but in our relation with
    ourselves, our lives, our poetry, our genius" (p 20; cf
    Churchill 1937-42 qu above pp 175-6 and Miller 1958 qu above
    p 64.)

Lane 1970: qu above p 70.

Johnson 1970: qu above p 56. Cf Marcus 1965.

Leavis 1970: qu above p 168.

Greaves, John (ed). Who's Who in Dickens. 1973. By the
    Secretary of the Dickens Fellowship. Cf Hardwick 1973: p 8
    above.

Winner 1974: p 112 above.

Tick 1974: p 104 above.

Thomas 1974: p 117 above.

Fantasy and the Grotesque

Bagehot 1858: p 13 above. "The original germ of Pickwick was
a 'Club of Oddities'. The idea was professedly abandoned;
but traces of it are to be found in all Mr Dickens's books.
It illustrates the professed grotesqueness of the characters
as well as their slender connection" (p 186 EL edn 1911;
cf Pritchett 1969 and Miller 1958 qu above pp 177, 64.)

James 1865: p 14 above. "In all Mr Dickens's works the
fantastic has been his great resource; and while his fancy
was lively and vigorous it accomplished great things. But
the fantastic, when the fancy is dead, is a very poor
business" (p 32 in PB edn.)

Harrison 1894-5: p 17 above. "...it may serve our immediate
purpose to say with Samuel Johnson that humour is 'grotesque
imagery'...an effort of the imagination presenting human
nature with some element of distortion or disproportion
which instantly kindles mirth. It must be imaginative; it
must touch the bed-rock of human nature; it must arouse
merriment and not anger or scorn. In this fine and most
rare gift Charles Dickens abounded to overflowing; and this
humour poured in perfect cataracts of 'grotesque imagery'
over every phase of life of the poor and the lower middle
classes of his time..." (p 132; see further below under
"Comedy and Satire".)

Saintsbury 1916: p 22 above. "...It cannot have taken many
people of any competence in criticism very long to discover
where...the secret of this 'new world' of Dickens lies.
It lies...in the combination of the strictest realism of
detail with a fairy-tale unrealism of general atmosphere...
nobody ever mastered better than Dickens...the Aristotelian
doctrine of the impossibility rendered probable or not
improbable" (p 312 1932 edn.)

Santayana 1921-2: p 23 above. "The most grotesque creatures
of Dickens are not exaggerations or mockeries of something
other than themselves; they arise because nature generates
them, like toadstools; they exist because they can't help i
as we all do..." (pp 546-7.)

Meynell, Alice. "...the grotesque man in literature is
immortal... His humours are strangely matched with
perpetuity..." (comparing Micawber and Falstaff, Essays,
1923, p 84; see further below under "Dickens and Shakespear

Cecil 1931-4: p 25 above. "...his was a fantastic imaginatic
He was fascinated by the grotesque..." (pp 33-4 FL edn.)

Fantasy and the Grotesque, cont.

Pope-Hennessy 1945: qu above p 138 under Dickens-Kuenzel 1841.
Relation of Dickens to Germany in "the world of phantasy."

Allen 1954: p 30 above. "So far as we can label him at all,
he was a fantasist, and he forces us to accept the world he
creates by the sheer compelling power of the intensity of
his imagination" (p 173 PB edn.)

Allott 1959: p 7 above. "Such an inclusive writer as Dickens
...damages the fabric of his fantasy-world by attempting to
portray...subjects which...emphasize his emotional and
intellectual weaknesses..." (pp 114-15.)

Dyson 1966: p 56 above.

Von Lempruch, Nils-Göran. Some Grotesque Characters in
Dickens's Great Expectations. Modern-Sprache 67 1973.

See further below.

Comedy and Satire

Court Mag 1837: p 9 above.

Lister 1838: p 9 above. "We have said that his satire was
not misanthropic. This is eminently true. One of the
qualities we most admire in him is his comprehensive
spirit of humanity..." (see further below under "Radical
and Reformer".)

Sydney Smith 1841: qu above p 10.

Horne 1844: p 12 above. "His works furnish a constant
commentary on the distinction between wit and humour; for
of sheer wit...there is scarcely an instance...while of
humour there is a fullness...which would be searched for in
vain...among all other authors." Cf Bagehot below.

Bagehot 1858: p 13 above. "Endless fertility in laughter-
causing detail is Mr Dickens's most astonishing peculiarity
... Writers have attained the greatest reputation for wit
and humour, whose whole works do not contain so much of
either as are to be found in a very few pages of his"
(pp 130-1 EL edn 1911.)

Masson 1859: qu above p 171.

Dallas, E.S. "The public insist upon seeing in Mr Dickens
chiefly the humorist; and, however great he may be in other
directions, they count all as nothing beside his rare
faculty of humour..." (anon review of Great Expectations,
Times 17 Oct 1861.)

Dickens. "...I have such an inexpressible enjoyment of what
I see in a droll light, that I dare say I pet it as if it
were a spoilt child" (letter to Bulwer Lytton 1865, qu
Forster 1872 bk 9 ch 1.)

Forster 1872-4: p 2 above. "His leading quality was
Humour..." (bk 9 ch 1; cf Dallas above.)

Hutton 1874: p 15 above. "...such a humorist as many
centuries are not likely to reproduce. But then humour of
this kind is not necessarily connected with any deep
knowledge of the heart and mind of man, and of such a
knowledge I can see little trace in Dickens" (cf Brindley
1843 qu above p 11.)

Lilly 1895: p 17 above.

Harrison 1895: p 17 above. "...before all things a great
humorist - doubtless the greatest of this century; for,
though we may find in Scott a more truly Shakespearean
humour of the highest order, the humour of Dickens is so
varied, so paramount, so inexhaustible, that he stands
forth in our memory as the humorist of the age" (p 131;
see further below under "Dickens and Scott".)

Gissing 1898: qu above p 62.

Gissing 1899: qu above p 42.

Swinburne 1902: p 19 above. "...the very greatest comic poet
or creator that ever lived" (p 29 1913 edn.)

Chesterton 1906: qu above p 42.

Jerome 1912: p 21 above. By one of Dickens's most famous
successors in humour and pathos.

James, Henry. "Who could pretend that Dickens was anything
but romantic, and even more romantic in his humour, if
possible, than in his pathos...?" (The New Novel, TLS 10
Mar & 2 Apr 1914; rp Selected Literary Criticism PB edn
p 364.)

Leacock 1916: qu above pp 22, 173.

Eliot, T.S. "...the old English humour, the terribly serious,
even savage comic humour, the humour which spent its last
breath in the decadent genius of Dickens" (Christopher
Marlowe, 1918; rp Selected Essays, 1932; p 123 1934 edn.
Cf Santayana 1921-2 and Churchill 1937-42.)

Santayana 1921-2: p 23 above. "...It is savage comedy..."
(on Squeers in Nickleby ch 5; cf Eliot above and Santayana
1921-2 qu pp 76, 174 above.)

Priestley 1925: qu above p 174.

Belloc 1927: p 24 above.

Maurois 1927: p 24 above. Cf Priestley 1925.

Forster 1927: p 24 above.

Priestley, J.B. English Humour. 1929.

Cecil 1931-4: p 25 above. "...perhaps the greatest humorist
that England has ever produced". In his "satiric humour",
"the wildness of the exaggeration is only equalled by its
effectiveness" (p 44 FL edn.)

Churchill 1937-42: p 26 above. "...this supreme type of
comedy, with its almost Shakespearean 'suggestiveness'..."
(p 367; cf pp 359, 366, 373.)

Orwell 1939-40: p 26 above. "...his remoteness from the
landowning-military-bureaucratic class incapacitates him
for full-length satire. He only succeeds with this class
when he depicts them as mental defectives" (pp 24-5 1946 edn.)

Pritchett 1942: p 28 above.

Pearson 1949: qu above p 44.

Carlton, W.J. The Story without a Beginning: An Unrecorded
Contribution by Boz to the Morning Chronicle. Dickensian
47 1951 pp 67-70. (Ref Chronicle 18 Dec 1834: his earliest
political satire.)

Pritchett, V.S. The Humour of Dickens. Listener 3 Jun 1954.
Cf Eliot, Santayana, Churchill above.

Crompton 1958: p 90 above.

Comedy and Satire, cont.

Churchill 1958: p 32 above under Ford. "If we use the term 'comedy' in its very widest sense, covering such examples as Volpone and Measure for Measure as well as Tom Jones and She Stoops to Conquer, then we can truly say that almost all Dickens's work is in this field. Comedy can be a very serious thing and have a very serious purpose behind it" (p 125; cf Eliot 1918, Santayana 1921, Churchill 1937.)

Cox 1959: p 39 above.

Coolidge, A.C. Dickens's Humour. Victorian Newsletter no 18 1960.

Ford and Lane 1961: p 7 above. "To grasp Dickens's meaning wholly, critics must grasp the meaning of his humour..." (intn.)

Davis 1963: p 33 above.

Schilling, B.N. The Comic Spirit. Detroit 1965.

Blount 1969: p 35 above.

Hodgart 1969: p 103 above. "...his best satirical passages often occur sandwiched between sentimental and melodramatic passages, and in novels whose overall vision of the world is other than a satirical one" (p 13; cf pp 228-32 and Churchill 1937-42 above.)

Pritchett 1969-70: p 35 above. "...the comedy of Dickens stands a great deal on its own because his genius belongs to a century of violent revolution... He represents, for me, his century's powerful release of an important psychological force" (p 19.)

Allen, Walter. The Comedy of Dickens. In Slater 1970: p 8 above. Cf Churchill 1937-42.

Miller, J.Hillis. The Sources of Dickens's Comic Art. NCF centenary no 1970.

Welsh 1971: p 36 above. "Dickens was a powerful satirist, perhaps the greatest of his time..." But his "purpose was never exclusively satirical" (cf Hodgart 1969 above.)

Kincaid 1971: p 56 above.

Manning, Sylvia Bank. Dickens as Satirist. New Haven 1971.

Ganz, Margaret. In DSA 1 1971.

<u>Comedy and Satire, cont.</u>

Kincaid 1972: p 36 above. Emphasizes that Dickens's humour
is at the heart of his technique and his vision of life,
no less important in Little Dorrit than in Pickwick.

Rabkin, Eric S. The Comedy and the Melodrama. Narrative
Suspense, Ann Arbor Mich 1973. Ch on Bleak House.
See further below under "Drama and Melodrama".

Carey 1974: p 37 above.

See further above under "Pickwick", "Chuzzlewit" etc.

<u>Sentiment and Sentimentality</u>

Lister 1838: qu above p 45.

Anon. Spectator 24 Nov 1838. "...sadly touching rather
than tearful..." (review of Oliver Twist.)

Hood 1840: qu above p 53. Cf Mrs Oliphant, Victorian Age in
Literature 1892 qu Collins 1971
Jeffrey 1841: qu above p 53.   p 91.

Robinson 1841: qu above p 53. Cf FitzGerald p 53.

Christian Remembrancer 1842: qu above p 54.

Janin 1842: qu above p 50.

Horne 1844: p 12 above. "...the heart-felt tears of tens
of thousands of readers..." (cf Jeffrey 1841.)

Dickens 2 Dec 1844. "If you had seen Macready last night,
undisguisedly sobbing and crying on the sofa as I read,
you would have felt, as I did, what a thing it is to have
power" (letter to his wife on the famous reading of The
Chimes ref p 68 above. Cf Maugham 1954 below.)

Jeffrey 1847: qu above p 74.

Thackeray 1847: qu above p 74.

Hallam, Henry. Letter to Mrs Brookfield 1847. "Everybody is
pretending that the death of Paul Dombey is the most
beautiful thing ever written. Milnes, Thackeray... own to
tears. I am so hardened as to be unable to look on it in

any light but pure business" (qu Pope-Hennessy 1945 p 272;
cf Dickens 1844 above and Maugham 1954 below.)

Anon (Coventry Patmore?).   North British Rev 7 1847.
"We might, indeed, were we so minded, find some flaws in
the beautiful sentimentalism of Paul's death-bed scene...
some little mawkishness of feeling...but we forbear"
(review of Dombey; cf Hutton below.)

Trollope, Anthony. The Warden. 1855. Dickens as Mr Popular
Sentiment in ch 15. See Lionel Stevenson, Dickens and the
Origin of The Warden, Trollopian 2 1947, and further below
under "Radical and Reformer" and "Dickens and Trollope".

Taine 1856: qu below under "Sex in Dickens".

Hutton, R.H. Spectator 1862. Criticizes "pathos feasting
on itself" in Dombey and "the absolute gluttony...with
which he spoons and stirs the subject of grief and death"
in The Old Curiosity Shop (qu Stang 1959: p 32 above.)

James 1865: p 14 above. "Miss Jenny Wren...belongs to the
troop of hunchbacks, imbeciles, and precocious children
who have carried on the sentimental business in all Mr
Dickens's novels; the little Nells, the Smikes, the Paul
Dombeys..." (p 32 in PB edn.)

Stott 1869: p 14 above. "We must confess to having found
little Paul Dombey and little Nell and Tiny Tim exceedingly
tiresome, and to have been glad to be rid of them on any
terms" (cf Hutton above.)

Anon.* New Monthly Mag 1870.   "That man must, indeed, have
a mind either thoroughly bedimmed with conceit, or entirely
degraded...who can see nothing tender and touching in the
narrative of the deaths of Paul Dombey or Little Nell, and
who rises unaffected from their perusal" (cf Wilde 1890
and Pearson 1949 below.)

Harte 1870: p 15 above.
"The fir-trees gathering closer in the shadows,
    Listened in every spray,
 While the whole camp, with 'Nell' on English meadows,
    Wandered and lost their way..."
Cf Pearson 1949 below and Orwell, Critical Essays p 111.

Buchanan 1872: p 15 above.   Cf Harte 1870.

*by William Mackay.   184

Lewes 1872: p 15 above. "He set in motion the secret springs
of sympathy by touching the domestic affections. He painted
nothing ideal, heroic; but all the resources of the bourgeois
epic were in his grasp" (cf Marx 1841-2 qu above p 138.)

Butler 1875: qu above p 125.

Wilde 1890: qu above p 54. See comment in Robert Bernard
Martin, The Triumph of Wit, 1974, pp 99-100.

Kitton 1897: qu above p 54.

Gissing 1898: p 17 above. "I do not think it worth while to
speak of Nancy, or of other lost creatures appearing in
Dickens. But read, I beg, that passage of Little Dorrit
where Amy herself and her idiot friend Maggy, wandering
about the streets at night, are addressed by a woman of the
town... and wonder that the same man whp penned this shocking
rubbish could have written in the same volume pages of a
truthfulness beyond all eulogy" (p 151 1924 edn; cf
Churchill 1937-42 below.)

Wilkins 1911: qu above p 54.

Kafka 1917: qu above p 81. Cf Dickens 1844 and Maugham 1954.

Huxley 1930: qu above p 55.

Cecil 1931-4: p 25 above; pp 30-2, 48-50 FL edn.

Leacock 1933: p 4 above. "Looking back now on what we think
of as Victorian sentimentality, we are apt to see only its
feebler aspects, its maudlin exaggeration, its joy in tears
... But in its day the tears were... needed... These were the
days of the unreformed factories, of the 'cry of the
children', of the little lives worn out unheeded... Tears
for imaginary children were to save the lives of real ones"
(pp 47-8; the last sentence should be read in italics and
would have won Dickens's gratitude and Lord Shaftesbury's
assent; see further below under "Radical and Reformer"
and "Dickens and Childhood".)

Kingsmill 1934: p 4 above. Cf Pearson 1949.

Churchill 1937-42: p 26 above; pp 358, 360-2, 368-9, 370.

Orwell 1939-40: qu above p 70. See also pp 42-3 1946 edn.

House 1941: p 27 above. Ch 2: Benevolence. Cf Leacock above.

Sentiment and Sentimentality, cont.

Pearson 1949: p 4 above. "...sentimentality is complementary
  to toughness and callousness, and an age that had grown fat
  on child-slavery, negro-slavery, the pillage of India, and
  many similar crimes, was easily melted by the sorrows of a
  pure and pretty girl... The man who could thus move his age
  was clearly a child of the age, and Dickens had a strain of
  ruthlessness in him which discharged itself in the
  sentimentality of his dream-figures" (pp 87-8; cf Kafka,
  Leacock, Maugham, also Wilson 1939-41.)

Churchill 1950: p 29 above; pp 111-13.

Lindsay 1950: p 5 above. See particularly pages where Lindsay
  discusses the influence of Bulwer Lytton on Dickens. And
  see further below under "Dickens and Bulwer Lytton".

Maugham 1954: p 30 above. "...his pathos leaves me cold...
  I have no doubt that Dickens was sincere, but it was an
  actor's sincerity; and that, perhaps, is why now, no matter
  how he piled up the agony, we feel that his pathos was not
  quite genuine and so are no longer moved by it" (pp 146-7
  PB edn; cf Dickens 1844.) See too Ruskin 1880 qu Collins
  1971 p 100.

Cockshut, A.O.J. Sentimentality in Fiction. Twentieth
  Century Apr 1957.

Churchill 1958: p 32 above under Ford; p 121.

Rees 1960: p 33 above.

Hardy 1961: p 33 above.

Furbank, P.N. "...much of the pathos in Dickens springs from
  just such anomalous relationships - the adult as child or
  the child as adult" (The Twentieth-Century Best-Seller. In
  The Modern Age ed Ford, PGEL 7 1961 pp 435-6.)

Senelick 1967: p 56 above.

Johnson 1970: qu above p 56. Cf Marcus 1965 qu p 56 and
  Pearson 1949 above.

Kincaid 1971: p 56 above.

Martin 1974: p 185 above under Wilde. Traces development of
  Victorian comedy from Dickensian sentimentality to the more
  intellectual comedy of late Victorian writers like Meredith,
  Butler, Wilde and Shaw.

Drama and Melodrama

Dickens 1858. "Every good actor plays direct to every good author, and every writer of fiction, though he may not adopt the dramatic form, writes in effect for the stage. He may write novels always, and plays never, but the truth and wisdom that are in him must permeate the art of which truth and passion are the life, and must be more or less reflected in that great mirror which he holds up to nature" (speech to the Royal General Theatrical Fund 29 Mar 1858 proposing the health of Thackeray who was in the chair.)

Ruskin 1860-2: qu above p 94. "...let us not lose the use of Dickens's wit and insight, because he chooses to speak in a circle of stage fire..." Cf Churchill 1937-42 and Axton 1966.

Sala, George Augustus. Sensationalism in Literature. Belgravia Feb 1868. See further below under "Dickens and Crime."

Ward 1882: qu above p 114.

Gissing 1898: qu above p 75. Cf Harrison 1894-5: "...it was only at times... that Dickens could keep clear of melodrama and somewhat stagey blue fire. And at times his blue fire was of a very cheap kind. Rosa Dartle and Carker, Steerforth and Blandois, Quilp and Uriah Heep, have a melancholy glitter of the footlights over them..." (pp 142-3).

Saintsbury 1916: qu above p 50. Cf Harrison above.

Eliot 1918: qu above p 181.

Santayana 1921-2: p 23 above. "Dickens entered the theatre of this world by the stage door..." Cf Quiller-Couch below.

Quiller-Couch 1922-5: p 23 above. "...His failing was that he did not quite trust his genius for the novel, but was persuaded that it could be bettered by learning from the drama - from the bad drama of his time" (p 46; cf Churchill 1937 but also Dickens 1858 above.)

Eliot 1927: p 24 above. "You cannot define Drama and Melodrama so that they shall be reciprocally exclusive... The Moonstone is very near to Bleak House..." (pp 431-2 1934 edn. The whole essay is very important for an understanding of this aspect of Dickens. It leads directly to Churchill 1937-42 which in turn leads directly or indirectly to more recent criticism such as Axton 1966.)

Maurois 1927: p 24 above.

187

Drama and Melodrama, cont.

Wagenknecht 1929: p 4 above. "The Speech of the Devil's Advocate" mentions most of what has been urged against Dickens by critics who have objected to his melodrama, sentimentality, and other weaknesses, real or imagined. Cf Cox 1958: p 31 above.

Cecil 1931-4: p 25 above. "There are passages in Nicholas Nickleby and Little Dorrit that would seem stagey to the readers of The Boy's Own Paper. When Dickens is not writing about Mr Crummles he sometimes seems to be writing a play for Crummles" (p 30 in FL edn; cf Saintsbury 1916, Quiller-Couch 1922, Churchill 1937.)

Churchill 1937-42: p 26 above. Amplifies Eliot 1918-27 and Quiller-Couch 1922-5 above. See particularly pp 361-7.

Orwell 1939-40: p 26 above; pp 37, 50-1 1946 edn.

Leavis 1948: p 29 above. "We may reasonably...see some Dickensian influence in Conrad's use of melodrama, or what would have been melodrama in Dickens; for in Conrad the end is a total significance of a profoundly serious kind" (p 29 in PB edn 1962; see further below under "Dickens and Conrad".)

Churchill 1951: p 30 above; ch 5. Cf Churchill 1937-42.

Maugham 1954: p 30 above. "The sensational novel has a bad name, but you cannot dismiss with a shrug of the shoulders a method which was practised by Balzac, Dickens and Dostoevsky" (p 297 PB edn.)

Coolidge, A.C. Dickens and the Philosophic Basis of Melodrama Victorian Newsletter no 20 1961.

Perry, J.O. The Popular Tradition of Melodrama in Dickens. Carleton Miscellany 4 1962. Cf Eliot 1927.

Davis 1963-6: p 33 above. Analyses debt of the early novels to contemporary theatrical conventions.

Garis 1965: p 34 above. Dickens's art "theatrical" in sense that we are constantly aware of him performing in a "theatre created by the insistent and self-delighting rhetoric of his voice."

Axton, W.F. Circle of Fire: Dickens's Vision and Style and the Popular Victorian Theatre. Lexington Ky 1966. Amplifies Ruskin 1860 and Quiller-Couch 1922.

Stage and Platform

Dickens. Letter to Frederick Yates Mar 1838. "... I propose
to dramatize Oliver for the first night of next season...
I am quite satisfied that nobody can have heard what I mean
to do with the different characters in the end, inasmuch as
at present I don't quite know myself" (House 1965 p 388.)
Nothing came of this proposed self-dramatization, but Oliver
was dramatized by Yates in 1839, preceded by five different
versions in 1838. See Malcolm Morley, Early Dramas of
Oliver Twist, Dickensian 43 1947 pp 74-9.

Dramatized versions of Dickens's novels and stories incl
The Peregrinations of Pickwick (1837); The Fortunes of Smike
(1840); The Old Curiosity Shop, or One Hour from Humphrey's
Clock (1840); Martin Chuzzlewit (1844); The Cricket on the
Hearth (1845; cf Orwell qu above p 70); Dombey and Son (1848);
Hard Times (1854); Little Dorrit (1856); A Christmas Carol
(1859); Oliver Twist (1869, with Irving as Sikes); Little
Emily (1869); Bardell v. Pickwick (1871); The Mystery of
Cloisterham (c1871); Jo (c1875); Lady Dedlock's Secret (1884);
The Only Way (1899, with Martin Harvey as Carton); Oliver
Twist (c1906, with Beerbohm Tree as Fagin); and David
Copperfield (c1920, with Bransby Williams as both Micawber
and Dan'l Peggotty). Film, radio and television versions
have included all the novels and many of the stories. See
articles in Dickensian by Malcolm Morley mentioned above
under "Pickwick" etc and note in Churchill 1958 p 142.

Dickens. The Story of Little Dombey. 1858; rp 1862; rp
Boston 1868.

Dickens. A Christmas Carol: The Public Reading Version.
Boston 1868; ed Philip Collins, New York 1972. With stage-
directions: "stern pathos" etc.

Field, Kate. Pen Photographs of Charles Dickens's Readings.
Boston 1868.

Dickens to a friend May 1870. "What do you think would be
the realization of one of my most cherished day dreams?
To settle down for the remainder of my life" - he died a
few weeks later - "within easy distance of a great theatre,
in the direction of which I should have supreme authority...
the players as well as the plays being absolutely under my
command" (qu Pearson 1949: p 4 above.)

Trollope 1870: p 15 above. "He would attempt nothing...which
he did not understand. But he was not on that account forced
to confine himself to literature. Everyone knows how he read
...As an actor he would have been at the top of his
profession..."

Forster 1872-4, Dent 1933, Pope-Hennessy 1945, Pearson 1949 and Johnson 1952 qqv above pp 2-5 give details of Dickens's amateur theatricals and public readings, as do many other sources like Field 1868 above and Dolby and Dexter below.

Kent, Charles. Charles Dickens as a Reader. 1872; rp 1971 intn Philip Collins.

Dolby, George. Charles Dickens as I Knew Him: The Story of the Reading Tours in Great Britain and America 1866-70. 1885. By his manager.

Pemberton, T.E. Dickens and the Stage. 1888.

Conway, Moncure. Autobiography. New York 1904. Incl impressions of Dickens as public reader: "in himself a whole stock company."

Hollingshead, John (ed). Readings from the Works of Charles Dickens: as arranged and read by himself. 1907.

FitzGerald, S.J.Adair. Charles Dickens and the Drama. 1910.

Williams, Bransby. Character Sketches from Dickens. 1910. By the actor who doubled Micawber and Peggotty c1920 (see above p 189) and who later played Dickens characters on BBC radio and television. Cf Churchill 1958 p 142.

Stonehouse, John Harrison (ed). Sikes and Nancy. 1921. Facsimile of Dickens's privately printed script used by him in his public readings. Ref Collins 1971 below.

Woollcott, Alexander. Mr Dickens Goes to the Play. 1923.

Playfair 1927: p 50 above.

Eliot 1927: p 24 above. Discusses The Frozen Deep.

Konig, K. Dickens und das Theater. Stettin 1932.

Klein, Herman. Musicians and Mummers. Describes Dickens's "masterpiece of characterisation" in his public reading of Fagin: "again and again he made his audience shudder" (qu Blacklands fwd Dent 1933 p 4 above.)

Muddock, J.E.Preston. Papers from an Adventurous Life. Incl impressions of Dickens's public readings. "There were no accessories of music or scenery, simply one man at a reading desk; but what a man!'" (qu Blacklands as above.)

Dexter, Walter. Dickens's Early Dramatic Productions.
Dickensian 33-4 1937-8.

Churchill 1937-42: p 26 above. "If we accept the proposition
that the dramatic genius which might have gone into
playwriting, had the theatre been in a more healthy state,
spent itself instead, like Fielding's, on the novel, then
we need to know why, on the face of it, Dickens would
appear likely to have been so _bad_ a dramatist..." (p 363;
cf Quiller-Couch qu above p 187.)

Dexter, Walter. For One Night Only: Dickens's Appearances
as an Amateur Actor. Dickensian 35-7 1939-41.

Wilson 1939-41: p 27 above. "Dickens had a strain of the
ham in him, and, in the desperation of his later life, he
gave in to the old ham and let him rip" (p 61 UP edn.)

Morley 1946: p 41 above under Reynolds. Cf Morley 1947
p 189 above under Dickens 1838 and further articles in
Dickensian listed under novels above. For USA see Morley,
Early Dickens Drama in America, Dickensian 1948 pp 155-6.

Fawcett, F.Dubrez. Dickens the Dramatist: On Stage, Screen
and Radio. 1952. Incl photos of stage and screen
productions.

Williams, Emlyn (ed). Readings from Dickens. 1953.
Intn Bernard Darwin. See Churchill 1958 p 142.

Churchill 1958: p 32 above under Ford; pp 123, 125, 142.

Finlay, I.F. Dickens in the Cinema. Dickensian 54 1958.
Lists films 1902-58.

Gordan, J.D. Reading for Profit. New York 1958. Lists
reading edns, prompt copies, etc.

Axton 1966: p 188 above.

Fluchère 1969: p 35 above.

Williams, Emlyn. Dickens and the Theatre. In Tomlin 1970:
p 8 above.

Powell, Dilys. In Slater Dickensian 1970: p 7 above. On the
Dickens films. Cf Finlay above.

Fitzsimons, Raymund. The Charles Dickens Show: An Account of
his Public Readings 1858-70. 1970.

Brannan, Robert Louis (ed). Under the Management of Mr
Charles Dickens: His Production of The Frozen Deep. 1970.
Cf Eliot 1927 above.

Dickens. Complete Plays and Selected Poems. 1970. Cf Dent
1933-5 pp 138-40 for details of The Village Coquettes (1836)
and The Strange Gentleman (1837) and House 1965-74 for
Dickens's letters on these early productions which incl
Is She His Wife? or Something Singular (1837). He himself
held no great opinion of these dramatic efforts. See
Dexter 1937-8 above.

Altick, Richard D. Victorian Studies in Scarlet. 1970.
Points out (p 97) connection between Dickens's public
readings of such items as Sikes and Nancy and the
Sensation Drama of the 1860s. Cf Quiller-Couch 1922-5.

Slater, Michael (ed). Treasures from the Suzannet Collection.
1970. Catalogue of Dickensiana from library of Comte Alain
de Suzannet incl some privately-printed desk copies used by
Dickens in his public readings.

Collins, Philip. Sikes and Nancy: Dickens's Last Reading.
TLS 11 Jun 1971. Cf Dolby 1885 pp 445-50.

Dickens. The Strange Gentleman and Other Plays. 1973.
Ed Jeffery Tillett. Cf Dickens 1970 above.

Wees, William C. Dickens, Griffith and Eisenstein: Form and
Image in Literature and Film. Humanities Assn Rev Fall 1973.

Collins, Philip. Dickens's Public Readings: Texts and
Performances. DSA 3 1974.

Basch, Francoise. "Oliver Twist is the novel of Dickens
that has most often been adapted for the stage. Episodes
such as the confrontation with Rose Maylie in the fortieth
chapter when Nancy... hastens towards the black waters of
the Thames, and finally her death, seem to have been written
for acting... Dickens, despite the violent reactions this
scene provoked in the audience and himself, refused to drop
it from his repertoire of dramatic readings. Contemporary
accounts describe him in the part of Nancy, alternating
between terror and supplication" (Relative Creatures:
Victorian Women in Society and the Novel 1837-67. 1974.
See further below under "Dickens and Crime" and "Sex in
Dickens").

Dickens the Journalist

Sala 1870: p 2 above. By one of Dickens's chief collaborators in Household Words and All the Year Round.

Forster 1872-4: p 2 above. School Days and Start in Life (bk 1 ch 3); Newspaper Reporting and Writing (bk 1 ch 4); New Literary Project (bk 2 ch 6); Christmas Books Closed and Household Words Begun (bk 6 ch 4); All the Year Round and Uncommercial Traveller (bk 8 ch 4). Cf Johnson 1952.

Kent, Charles. Charles Dickens as a Journalist. The Journalist 1879.

Dickens, Charles jr. Dickens as an Editor. English Illustrated Mag Aug 1889.

McCarthy, Justin and Sir John R.Robinson. The Daily News Jubilee. 1896. Dickens was the first editor of the News, 1846; his father was head of the reporting staff 1846-8.

Collet, Collet Dobson. History of the Taxes on Knowledge. 1899; abr Thinker's Library 1933. Ch 9 incl "acquittal of Dickens's Household Narrative" - the threepenny monthly supplement to Household Words called A Narrative of Events - from having to pay newspaper stamp duty.

Matz, B.W. Dickens as a Journalist. Fortnightly Rev May 1908. Matz ed Miscellaneous Papers, 1908, for the Gadshill edn 1897-1908. Also incl in National edn 1906-8 and Centenary edn 1910-11.

Escott, T.H.S. Masters of English Journalism. 1911.

Lehmann, R.C.(ed). Charles Dickens as Editor: Letters to W.H.Wills. 1912. Wills was assistant editor of Household Words and All the Ywar Round.

Fitzgerald, Percy. Memories of Charles Dickens, with an Account of Household Words and All the Year Round and of the Contributors thereto. Bristol 1913.

Crotch 1913: see below under "Radical and Reformer".

Saintsbury 1916: qu above p 84.

Carlton, William J. Charles Dickens, Shorthand Writer. 1926. Cf Forster above.

Dent 1933: p 4 above; ch 2.

Dickens the Journalist, cont.

Dexter, Walter.   Charles Dickens: Journalist.   Nineteenth
    Century & After Jun 1934.
    Dickens and the Morning Chronicle.   Fortnightly Nov 1934.

Churchill 1937-42: qu above p 114.

Grubb, Gerald G.   Charles Dickens's First Experience as a
    Parliamentary Reporter.   Dickensian 1940 pp 211-18.

House 1941: p 27 above; passim.

Churchill, R.C.   Dickens as Journalist.   Scrutiny 10 pp 304-7.
    Review of House above.   "Mr House is obviously aware that
    the separation between Dickens as journalist and Dickens
    as novelist is necessary for reasons other than those of
    convenience..." (p 304).   "...of the mass of writing
    about Dickens...a disproportionately large amount has
    been devoted to his 'interest in social reform'...But few
    critics...have considered this aspect of Dickens's work
    from the point of view of Dickens as a novelist, taking his
    success therein to be part of his artistic achievement"
    (pp 305-6) - an argument developed at more length in
    Churchill 1937-42 and Churchill 1958.   See further below
    under "Radical and Reformer".

Grubb, Gerald G.   Dickens and the Daily News.   NCF 6-7 1952-3.

Collins, Philip.   The Significance of Dickens's Periodicals.
    REL 2 1961.

Brown 1963: p 33 above.

Hibbert 1967: p 5 above.   The early reporting and journalism.

Stone, Harry (ed).   The Uncollected Writings of Charles
    Dickens.   2 vols 1969.   From Household Words 1850-9.

Q.D.Leavis 1970: p 36 above.   "The Dickens who wrote his
    excellent journalistic pieces...was not the Dickens who
    wrote the novels or those parts (the most) of them which
    make them works of art" (cf Churchill 1937-42 p 114 above.)

Lohrli 1974: p 85 above.

See further above under "Household Words" etc.

Radical and Reformer

Maginn 1836: qu above p 9.   Cf William Howitt, People's
         Journal 3 Jun 1846 qu Collins
                                   1971.
Dickens.   Letter to Edward Marlborough Fitzgerald (?)
    29 Dec 1838.   "I went...to Manchester, and saw the worst
    cotton mill.   And then I saw the best... There was no great
    difference between them.   I was obliged to come back
    suddenly on some matters connected with the publication of
    Oliver Twist... I am going down again...into the enemy's
    camp and the very headquarters of the Factory System
    advocates... I have seen enough for my purpose, and what
    I have seen has astonished and disgusted me beyond all
    measure.   I mean to strike the heaviest blow in my power
    for those unfortunate creatures, but whether I shall do so
    in Nickleby or wait some other opportunity I have not yet
    determined" (qu Pope-Hennessy 1945 p 107 from Hodder's
    Life of Lord Shaftesbury.   She gives recipient as the poet
    Edward FitzGerald.   House 1965 p 483n thinks it more
    probable that it was the Irish journalist and writer of
    political verse E.M.Fitzgerald.   Dickens knew both men,
    but probably not the poet till the 1840s.)

New Moral World 1840: qu above p 38.

Marx 1841-2: qu above p 138.   Cf letter to Engels about
    Dickens's "graphic and eloquent pages" which have "issued
    to the world more political and social truths than have been
    uttered by all the professional politicians, publicists and
    moralists put together" (qu Lucas 1970: p 36 above.)

Whitman Feb 1842: qu above p 11.   See further below under
    "Dickens and Walt Whitman".

Webster, Daniel.   Speech at Boston 1842 saying Dickens had
    "done more to ameliorate the condition of the English poor
    than all the statesmen that Great Britain had sent into
    Parliament" (qu Pope-Hennessy 1945 p 160; cf Marx above,
    but see House 1941 below.)

Felton 1843: p 11 above.   Compares Dickens's correction of
    "ancient abuses" with Channing's.

Martineau, Harriet.   "His sympathies are on the side of the
    suffering and the frail; and this makes him the idol of
    those who suffer, from whatever cause.   We may wish that he
    had a sounder social philosophy, and...could show us
    something of the necessity and blessedness of homely and
    incessant self-discipline, and dwell a little less fondly on
    the grosser indulgences..." (History of the Thirty Years'
    Peace, 1849; fully qu House 1941 pp 74-5 qv.)

Dickens. Household Words first no.   30 Mar 1850.   Announced
journal as "the gentle mouthpiece of reform".

Working Man's Friend 1852: p 12 above.

Dickens. Speech at Birmingham 6 Jan 1853. "...And my creed
in the exercise of that profession is that Literature
cannot be too faithful to the people in return - cannot too
ardently advocate the cause of their advancement, happiness
and prosperity..." (qu fully Wall 1970 pp 92-3.)

Denman 1853: qu above p 87.

Dickens. Introductory words before a reading of the Carol
at Birmingham 30 Dec 1853. Said how important he thought it
was that workers should take their share in management,
how essential to the healthy life of the whole community.
See further Birmingham Post 6 Jun 1970.

Anon. Blackwood's Mag Jun 1855. "...He is a man of very
liberal sentiments...one of the advocates in the plea of
Poor versus Rich, to the progress of which he has lent no
small aid in his day. But he is, notwithstanding, perhaps
more distinctly than any other author of the time, a class
writer, the historian and representative of one circle in
the many ranks of our social scale. Despite their descents
into the lowest class, and their occasional flights into the
less familiar ground of fashion, it is the air and breath of
middle-class respectability which fills the books of Mr
Dickens" (qu House 1941 p 152; cf Orwell 1939-40 below.)

Stephen 1857: p 13 above. "Imprisonment for debt on mesne
process was doomed, if not abolished, before he wrote
Pickwick; the Court of Chancery was reformed before he
published Bleak House; in his attacks on Parliament he...
was utterly and hopelessly wrong". Cf House 1941 pp 222-3:
"...in his major campaigns he did not succeed...No genuine
attempt to meet his objections to the Poor Law was made
till the appintment of the Royal Commission of 1905.
Private persons were still imprisoned for debts over £20
until 1861, and imprisonment for debt was not formally
abolished before 1869..." Cf Chaplin 1964 qu above p 48.

Bagehot 1858: p 13 above. "Mr Dickens's political opinions
have subjected him to a good deal of criticism, and to some
ridicule... His is what we may call the 'sentimental
radicalism'... Nothing can be better than the description
of the poor debtors' gaols in Pickwick or of the old
parochial authorities in Oliver...It is painful to pass
from these happy instances of well-used power to the glaring
abuses of the same faculty in Mr Dickens's later books"
(pp 189-91 EL edn 1911.)

Radical and Reformer, cont.

Masson 1859: p 13 above. "There is scarcely a social question
on which he has not touched; and there are few of his novels
in which he has not blended the functions of a social and
political critic with those of the artist, to a degree
detrimental, as many think, to his genius in the latter
capacity... And yet how much we owe to Mr Dickens for this
very opinionativeness.'... The Administrative Reform
Association might have worked for ten years without
producing half of the effect which Mr Dickens has produced...
by flinging out the phrase 'The Circumlocution Office'... "

Ruskin 1860-2: qu above p 94.

Jowett 1870: p 15 above. "He whom we mourn was the friend of
mankind... the enemy of every form of meanness and oppression
... We feel that a light has gone out" (qu Forster bk 11
final para.)

Shaftesbury, Lord. 1870. "He was set, I doubt not, to rouse
attention to many evils and many woes. God gave him a
general retainer against all suffering and oppression"
(qu Pope-Hennessy 1945 p 485.)

Trollope 1870: p 15 above. "I never heard any man call
Dickens a radical; but if any man ever was so, he was a
radical at heart, believing entirely in the people, writing
for them, speaking for them, and always desirous to take
their part as against some undescribed and indiscernible
tyrant, who to his mind loomed large as an official rather
than an aristoratic despot" (cf Orwell below.)

Shepherd, R.H.(ed). The Speeches of Charles Dickens 1841-70.
1870; rv 1884; new edn nd intn Bernard Darwin. Cf Fielding
1960 below.

Anon. Temple Bar 1873. "...that Mr Dickens was rather more
than less unfortunate than other people when, like them,
he talked of things he did not understand is abundantly
proved by... the invariable association of rank with folly
and power with incompetence in all his works" (cf Stephen
1857 and Orwell 1939.)

Butler 1875: p 125 above. See comment by Dickens on
Dr Arnold.

Canning 1880: p 16 above.

Ruskin 1880-1: p 16 above. Cf Ruskin 1860-2.

Maine, Sir Henry. "It does not seem to me a fantastic
assertion that the ideas of one of the great novelists of
the last generation may be traced to Bentham... Dickens,
who spent his early manhood among the politicians of 1832
trained in Bentham's school, hardly ever wrote a novel
without attacking an abuse..." (Popular Government, 1885;
qu House 1941 p 36 who comments that this suggestion was
taken up by A.V.Dicey in his Law and Opinion in England,
1905, "who accepted it without criticism; but he used it
as a step in his argument that the Benthamite
individualism of the 'thirties was already being
abandoned in the 'fifties by those who had formerly held
it. He took it as true that the young Dickens was a
Benthamite radical; but he then quoted Hard Times to show
that the man who was in 1846 'the editor of the organ of
the Manchester school' had become by 1854 'the satirist
and the censor of political economy and utilitarianism'.
He took the alteration to be 'unconscious'; but a closer
reading of Dickens would have reminded him that Mr Filer
appeared in 1843. For Dickens was consistently the
indignant satirist and censor of the 'classical'
economists; but this need not mean that he was never in
any sense a Benthamite" (cf Dickens 1838 qu above p 195;
Chesterton 1913 qu above p 69 - "he wrote against Mr
Gradgrind long before he created him" - and more recent
critics such as Churchill 1937-42, Leavis 1947 and Slater
1970 qu above p 69.)

Cazamian, Louis. Le Roman social en Angleterre 1830-50:
Dickens, Disraeli, Mrs Gaskell, Kingsley. Paris 1904.
Qu Wall 1970 pp 240-3 and Basch 1974.

Baillie-Saunders, Margaret. The Philosophy of Charles
Dickens: A Study of his Life and Teaching as a Social
Reformer. 1905.

Chesterton 1907-11: p 20 above. "For the first half of the
century Dickens and all his friends were justified in
feeling that the chains were falling from mankind. At any
rate, the chains did fall from Mr Rouncewell the Ironmaster. And when they fell from him he picked them up
and put them upon the poor" (p 177 1933 edn; cf Maine
above and Chesterton qu under "Oliver Twist", "The Chimes"
and "Hard Times".)

Pugh, Edwin. Charles Dickens: The Apostle of the People.
1908. Cf Crotch below.

Radical and Reformer, cont.

Walters, J.Cuming. Phases of Dickens: The Man, his Message
and his Mission. 1911.

Escott 1912: p 21 above.

Shaw 1912: qu above p 95.

Chesterton 1913: p 21 above. "He had no particular plan of
reform... He didn't like the Unrivalled Happiness which Mr
Roebuck praised; the economic laws that were working so
faultlessly in Fever Alley; the wealth that was accumulating
so rapidly in Bleeding Heart Yard. But, above all, he
didn't like the mean side of the Manchester philosophy:
the preaching of an impossible thrift and an intolerable
temperance... And this meanness of the Utilitarians had
gone very far - infecting many finer minds who had fought
the Utilitarians... he attacked the cold Victorian
compromise... He was attacking something which we will
call Mr Gradgrind..." (pp 33-4 OPUS edn; cf Martineau and
Maine above). "If in your sympathy for Mr Rouncewell you
call Dickens the champion of a manly middle-class
Liberalism against Chesney Wold, you will suddenly
remember Stephen Blackpool - and find yourself unable to
deny that Mr Rouncewell might be a pretty insupportable
cock on his own dunghill..." (p 53). "In Hard Times he
realized Democracy at war with Radicalism; and became,
with so incompatible an ally as Ruskin, not indeed a
Socialist, but certainly an anti-Individualist" (p 56).

Crotch, William Walter. Charles Dickens: Social Reformer.
1913. Crotch also wrote The Pageant of Dickens (1915);
The Soul of Dickens (1916); The Secret of Dickens (1919);
and The Touchstone of Dickens (1920). He was one of the
originators of the Dickens Fellowship and was President
1915-20. On the invitation of Sir Hall Caine he revived
Household Words (ref Who's Who 1945 edn.)

Santayana 1921-2: p 23 above. "Perhaps, properly speaking,
he had no ideas on any subject; what he had was a vast
sympathetic participation in the daily life of mankind;
and what he saw of ancient institutions made him hate them,
as needless sources of oppression, misery, selfishness, and
rancour. His one political passion was philanthropy,
genuine but left only on its negative, reforming side..."

Radlov: p 142 above.

Inge 1922: p 23 above. Cf Chesterton 1913.

Radical and Reformer, cont.

Quiller-Couch 1922-5: p 23 above. "...a great and genuine
early-Victorian radical, something better than any
politician; an unbribed and unbribable writer, immensely
potent, with a pen...dedicated to war against social
abuses" (p 12). "...he hated Jeremy Bentham and all his
works" (p 74). Cf The Victorian Background op cit pp 158-79.

Clark, Cumberland. Dickens and Democracy and Other Studies.
1926. Incl Dickens's essay The Condition of the Working
Classes and his letter to Southwood Smith on The Condition
of the Poor.

Payne, Edward and H.Harper. The Charity of Charles Dickens.
Boston 1929.

Cecil 1931-4: p 25 above. "...something more than an artist.
He is also a prophet...out to expound...a view of life, a
scale of values... Class distinctions...were especially
hateful to him because they checked the natural free
current of benevolence which should flow from one man to
another..." Like "the old moralities", his novels "have
their universal application", their "universal truth"
(pp 55-7 FL edn.)

Chancellor 1932: p 25 above.

Baldwin, Stanley. "...one of the greatest creative geniuses
of all times... the first man who had a conception of the
so-called 'lower orders' and could treat them as men and
women with character, not as characters..." (The Chronicler
of the People of England; qu Blacklands fwd Dent 1933 qv.)

Dent 1933: p 4 above. "...like all great reformers, he saw
the uselessness of palliatives, and searched for fundamental
causes... His anger became directed against the indifference
and hypocrisy, the blindness and selfishness of society"
(p 150 1935 edn; cf pp 10-14, 23-5.)

Young, G.M. "Dickens's ideal England was not very far from
Robert Owen's. But it was to be built by some magic of
goodwill overriding the egoism of progress; not by law,
and most emphatically not by logic... In all Dickens's
work there is a confusion of mind which reflects the
perplexity of his time; equally ready to denounce on the
grounds of humanity all who left things alone, and on the
grounds of liberty all who tried to make them better"
(Early Victorian England II pp 455-6 qu House 1941 p 201n.
See House's comment and cf New Moral World 1840 qu above
p 38.)

Radical and Reformer, cont.

Young, G.M. "...The political satire of Dickens is tedious
and ignorant. But it registers, what Past and Present
conveys more passionately, the disillusionment which
followed on the hopes of 1830..." (Victorian England:
Portrait of an Age, 1936, p 29; cf Chesterton 1913 and see
further below under "Dickens and Carlyle".)

Shaw 1937: p 26 above. "Dickens never regarded himself as a
revolutionist, though he certainly was one. His implacable
contempt for the House of Commons...never wavered from the
account of the Eatanswill election and of Nicholas
Nickleby's interview with Pugstyles to the Veneering
election in Our Mutual Friend..."

Jackson 1937: p 26 above. Points out (p 253) that many of
Dickens's characters are, as it were, "flattened" by
capitalist society. Cf Forster 1927 and Orwell 1939 and
defence of Jackson's general position by Barbara Hardy in
Slater 1970 pp 37-40.

Churchill 1937-42: p 26 above. "...he is not less of a
novelist because he is concerned so directly with social
issues; on the contrary, he gains in stature as a writer,
as an artist, by the manner in which he presents his
criticism. If this were not so, such parts of his work
would be as dead now as other nineteenth-century 'novels
with a purpose'. The gift, the gift of the artist, for
perceiving the fundamental beneath the particular, saves
him" (p 374.)

Dobrée and Batho 1938: p 26 above. "Where Dickens touched
upon social reform, anywhere in fact where he began to
think, he falls below the level of the second-rate,
though the generous indignation that he shows is worthy
of a full and complete man" (cf Quiller-Couch above.)

Christie 1939: p 26 above

Orwell 1939-40: p 26 above. "In Oliver Twist, Hard Times,
Bleak House, Little Dorrit, Dickens attacked British
institutions with a ferocity that has never since been
approached..." (p 8 1946 edn.) "His radicalism is of the
vaguest kind, and yet one always knows that it is there"
(p 53; cf Trollope 1870.)

Wilson 1939-41: p 27 above. "Of all the great Victorian
writers, he was probably the most antagonistic to the
Victorian Age itself..." (pp 26-39 UP edn; cf Chesterton
1913 above.)

Radical and Reformer, cont.

House 1941: p 27 above. "He seemed topical to thousands: he
     was not too topical for them to see the point, nor too
     advanced to have the public conscience on his side... He
     shared a great deal of common experience with his public...
     and caught exactly the tone which clarified and reinforced
     the public's sense of right and wrong, and flattered its
     moral feelings" (pp 41-2). "It means very little that
     Dickens called himself a Radical or that Bagehot called him
     one, if the word must be tied down to some exact
     significance..." (pp 171-2). Cf Chesterton 1913.

Trevelyan, G.M. English Social History. New York 1942;
     London 1944; pp 507-8, 522, 538-9 (Oliver Twist), 544-5.

Cruikshank, R.J. Dickens and Early Victorian England.   1949.

Lindsay 1950: p 5 above.

Churchill 1950: p 29 above.   Ch 3.

Johnson 1952: p 6 above.

Johnson 1952: p 5 above. "Johnson's criticism of the novels,
     which is hived off into separate chapters, emphasizes
     Dickens's force as a critic of his society" (Wall 1970 p 318

Kettle, Arnold. In Ford 1958: p 32 above. "You cannot
     describe Bleak House...or even Oliver Twist or Hard Times,
     as a 'social-problem novel'. But that is exactly what Sybil
     or North and South or Alton Locke is..." (The Early Victoria
     Social-Problem Novel, p 170; cf Churchill 1937-42 qu above
     and Kettle 1951-3 and see further below under "Dickens and
     Disraeli" and "Dickens and Mrs Gaskell".)

Pritchett, V.S. The Great Reformist. New Statesman 1 Oct 196

Fielding, K.J.(ed). The Speeches of Charles Dickens. Oxford
     1960. Largely supersedes Shepherd 1870 qv.

Brown 1963: p 33 above.

Collins 1963: see below under "Dickens and Education".

Williams, Raymond. Social Criticism in Dickens: Some Problems
     of Method and Approach. CQ 1964.

Peyrouton, Noel C. Dickens and the Chartists. Dickensian 60
     1964. Cf Spence below.

Radical and Reformer, cont.

Dabney 1967: p 34 above.

Smith 1969: p 35 above.

Brown 1970: p 36 above.

Williams 1970: p 78 above. "...the remarkable emergence,
   at that critical moment, of a great radical novelist"
   (p 34; but cf Dickens 1838 and Chesterton 1907-11 and 1913
   for earlier radical development.)

Brown, Ivor. Dickens as a Social Reformer. In Tomlin
   1970: p 8 above. Cf Brown 1963 and 1970 above.

Lucas 1970: p 36 above. "...the great truth-teller and
   conscience of his age" whose novels provide "central
   statements and judgments of Victorian England". Cf
   Chesterton 1913, Wilson 1939, Brown 1963.

Williams, Raymond. Dickens and Social Ideas. In Slater
   1970: p 8 above.

Slater 1970: qu above p 69. Cf House 1941.

Lucas, John (ed). Literature and Politics in the Nineteenth
   Century. 1971. Incl essay by William Myers on the
   radicalism of Little Dorrit. Cf Stephen 1857 and Snow 1970
   qu above under "Dorrit".

Keating 1971: p 36 above. "Excepting the shadowy Daniel
   Doyce, the intellectual working man and the superior
   artisan are entirely absent from his novels" (cf Orwell).

Spence 1973: qu above p 58.

Oddie 1973: p 98 above. See ch on The People: Revolution
   and Radicalism. And further below under "Dickens and
   Carlyle".

Gold, Joseph. Charles Dickens: Radical Moralist. Oxford
   1974. See further below under "Dickens and Religion".

Basch 1974: p 192 above; pp 131, 207-8. See further below
   under "Dickens and Education" and "Sex in Dickens".

Craig 1974: p 98 above.

Dickens and Childhood

Hood 1840: p 51 above. "As for Little Nelly herself, we
should say that she thinks, speaks and acts in a style
beyond her years, if we did not know how poverty and
misfortune are apt to make advances of worldly knowledge
to the young at a most ruinous discount - a painful
sacrifice of the very capital of childhood."

Robinson 1841: p 53 above.

Dostoevsky 1846-8: p 54 above.

Dickens 1847: p 2 above. "No words can express the secret
agony of my soul..." Cf Copperfield ch 11 and Orwell 1939,
Wilson 1939, Maugham 1954 below.

Druzhinin 1849: p 141 above. See further below under
"Dickens and Dostoevsky".

Thackeray 1852: p 150 above. "All children ought to love
him. I know two that do, and read his books ten times for
once that they peruse the dismal preachments of their father
I know one who... at ten years of age said 'I like Mr
Dickens's books much better than your books, papa' and
frequently expressed her desire that the latter author
should write a book like one of Mr Dickens's books.
Who can? ... " (pp 284-5 loc cit.)

Higginson, T.W.(ed). Child-Pictures from Dickens. Boston
1868, London 1885. Incl prefatory note by Dickens.

Buchanan 1872: p 15 above. "Charles Dickens, having crushed
into his childish experience a whole world of sorrow and
humorous insight, so loaded his soul that he never grew any
older... He saw all from a child's point of view - strange,
odd, queer, puzzling..." (cf Evans, Orwell, Priestley etc
below.)

Langton 1883: p 3 above.

Gissing 1898 and 1899: pp 17-18 above. Points out Dickens's
originality in his treatment of children. Cf Orwell 1939.

Gissing 1901: p 19 above.

Chesterton 1906: p 20 above.

Munro 1908: p 20 above. See further below under "Dickens and
Daudet".

204

Powys 1912: p 21 above.

Meynell 1912: p 21 above.

Watts-Dunton 1912-13: p 21 above.

James 1913: p 22 above.   Cf Gissing 1901.

Leacock 1916: p 22 above.

Phelps 1916: p 22 above.   "He regarded his own childhood
  with considerable and justifiable self-pity; but his
  unfathomable tenderness is shown with especial force
  toward all children.   The sufferings of little boys and
  girls made to him an irresistible appeal; and he felt that
  the death of a child was the most tragic event in nature,
  as Poe thought the death of a young girl the most
  poetically and romantically beautiful.   Dickens insisted
  on the inherent dignity of childhood - a dignity constantly
  outraged both by the selfishness and by the condescension
  of adults" (p 107.)

Woolf 1919: p 23 above.

Santayana 1921: p 23 above.   "He was a waif himself, and
  utterly disinherited... like a sensitive child, with a
  most religious disposition, but no religious ideas..."
  See further below under "Dickens and Religion" and
  "Dickens and Christmas".

Quiller-Couch 1922-5: p 23 above.   "...you will never
  understand Charles Dickens until you realize...how
  indignantly the genius in this child of the blacking-
  warehouse felt the shame of its lot..." (pp 59-61; cf
  Wilson 1939 below.)

Maurois 1927: p 24 above.

Wagenknecht 1929: p 4 above.

Cecil 1931-4: p 25 above.   "...an extraordinary understanding"
  of children... "The first halves of Great Expectations and
  David Copperfield are among the profoundest pictures of
  childhood in English letters" (p 51 FL edn; cf Wilson 1970
  below.)

Dent 1933: qu above p 55.

Leacock 1933: qu above p 185.

Dickens and Childhood, cont.

Kingsmill 1934: p 4 above.

Orwell 1939–40: p 26 above. "No one...has written better about childhood than Dickens... no novelist has shown the same power of entering into the child's point of view..." (pp 17–19 1946 edn.)

Wilson 1939–41: p 27 above; pp 4–8 UP edn.

Evans 1940: qu above p 154.

House 1941: p 27 above. "...Dickens hated any charity that had a stigma: Dombey's charity to Rob the Grinder, which made him wear a uniform that brought flocks of jeering boys round his heels, was nearly as bad in Dickens's mind as the kindness of a Board of Guardians..." (p 78; cf Phelps 1916 qu above.)

Leavis 1947: p 96 above. See further below under "Dickens and Education".

Sackville-West, Edward. Dickens and the World of Childhood. Inclinations, 1949.

Brown, Ivor. Shakespeare. 1949. Compares boyhoods of Shakespeare and Dickens: "Both boys witnessed parental decline and humiliating sense of poverty... Both were self-educated in the sense that both possessed and exercised the greatest gift obtainable by any writer, what Dickens called 'the key of the street'" (pp 92–3; see further below under "Dickens and Shakespeare".)

Lindsay 1950: p 5 above.

Rooke, E. Fathers and Sons in Dickens. Essays & Studies ns 4 1951.

Johnson 1952: p 5 above.

Allen 1954: p 30 above; pp 163–6 PB edn.

Maugham 1954: p 30 above. "... I do not believe that the experience" in the blacking warehouse "caused him anything like the suffering that in after years...he persuaded himself that it had; and I believe even less that...it had a decisive effect on his life and work" (p 131 PB edn; cf Dickens 1847, Forster 1872, Quiller-Couch 1922, Wilson 1939 Johnson 1952 etc.)

Dickens and Childhood, cont.

Coveney, Peter. Poor Monkey: The Child in Literature. 1957; rv as The Image of Childhood, 1967. Incl ch The Child in Dickens.

Churchill 1958: p 32 above under Ford. Childhood in Dickens and Butler (pp 344-6; see further below under "Dickens and Charles Reade" and "Dickens and Butler".)

Wilson 1960: p 33 above. Cf Gissing 1901.

Priestley 1960: p 33 above. "...here we shall do well to remember Baudelaire's 'Genius is childhood recaptured at will', for in Dickens's creative genius there is a direct access to childhood, to the fantastic world that imaginative children know..." (p 235 PB edn.)

Cockshut 1961: p 33 above.

Leavis 1962: see above under "Dombey".

Reid 1962: p 33 above.

Collins 1963: see below under "Dickens and Education".

Wilson 1963: p 34 above.

Marcus 1964: p 34 above.

Hibbert 1967: p 5 above.

Greene 1969: see above under "Oliver Twist".

Wilson, Angus. Dickens on Children and Childhood. In Slater 1970: p 8 above.

Lane, Margaret. Dickens on the Hearth. Ibid.

Allen, Walter. Discusses connection between Dickens's retention of "the child's-eye view of human beings" and "the nature of his comedy" (Slater 1970 pp 10-11; cf Priestley 1960 above.)

Leavis 1970: p 36 above. Chs on Dombey, Copperfield, Hard Times and Little Dorrit.

Churchill 1973-4: p 37 above.

Horsman 1974: p 79 above. Intn pp xxiv-xxv ref W.J.Carlton, Dickensian 1962 p 89.

Dickens and Education

Dickens 1848. "Of the monstrous neglect of education in
England, and the disregard of it by the State as a means
of forming good or bad citizens, and miserable or happy
men, private schools long afforded a notable example... "
(pref cheap edn Nickleby.)

Dickens 1855: qu above p 93.

Taine 1856: qu above p 93.

Bagehot 1858: see below under "Dickens and the Universities".

Arnold 1881: p 80 above. "Intimately, indeed, did Dickens
know the middle class... Intimately he knew its bringing up.
Mr Creakle and Salem House are immortal... Mr Murdstone may
be called the natural product of a course of Salem House...'"
(qu more fully Wall 1970 pp 215-7; Arnold compares English
education as exemplified in Copperfield with "the public
schools of Germany"; cf Dickens on Dr Arnold qu above p 125)

Hughes, J.L. Dickens as an Educator. New York 1900.

More 1908: p 20 above.

Chesterton 1913: p 21 above. "Matthew Arnold, trying to
carry into England constructive educational schemes which
he could see... all over the Continent, ... invoked the aid
of Dickens... " (pp 35-6 OPUS edn; ref is to Arnold 1881 qu
above.)

Shaw, Bernard. Treatise on Parents and Children. 1914.
Pref Misalliance etc. See p xx.

Hughes, J.L. Personal Reminiscences relating to Dickens.
Journal of Education 101 1925.

Humphreys, Arthur. Charles Dickens and his First
Schoolmaster. Manchester 1926. This was Rev William
Giles (1798-1856): see letter to him in House 1965 p 429.

Blacklands 1933: p 4 above under Dent. "It is because
Dickens reflected so admirably the zeitgeist - the spirit
of the age - that his work is so useful educationally. "

Dent 1933: p 4 above; see particularly pp 45-7, 69-72, 77-9,
173-8, 339-40, 359-60, 447 in 1935 edn. Author was editor
of Times Educational Supplement.

Leacock 1933: p 4 above.

Dickens and Education, cont.

Shaw 1937: p 26 above. "...he escaped the school and
 university routine which complicates cultural Philistinism
 with the mentality of a Red Indian brave... But there are
 homes in which a mentally acquisitive boy can make contact
 with the fine arts... Now the Dickenses seem to have been
 complete barbarians..."

Orwell 1939-40: p 26 above. "Except for the universities
 and the big public schools, every kind of education then
 existing in England gets a mauling at Dickens's hands..."
 (pp 19-21 1946 edn.)

House 1941: p 27 above; pp 10, 99, 223.

Leavis 1947: see above under "Hard Times".

Manning, John. Dickens and the Glasgow System.
 School & Society 83 1956.

Clinton-Baddeley 1957: p 51 above.

Fielding 1957: p 97 above.

Manning, John. Dickens on Education.   Toronto 1959.

Collins, Philip. Dickens and the Ragged Schools.
 Dickensian 55 1959. Cf Forster 1872 bk 4 ch 1 and Pope-
 Hennessy 1945 p 143.

Collins, Philip. Dickens and Adult Education.   Leicester
 1962. Cf Forster 1872 bk 4 ch 3.

Brown 1963: p 33 above.

Collins, Philip. Dickens and Education.   1963; rv 1964.
 The most detailed study.

Blount, Trevor. Poor Jo, Education and the Problem of
 Juvenile Delinquency.   MP 62 1965.

Hibbert 1967: p 5 above.

Basch 1974: p 192 above; p 141.

See further below under "Dickens and the Universities".

Dickens and the Universities

Fraser's Mag 1842: p 59 above.   "Does Mr Dickens know anything of our universities?" (ref praise of Harvard in American Notes ch 3 at implied expense of Oxford and Cambridge.)

Bagehot 1858: p 13 above.   "A few pedantic critics have regretted that Mr Dickens had not received what they call a regular education... We believe they mean to regret that he had not received a course of discipline which would probably have impaired his powers... It would have been absurd to have shut up his observant youth within the walls of a college..." (pp 193-5 EL 1911; cf Dickens 1847 and Shaw 1937.)

Quiller-Couch 1922-5: p 23 above.   Lectures at Cambridge praising Dickens as a literary artist of the highest calibre.   See under "Literary Artist" etc above.

Forster 1927: p 24 above.   Clark Lectures at Trinity College, Cambridge.   "...and yet there is this wonderful feeling of human depth..."

Cecil 1931-4: p 25 above.   Lectures at Oxford largely confirming high estimate of Dickens by Quiller-Couch at Cambridge.

Leacock 1933: p 4 above.   "...in all schools and colleges where literature is taught...the name of Dickens has not yet been put where it belongs.   Whole courses are devoted to Shakespeare, a man...of far lesser genius" (p 307.)

Blacklands 1933: p 4 above under Dent.   "He was of 'the common people', he loved them, and he wrote for them. Whereas many other eminent followers of the same profession have had academic honours thrust upon them... no such distinction fell to the lot of the creator of David Copperfield" (p 17 1935 edn.)

Churchill 1937-42: p 26 above.   Paper read to literary society of Downing College, Cambridge.

Wilson 1939-41: p 27 above.   "...literary men from Oxford and Cambridge...have rather snubbingly let him alone..." (p 1 UP edn; cf Leacock above but Wilson ignored Quiller-Couch, Cecil etc.)

Sampson 1941: p 28 above.   Amplifies and extends Saintsbury 1916 in appreciation of Dickens and compares him with Shakespeare.

Dickens and the Universities, cont.

Leavis 1947: p 96 above.

Butt 1948: p 29 above.

Wilson 1959: p 32 above.

Peyrouton 1965: p 1 above.

House 1965: p 6 above.

Tillotson 1966: p 34 above.

Tomlin 1970: p 35 above.

Nisbet 1970: p 35 above.

Snow 1970: p 8 above under Slater. "Personally, I do not
remember hearing one genuinely favourable comment on
Dickens as a writer. As a rule, he was passed over as not
suitable for serious literary discussion" (p 137n). Snow
refers to his Cambridge days in the late 1920s, making an
exception of Quiller-Couch. Churchill observed much the
same attitude towards Dickens at Cambridge 1935-8 but did
something about it - Churchill 1937 above - whereas Snow
seems to have been silent till recent years.

Churchill 1974: p 23 above under Quiller-Couch. Points out
how much Quiller-Couch was a pioneer, both in Dickensian
criticism and in the relating of Victorian literature to
Victorian society.

See also under "Journals" above. Neither Leacock nor
Edmund Wilson would have cause to grumble today.

Dickens and Religion

Dickens. Letter to Mrs Godfrey 25 Jul 1839. Final para.
See House 1965 p 568 and cf Orwell 1939 below.

Townshend 1840: p 10 above.

Collins 1842: qu above p 11.

Anon. Christian Examiner, Boston, Mar 1842 (qu House 1941
p 112.)

Dickens and Religion, cont.

Dana, Richard Henry jr.   "His forces are all light infantry...
not many heavy pieces...the scientific corps is deficient,
and I fear there is no chaplain in the garrison..."
(Journal 5 Feb 1842 qu House 1974 p 38n.)

Christian Remembrancer 1842: p 54 above.   "His religion,
whenever any is introduced, is for the most part such mere
pagan sentimentalism that we should have been better pleased
by its absence... The Clergy are never introduced otherwise
than with a sneer..." (cf Dickens 1847 below.)

Dickens 1847.   "Lest there should be any well-intentioned
persons who do not perceive the difference...between religion
and the cant of religion...let them understand that it is
always the latter, and never the former, which is satirized
here" (pref cheap edn Pickwick.)

Mrs Oliphant 1853.   Considered the portrait of Chadband in
Bleak House to be "a libel upon the preachers of the poor".
Cf Jowett 1870, Stephen 1902, House 1941.

Anon.   Dickens's Use of the Bible.   Temple Bar Sep 1869.

Jowett 1870: p 15 above.   "Works of fiction, indirectly, are
great instructors of this world; and we can hardly exaggerate
the debt of gratitude which is due to a writer who has led us
to sympathize with these good, true, sincere, honest English
characters of ordinary life, and to laugh at the egotism,
the hypocrisy, the false respectability of religious
professors and others" (qu Forster 1872 bk 11 ch 3.)

Stanley 1870: p 15 above.   Cf Dickens on Stanley's Arnold
qu above p 125.

Anon.   Fraser's Mag Jul 1870.   "He spent no thought on
religious doctrines or religious reforms, but regarded the
Sermon on the Mount as good teaching, had a regard for the
village church and churchyard, and quarrelled with nothing
but intolerance" (qu House 1941 p 112.   Cf Dickens on the
New Testament qu Forster 1872 bk 11 ch 3.)

Austin 1870: p 15 above.

Ham 1870: p 15 above.

Forster 1872-4: p 2 above; bk 11 ch 3.   Dickens's own views
on religion quoted from his letters.   Cf Orwell 1939 below.

Mackenzie, C.H.(ed).   The Religious Sentiments of Charles
Dickens.   1884.

Cuyler, Rev Theodore L.   Intensely admired Dickens but
regretted he "could utterly ignore Christianity" in his
novels (Recollections of a long Life, c1900, qu House 1974
p 357n.)

Stephen, Leslie.   "Stiggins and Chadband and their like are
wonderful caricatures, but imply a very summary 'analysis'...
George Eliot had gone much further than Dickens in explicit
rejection of the popular religion... but she found her ideal
heroine in one of its typical representatives" (George Eliot,
EML 1902 p 69; see further below under "Dickens and George
Eliot".)

Pike, Clement E.   Charles Dickens and Unitarianism.
Unitarian Monthly Feb 1912.   Dickens began to attend
Essex Street chapel soon after his return from America in
1842 and later attended the Unitarian Chapel in Little
Portland Street.   See William J.Roffey, Essex Street Chapel,
Dickensian 22 1926.

Chesterton 1913: qu above p 67. Cf Phelps below.

Phelps 1916: p 22 above.   "...one of the most powerful allies
of Christianity that English literature has ever produced.
The whole foundation of his works is the love of God and
the love of man" (p 70.)

Santayana 1921-2: p 23 above.   "It is remarkable... how
insensible Dickens was to the greater themes of the human
imagination - religion, science, politics, art... The
political background of Christendom is only, so to speak,
an old faded back-drop for his stage; a castle, a frigate,
a gallows and a large female angel with white wings
standing above an orphan by an open grave - a decoration
which has to serve for all the melodramas in his theatre,
intellectually so provincial and poor" (cf Chesterton 1913
and see further below under "Dickens and Christmas".)

Quiller-Couch 1922-5: p 23 above.   "Dickens... had little use
for religious forms or religious mysteries... he carried
his own religion about with him... Religious formulae...
he hated... he had little use for ministers of religion...
As for sacred edifices... Dickens uses them as picturesque,
romantic, mouldy, just as suits his convenience" (pp 72-3;
cf Orwell below.)

Stevens, J.S.   Dickens's Use of the English Bible.
Dickensian 21 1925.   Cf Shaw qu above p 86.

Dickens and Religion, cont.

Procter, W.C. Christian Teaching in the Novels of Dickens.
1930. Cf Phelps 1916 above.

Kent, William. Dickens and Religion. 1930. An agnostic
view. Cf Orwell 1939 below and R.C.Churchill, English
Literature and the Agnostic, 1944, p 18.

Shaw 1937: qu above p 86. Shaw concludes that though Dickens
took his children "for a time at least" to "churches of the
Unitarian persuasion, where they could be both sceptical and
respectable" - cf Pike 1912 above - "it is hard to say what
Dickens believed or did not believe metaphysically or meta-
politically." Cf Santayana 1921. Dean Inge 1922 (p 23
above) remarked that "the number of great subjects in which
Dickens took no interest whatever is amazing".

Connell, J.M. The Religion of Dickens. Hibbert Journal 36
1938.

Orwell 1939-40: p 26 above; pp 53-5 1946 edn.

House 1941: qu above p 73. And see ch 5 passim.

Pope-Hennessy 1945: p 4 above. His relations with
Unitarians in Boston and London (p 165).

Shettle, G.T. Dickens and the Church. 1946.

Wilson 1950: p 30 above.

Johnson, Edgar. Dickens, Fagin and Mr Riah. Commentary 9
1950. Cf Rosenberg 1960 and Marcus 1962.

Greene 1951: qu above p 47. The "Manichaen world" of Oliver
Twist. Cf Santayana 1921 above and James 1957 below.

Trilling 1953: p 103 above.

James, G.I. Dickens: An Essay in Christian Evaluation.
Blackfriars Nov 1957. Cf Greene 1951.

Lane, Laurie jr. Dickens's Archetypal Jew. PMLA 73 1958.
Cf Johnson 1950 and Marcus 1962.

Bishop 1959: p 48 above.

Stone, Harry. Dickens and the Jews. Victorian Studies 2
1959. Cf Johnson above.

Rosenberg, E.   From Shylock to Svengali: Jewish Stereotypes
  in English Fiction.   Stanford 1960.   Incl Fagin.

Auden 1962: qu above p 44.   Cf Greene 1951.

Marcus, Steven.   Who is Fagin?   Commentary 34 1962.

Peyrouton, Noel C.   Dickens and the Christian Socialists.
  Dickensian 58 1962.

Fielding, K.J.   Dickens's Novels and the Discovery of the
  Soul.   Aryan Path 33 1962.

Blount, Trevor.   The Chadbands and Dickens's View of
  Dissenters.   MLQ 25 1964.

Hodgart 1969: p 103 above; p 231.

Welsh 1971: p 36 above.   Christian concepts in the novels
  "inescapably there and yet finally elusive".

Hornback, Bert G.   Noah's Arkitecture: A Study of Dickens's
  Mythology.   Columbus Ohio 1973.

Gold 1974: p 203 above.   "We find God in every novel..."
  Cf Greene 1951 qu above p 47.   "... The Struggle of all
  Dickens's heroes is an attempt to apprehend a great Divine
  system and their relation to it".   Or alternatively, of
  course, to marry the heroine and live happily ever after:
  see Orwell 1939 pp 42-3.

Dickens and Christmas

Jerrold 1845: qu above p 12.

Watts-Dunton, Theodore.   Records that he was passing through
  the London streets on the day after Dickens's death in June
  1870 and heard a child inquire: "Will Father Christmas die
  too?"   (qu more accurately in Collins 1971 p 502.)

Forster 1872-4: p 2 above.   Dickens's identity with Christmas:
  bk 4 ch 2.   See also bk 11 ch 3.   Cf Pope-Hennessy 1945 pp
  309-10.

Kitton 1890: p 66 above.

Dickens and Christmas, cont.

Cazamian 1904: p 198 above.   "No one has known better how to
express the traditional feelings of a whole people....The
Christmas stories make the connection in Dickens between
Christianity and social doctrine clearly discernible."

Saintsbury 1916: p 22 above.   Observes that Washington Irving
wrote Bracebridge Hall "when Dickens was at the blacking
manufactory" but adds that there is something to be said
for the popular identification of Dickens and Christmas.
"The idea of Christmas as a season of good feeding and
good feeling was congenial to all Dickens's best
characteristics, though it may have slightly encouraged
some of his weaknesses" (p 323 1932 edn.)

Santayana 1921-2: p 23 above.   "In reviving Christmas,
Dickens transformed it from the celebration of a
metaphysical mystery into a feast of overflowing simple
kindness and good cheer; the church bells were still there
- in the orchestra; and the angels of Bethlehem were still
there - painted on the back-curtain."

Quiller-Couch 1922-5: p 23 above; pp 16-19.

Chesterton, G.K.   Dickens and Christmas.   BBC radio talk,
c1930.

Dent 1933: p 4 above; pp 276-81.

House 1941: p 27 above; pp 52-4.

House 1969: qu above p 40.

Welsh 1971: p 36 above.

Dickens and Sport

Dickens 1847.   "The idea propounded to me was...that a 'Nimrod
Club'...were to go out shooting, fishing, and so forth...
getting themselves into difficulties through their want of
dexterity... I objected...that although born and partly bred
in the country I was no great sportsman...and that I should
like to take my own way, with a freer range of English scene
and people..." (pref cheap edn Pickwick; cf Quiller-Couch
and Orwell below.)

Forster 1872-4: p 2 above.   Describes the cricket matches etc
at Gadshill (bk 11 ch 3.)

Dickens and Sport, cont.

Dibelius, Wilhelm. Pierce Egan und Dickens. Archiv 124 1910.
Cf Child below.

Child, Harold. Caricature and the Literature of Sport.
CHEL Vol XIV 1916. Dickens and Surtees (pp 233-4 1932 edn.)

Santayana 1921-2: p 23 above. "Dickens tells us little of
English sports, but he shares the sporting nature of the
Englishman, to whom the whole material world is a playing-
field... His art is to sport according to the rules of the
game, and to do things for the sake of doing them, rather
than for any ulterior motive."

Quiller-Couch 1922-5: p 23 above. "...Pickwick, in its first
conception, was to deal with the adventures and misadventures
of a Sporting Club after the fashionof the Handley Cross
series by Surtees... The Pickwickian sportsmen had to
decline that competition very soon" (pp 36-7; cf Orwell
below.)

Lambert, S.W. When Mr Pickwick Went Fishing. New York 1925.
Discusses Seymour's claim to have originated the "sporting
transactions" of the Pickwick Club.

Ley, J.W.T. Dickens and Surtees. Dickensian 27 1931.

Darwin 1933: p 4 above.

Orwell 1939-40: p 26 above. "...one side of nineteenth-century
life - the boxing, racing, cockfighting, badger-digging,
poaching, rat-catching side of life, so wonderfully embalmed
in Leech's illustrations to Surtees - is outside his scope"
(p 39 1946 edn). But Toots in Dombey sponsors the Game-
Chicken, as Ukridge sponsors Battling Billson in P.G.
Wodehouse, Lord Emsworth and Others, 1937, ch 8.

House 1941: p 27 above. "...in his mind the England of
cricket in the clergyman's field had never died out; it did
not need reviving; it merely needed the chance to keep
alive..." (p 130; cf Churchill 1958 below.)

Churchill, R.C. "...the 'muscular Christian' of Victorian
times...knew a fact or two beyond the reach of Mr Gradgrind
..." (Sixty Seasons of League Football, 1958, p 6; cf Hard
Times ch 8 in bk 3, final paras.)

Collins, Philip. Dickens and Popular Amusements. Dickensian
61 1965.

Brown 1970: p 36 above.

John Arlott (BBC 1973) and others have observed that in the
    famous cricket match in Pickwick Dickens gives the impression
    that the fielding side as well as the batting side should be
    scoring: "...when Dumkins was caught out, and Podder stumped
    out, All-Muggleton had notched some fifty-four, while the
    score of the Dingley Dellers was as blank as their faces"
    (ch 7.)

Dickens and the Stage-Coach

Forster 1872-4: p 2 above; bk 1 ch 4.

Harris, Stanley. Old Coaching Days. 1882.

Gissing 1898: qu Orwell 1939 below.

Matz 1922: p 43 above.

Quiller-Couch 1922-5: p 23 above; pp 37, 69-70.

Orwell 1939-40: p 26 above. "As Gissing remarks, Dickens
    nowhere describes a railway journey with anything like the
    enthusiasm he shows in describing journeys by stage-coach.
    In nearly all of his books one has a curious feeling that
    one is living in the first quarter of the nineteenth
    century..." (pp 39-40 1946 edn; cf House below.)

House 1941: p 27 above. "...'The old coaching days' are
    largely the literary creation of Dickens, De Quincey and
    Tom Hughes..." (p 26; see also pp 18-19, 23-5.)

Trevelyan 1942-4: p 202 above. Points out that Bradshaw's
    Railway Time-Table was first issued in 1839 while Nickleby
    was still appearing. "Not only the canals, but the stage-
    coaches were doomed" with the coming of the railway age.
    " Mr Weller senior's occupation was gone" (p 531). "And he
    had only just been born.'" (Churchill below.)

Churchill 1958: p 32 above under Ford. See pp 124-5, 141.

House 1969: qu above p 40.

See further below under "Dickens and the Railway Age".

Dickens and the Railway Age

Dickens's brother Alfred Lamert Dickens (1822-60) worked as
a surveyor on the Birmingham and Derby Railway. Dickens
wrote of railways in Bentley's Miscellany (1839), Master
Humphrey's Clock, Martin Chuzzlewit, Dombey and Son,
Household Words (1851), The Lazy Tour of Two Idle
Apprentices (with Wilkie Collins, 1857), Our Mutual Friend,
Mugby Junction (1866) and Edwin Drood. See T.W.Hill,
The Staplehurst Railway Accident, Dickensian 38 1942;
Gerald G.Grubb, Dickens and his brother Fred, Dickensian
50 1954; and House 1941 below.

Athenaeum 1846: qu above p 74.

Ruskin, John. "Dickens was a pure modernist - a leader of
the steam-whistle party par excellence - and he had no
understanding of any power of antiquity except a sort of
jackdaw sentiment for cathedral towers... His hero is
essentially the ironmaster; in spite of Hard Times, he has
advanced by his influence every principle that makes them
harder..." (letter to Charles Eliot Norton 19 Jun 1870 qu
Wall 1970 p 191.)

Forster 1872-4: p 2 above. Bk 3 ch 4; bk 4 chs 4-7.

Harrison 1894-5: p 17 above. The humour "without
caricature" of Swift, Fielding, Hogarth, Sterne and
Goldsmith "has been more rarely imparted to their
successors in the age of steam" (p 132.)

Gissing 1898: qu above p 218 under Orwell.

Chesterton 1913: qu above p 136.

Quiller-Couch 1922-5: p 23 above; p 38.

Leacock 1933: p 4 above; pp 244-5.

Orwell 1939: qu above p 218.

House 1941: p 27 above; pp 137-46.

Trevelyan 1942: qu above p 218.

Allen 1954: p 30 above. "...the railways killed the
picaresque novel..." (p 170 PB edn.)

Churchill 1958: qu above p 218 under Trevelyan.

Smith 1959: p 32 above.

Dickens and the Railway Age, cont.

Atthill, R.   Dickens and the Railway.   English 13 1961.

Collins, Philip.   Queen Mab's Chariot among the Steam
Engines.   English Studies 42 1961.

Sussman, H. L.   Victorians and the Machine.   Cambridge Mass
1968.

Williams 1970: p 78 above; pp 30-4.   Cf House 1941.

Welsh 1971: p 36 above.

Oddie 1973: p 98 above; ch on Mechanism.   See further below
under "Dickens and Carlyle".

Horsman 1974: p 79 above.   "In the objective view of ch 15,
the railway had energized a whole neighbourhood 'like its
life blood'; now it becomes a similitude of Death when
seen through Mr Dombey's eyes once Toodle has reminded him
of his defeated hopes" (pp xxx-xxxi).

Nelson, Harland S.   Staggs's Gardens: The Railway Through
Dickens's World.   DSA 3 1974.

Dickens and Crime

Hogarth 1836: qu above p 38.

Lister 1838: p 45 above.   "He never endeavours to mislead our
sympathies - to pervert plain notions of right and wrong -
to make vice interesting in our eyes" (cf Thackeray below.)

Thackeray 1839-40: qu above p 45.

Forster 1841-72: qu above p 45.

Horne 1844: p 12 above.   "The author hunts down the victim,
like a wild beast...It is not 'Sikes, the murderer' of whom
we think... it is...that one worn and haggard man with all
the world against him..." (cf Taine 1856 on Jonas qu above
p 62.)

Tellkampf 1859: p 60 above.

Sala 1868: p 187 above.

Ruskin 1880: p 16 above.   "In the single novel of Bleak House
there are nine deaths...carefully wrought out or led up to,
either by way of pleasing surprise...or finished in their
threatenings and sufferings, with as much enjoyment as can
be contrived in the anticipation, and as much pathology as
can be concentrated in the description..." (cf Wilson and
Priestley below.)

Trumble, A.   In Jail with Dickens.   1896.   From Pickwick to
Little Dorrit.

Gissing 1898: p 17 above.   "...casting about him for a new
story" in 1870, Dickens "saw murder at the end of every
vista."

Fyfe, T.A.   Dickens and the Law.   Edinburgh 1910.

Holdsworth, Sir William.   Charles Dickens as a Legal
Historian.   New Haven 1928.   Recommended in House 1941 as
"the best book on the subject.". House p 31 qu Holdsworth on
Bleak House.

Dent 1933: qu above p 43.

Squires, P.C.   Dickens as Criminologist.   Journal of Criminal
Law 29 1939.

Orwell 1939-40: p 26 above.   "The only officials whom Dickens
handles with any kind of friendliness are, significantly
enough, policemen" (p 23 1946 edn; cf pp 29, 45, 48.)

Wilson 1939-41: p 27 above.   One of main themes of essay is
Dickens's interest in prsons and prisoners: "probing of the
psychology of the murderer".   See pp 13-21, 48-9, 75-87,
92-3 UP edn.   But cf Fielding 1953 (p 1 above) pp 36-7.

House 1941: p 27 above.   See pp 10, 32, 43, 201-2.

Pritchett 1946: qu above p 120.

House 1947: qu above p 77.

Aldington 1948: p 4 above.   The Underworld of Young Dickens.

Lindsay 1950: p 5 above.

Symons 1951: p 5 above.

McMaster, R.D.   Dickens and the Horrific.   Dalhousie Rev 38
1954.

Dickens and Crime, cont.

Lucas, Audrey. Oliver Twist and the Newgate Novel.
  Dalhousie Rev 1954.

Miller 1958: p 31 above.

Priestley 1960: p 33 above. "...the fascination that murder
  had for him..." (p 237 PB edn; cf Wilson 1939 and House
  1947.)

Wilson, Angus. Evil in the English Novel. Northcliffe
  Lectures, 1961.

Collins, Philip. Dickens and Crime. 1962; rv 1963. The
  most detailed treatment of the subject.

Reid 1962: p 33 above.

Bayley 1962: p 48 above. "Like Oliver reading the tales of
  crime in Fagin's den, Dickens 'prayed heaven to spare him
  from such deeds'. He came later, at the time of his
  readings from Oliver Twist, to have a clear and horrifying
  awareness of his split personality: he dreaded himself, and
  the possibility that he might be exiled by his own doing
  into the world of the murderer and the social outcast..."
  (cf Edmund Wilson above.)

Hollingsworth 1963: p 48 above.

Steig, M. The Whitewashing of Inspector Bucket. Papers of
  Michigan Academy of Science, Arts & Letters 50 1965.
  Cf Saintsbury 1916 p 329.

Tillotson 1966: p 48 above.

Dyson 1967: p 58 above.

Carey 1974: p 37 above. Dickens and Violence (ch 1);
  Dickens and Order (ch 2). In ch Corpses and Effigies
  Carey shows how fascinated Dickens was with such things.
  It should be remarked, however, in regard to the number of
  wooden legs in the novels (which Carey and others see as
  so psychologically significant) that in Dickens's youth,
  immediately after the Napoleonic Wars, such appendages
  were by no means uncommon both in Chatham and in Woolwich.

Basch 1974: p 192 above. Dickens's Sinners (ch 12).

See further above under "Oliver Twist", "Edwin Drood" etc.

Sex in Dickens

Dickens 1837. The author "trusts that, throughout this book, no incident or expression occurs which could call a blush into the most delicate cheek..." (pref Pickwick; cf Our Mutual Friend bk 1 ch 11 and Taine 1856 below.)

Lister 1838: p 9 above. "The reader is led through scenes of poverty and crime...and yet we recollect no passage which ought to cause pain to the most sensitive delicacy, if read aloud in female society."

Mill 1854: qu above p 87.

Taine 1856: p 13 above. "Dickens, like all English novelists, is hopelessly respectable (in the English sense). He and his fellows work under a formula: 'Be moral. All your novels must be such as may be read by young girls...'"

Bagehot 1858: p 13 above. "...Mr Dickens's great, we might say complete, inability to make a love-story... The excruciating writing which is expended on Miss Ruth Pinch passes belief..." Goes on to compare Dickens and Thackeray in their treatment of sexual matters, approving of Dickens for "what we may fairly call an instinctive purity of genius" (pp 186-8 EL edn 1911; see further below under "Dickens and Thackeray").

Anon (R.H.Hutton) 1869: p 157 above. "...it is singular how very little of passion there is in him. There is more passion in Charles Lamb..." "...Almost all creative humorists tend to the impure - like Swift and Smollett, even Fielding... But Dickens uses his unlimited powers of observation...without ever being attracted for a moment towards any prurient or unhealthy field of laughter..."

Anon. Sunday Times 12 Jun 1870. "His inspiration was ever pure. His thoughts and aims and sympathies were delicate, refined, clean... he never wrote a line which his daughter would blush to read aloud..." (qu Collins 1971 p 513; cf Mowbray W.Morris, Fortnightly Rev 1 Dec 82, qu ibid p 611.)

Harrison 1894-5: p 17 above. "There is another quality in which Charles Dickens is supreme - in purity... in forty works and more you will not find a page which a mother need withhold from her grown daughter" (p 134.)

Rideal, Charles F. Charles Dickens's Heroines and Womenfolk. 1896.

Gissing 1898: qu above p 185.

Sex in Dickens, cont.

James, Henry. "I cannot so much as imagine Dickens and Scott
without the 'love-making' left, as the phrase is, out..."
(The Future of the Novel, 1899; rp Selected Literary
Criticism, p 225 PB edn.)

Howells, William Dean. Heroines of Fiction. New York 1901.

Gosse, Edmund. Father and Son. 1907. Records he was
allowed in his childhood to read some Dickens, because his
strict Evangelical father, the naturalist Philip Henry
Gosse FRS, held that Dickens "exposes the passion of love
in a ridiculous light".

Shaw, Bernard. "It was left to an abnormal critic like George
Gissing to point out the glaring fact that in the collection
of life studies of Victorian women to be found in the novels
of Dickens, the most convincingly real ones are either
vilely unamiable or comically contemptible; whilst his
attempts to manufacture admirable heroines by idealizations
of home-bred womanhood are not only absurd but not even
pleasantly absurd: one has no patience with them" (pref
Getting Married, 1908; Standard edn 1932 p 192.)

Moses, Belle. Charles Dickens: His Girl-Heroines. 1911.

Chesterton 1913: p 21 above. "Dickens did not claim the
licence of diction Fielding might have claimed in
repeating the senile ecstasies of Gride (let us say)
over his purchased bride: but Dickens does not leave the
reader in the faintest doubt about what sort of feelings
they were..." (p 43 OPUS edn.)

Meynell, Alice. "In that time there was, moreover, one great
humorist, one whom I infinitely admire; he, too, I am
grieved to remember, bore his part willingly in vulgarizing
the woman; and the part that fell to him was the
vulgarizing of the act of maternity. Woman spiteful...
woman incoherent...woman feigning sensibility - in none of
these ignominies is woman so common and so foolish for
Dickens as she is in child-bearing" (Victorian Caricature,
Essays 1923 p 162.)

Orwell 1939-40: p 26 above. "One thing which Dickens seems
to have recognized...is the sadistic sexual element in
flogging" (p 19 1946 edn.) "Agnes...the most disagreeable
of his heroines, the real legless angel of Victorian
romance, almost as bad as Thackeray's Laura" (p 54; cf p 51)

Wilson 1939-41: p 27 above.

Maly-Schatter 1940: p 27 above.

House 1941: p 27 above; pp 120-1, 154, 215-8.

Oehlbaum 1944: p 28 above.

Alain 1945: p 28 above.

Lemonnier 1946: p 4 above.

Pearson 1949: qu above p 186.

Lindsay 1950: p 5 above.

Symons 1951: p 5 above. Considers it "a deep defect of
   spirit" that in the novels there is an absence of any adult
   relationship between a man and a woman.

Monod 1953: p 30 above.

Lindsay, Jack. Dickens and Women. Twentieth Century Nov 1953.

Churchill, R.C. "If the Victorians can beat us in appreciation
   of literature, we have the edge in our profound sexual
   knowledge of Victorian authors..." (Spectator 11 Dec 1959
   review of Aylmer 1959 qv under "Dickens and Ellen Ternan"
   below.)

Dupee 1960: p 33 above.

Wilson, Angus. The Heroes and Heroines of Dickens. REL 2
   1961. "The contemporary censorship...went along with,
   rather than against, Dickens's natural inclinations"
   (cf Bagehot above.)

Stedman, Jane W. Child-Wives of Dickens. Dickensian May 1963
   pp 112-18.

Deneau, D.P. The Brother-Sister Relationship in Hard Times.
   Dickensian Sep 1964 pp 173-7.

Jarmuth, S.L. Dickens's Use of Women in his Novels. New
   York 1967. Cf Audrey Lucas, Some Dickens Women, Yale Rev
   1940 pp 706-28.

Dabney 1967: p 34 above.

Senelick 1967: p 56 above.

Lane 1970: qu above p 70.

Sex in Dickens, cont.

Wilson 1970: p 35 above. Remarks on "the absence of any real
sympathy with, or understanding for, women" in the novels.
Cf Miles 1974 below.

Dyson 1970: p 35 above. Incl discussion of sexual attitudes
in Copperfield.

Johnson, Pamela Hansford. The Sexual Life in Dickens's Novels.
In Slater 1970: p 8 above. Quilp "one of the most sensual
of Dickens's creations...doubtless a sexual athlete... is
the burning pipe a sexual symbol?" (p 176.)

Hardy, Barbara. In NCF centenary no, 1970.

Holloway 1970: p 78 above.

Welsh 1971: p 36 above.

Faulkner, Peter. The Historical Perspective. The Arts in a
Permissive Society, ed Christopher Macy, 1971. Discusses
Dickens's attitude towards restraints of Victorian morality
(pp 31-4). Cf Wilkie Collins's reaction to Forster's
assertion that there is hardly a page of Dickens which could
not be placed in the hands of a child: "If it is true,
which it is not, it would imply the condemnation of
Dickens's books as works of art, it would declare him to be
guilty of deliberately presenting to his readers a false
reflection of human life... means that the novelist is
forbidden to touch on the sexual relations which literally
swarm about him..." (qu Robinson, Wilkie Collins, 1974 edn
pp 235-6.)

Stone, Harry. The Love Pattern in Dickens's Novels.
DSA 1971.

Brown, Arthur Washburn. Sexual Analysis of Dickens's Props.
New York 1971. Discusses alleged Freudian implications of
cribbage, wooden legs etc in Old Curiosity Shop, Barnaby,
Dombey, Our Mutual Friend and other novels. Cf comment on
Carey 1974 p 222 above.

Carey 1974: pp 37, 222 above. Ch on sex in Dickens incl
new interpretation of Copperfield ch 53 in which Agnes is
alleged to be "pointing upwards", not towards Heaven, as
was formerly thought, "but towards the bedroom".

Anon. TLS 26 Jul 1974. Review of Oscar Wilde reprint
alludes to "Louisa Gradgrind's phallic smokestacks".
Cf Johnson 1970 and Carey 1974 above.

Moore, Katharine. Victorian Wives. 1974. Incl discussion
    of wives in Dickens's novels.

Pope, Katherine V. Women in Dickens. DSN 5 1974.

Miles, Rosalind. "...can we truly say that Dickens, for
    instance, with all his tremendous imaginative energy, all
    his reserves of satire and sentiment, of love, bluster, and
    despair, ever got across to the side signposted 'female'?"
    (The Fiction of Sex, 1974, p 14.) "It is axiomatic in
    Dickens that women who concern themselves with extra-
    domestic issues must be failures as mothers... Females, to
    Dickens, must be pretty and pleasant or they are not
    females, and every one of his books contains some
    expression of the compendium of his prejudices..." (p 118.)

Basch 1974: p 192 above. The Myth in the Novel (ch 4);
    Charles Dickens's Anti-Woman (ch 8); Dickens's Sinners
    (ch 12). "The novels of Dickens are full of the mythic
    wife-mother, portrayed either in complete achievement or
    its opposite; both extremes being equally unrealistic,
    socially and psychologically. ." (p 53).

Dickens and Ellen Ternan

The branch of learning known as Ellen Ternan Studies, which
    has not yet entirely superseded the study of Dickens's
    novels, should always be taken with a grain of salt,
    particularly when attempts are made to draw literary
    conclusions from the liaison.

Wright, Thomas. Daily Express 3 Apr 1934. Amplified below.

Wright 1935: p 4 above.

Thomas Wright of Olney: An Autobiography. 1936. Ch 14 incl
    further details.

Storey 1939: p 4 above.

Wilson 1939-41: p 27 above; pp 61-6 UP edn.

Pope-Hennessy 1945: p 4 above; ch 23.

Lemonnier 1946: p 4 above.

Dickens and Ellen Ternan, cont.

Pearson 1949: p 4 above. Pearson's intention being "to note what is biographically revealing in each work as we come to it", the reader is forewarned in regard to novels contemporary with the Ternan affair. "An entertaining game to play" commented the TLS reviewer (9 Sep 49), "also a dangerous one in that it may be carried to tiresome and sometimes rather absurd lengths. "

Lindsay 1950: p 5 above.

Rolfe, F.P. Dickens and the Ternans. NCF 4 1950.

Johnson 1952: p 5. "...his association with Ellen Ternan... seen in tolerant perspective" (Wall 1970 p 318.)

Nisbet, Ada. Dickens and Ellen Ternan. Berkeley 1952; Cambridge 1953. Fwd Edmund Wilson. See Edgar Johnson, NCF Mar 1953 pp 296-8.

Fielding 1953: p 1 above. Revelations and Interpretations (ch 4); Recent Biography (ch 5.)

Adrian 1957: p 5 above.

Aylmer, Felix. Dickens Incognito. 1959. Cf comments by R.C.Churchill (Spectator 11 Dec 59) and Graham Storey (Sunday Times 13 Dec.)

Du Cann, C.G.L. The Love-Lives of Dickens. 1961.

Elsna, Hebe. Unwanted Wife: A Defence of Mrs Charles Dickens. 1963. Emphasizes Catherine's dignity and forbearance in contrast with Dickens's behaviour at the time of the separation.

Wagenknecht 1965: p 5 above.

Johnson 1970: p 226 above; pp 181-2, 183, 186, 193.

Basch 1974: p 192 above; pp 60, 148, 151.

CRITICAL COMPARISONS

Dickens and Aristophanes

Hutton 1869: p 157 above. "We doubt if there ever were so
  great a humorist in the world before, Aristophanes and
  Shakespeare not excepted."

Santayana 1921-2: qu above p 47.

Dickens and Dante

Quiller-Couch 1922-5: p 23 above; pp 27, 93.

Eliot 1927: qu above p 175.

Trilling 1953: qu below p 235.

Dickens and Langland

Quiller-Couch 1922-5: qu above p 128.

Trilling 1953: qu below p 235.

Dickens and Chaucer

Bagehot 1858: p 13 above. Compares Chaucer's "ordered and
  symmetrical comprehension" with the "overteeming imagination"
  and "irregular and unsymmetrical genius" of Shakespeare and
  Dickens (pp 166-9 EL edn 1911.)

Swinburne 1908: p 20 above. "Neither Chaucer nor Molière has
  ever breathed life into a child of his genius...more sure of
  immortality" than "the incomparable Mr Bucket" (p 11.)

Quiller-Couch 1922: p 23 above. "...always in the straight
  line of Chaucer, Ben Jonson, Dryden, Fielding, a preacher of
  man's dignity in his full appetite..." (p 19.)

Butt and Tillotson 1957: p 31 above. "Through serial
  publication an author could recover something of the
  intimate relationship between story-teller and audience

which existed in the ages of the sagas and of Chaucer; and
for an author like Dickens, who was peculiarly susceptible
to the influence of his readers, this intimate relationship
outweighed the inherent disadvantages of the system. "

Allen, Walter.   In Slater 1970: p 8 above.   "In the presence
of this fantastic prodigality, this superabundance of
invention, all that can be said, though I think even more
justly, is what Dryden said of Chaucer: 'Here is God's
plenty. '" (p 27.)

Holloway, John.   Ibid 1970.   Compares Old Curiosity Shop and
Prioress's Tale (p 60.)

Dickens and Cervantes

Irving 1841: qu above p 42.   Cf Metropolitan Mag Jan 1837
                              qu Collins 1971 p 31.
Dickens 1841.   "Cervantes laughed Spain's chivalry away, by
showing Spain its impossible and wild absurdity.   It was my
attempt, in my humble and far-distant sphere, to dim the
false glitter surrounding something which really did exist,
by showing it in its unattractive and repulsive truth"
(pref 3rd edn Oliver Twist.)

Dickens 1847: p 2 above.   Don Quixote among his youthful
reading.

Dostoevsky 1868.   "Of the good types in Christian literature,
the most perfect is Don Quixote.   But he is good only
because at the same time he is ridiculous.   The Pickwick of
Dickens (an infinitely weaker conception...but still
immense) is also ridiculous and succeeds in virtue of this.
A feeling of compassion is produced... This rousing of
compassion is the secret of humour" (letter qu E.H.Carr,
Dostoevsky, 1931, pp 159-60 1962 edn.)

Gissing 1898: p 17 above.   "Dickens is good reading for all
times of life, as are all the great imaginative writers.
Let him be read by children together with Don Quixote.
But who can speak with authority of Cervantes who knows him
only from an acquaintance made at ten years old?..." (ch 5.)

Santayana 1921-2: p 23 above.   "...facts, however serious
inwardly, are always absurd outwardly; and the just critic
of life sees both truths at once, as Cervantes did in Don

Dickens and Cervantes, cont.

Quixote... Dickens saw the absurdity, and understood the
life; I think he was a good philosopher. "

Shaw 1937: p 26 above. "Dickens mentions the delight with
which he discovered in an attic a heap of eighteenth-century
novels.   But Smollett was a grosser barbarian than Dickens
himself; and Don Quixote and The Arabian Nights, though
they gave the cue to his eager imagination, left him quite
in the dark as to the philosophy and art of his day... "

Auden 1962: qu above p 44.

Dickens and Marlowe

Eliot 1918: qu above p 181.

Dickens and Shakespeare

Hunt 1838: qu above p 9.

Landor 1841: qu above p 10.

Caledonian Mercury 1841: qu above p 11.

Parley 1841: qu above p 11.

Jeffrey, Landor, Hall 1841: qu above p 53.

Ludwig 1860: qu above pp 94, 100.

Trollope 1870: qu above p 172.

Hutton 1870: qu above p 229.

Forster 1872-4: p 2 above; bk 6 ch 2 para 8.   Cf Bagehot
1858 qu above p 229.

Swinburne 1882: qu above p 16.

Harrison 1894-5: qu above pp 164, 180.

Gissing 1898-1901: qu above pp 42, 62, 172.

Dickens and Shakespeare, cont.

Swinburne 1902: qu above pp 62, 101, 109, 160.

Wells 1911: qu above p 52.

Phelps 1916: qu above p 142.

Dibelius, Wilhelm. Dickens und Shakespeare. Shakespeare-
  Jahrbuch 52 1916.

Santayana 1921-2: qu above p 47.

Quiller-Couch 1922-5: p 23 above. "I do not see what
  English writer we can choose to put second to Shakespeare
  save Charles Dickens. I am talking of sheer creative
  power..." (p 20; cf p 128 above and view of Sir James
  Barrie c1910 qu TLS 4 Jun 1970 that Dickens in creative
  power "stands next to Shakespeare".)

Priestley 1925: qu above p 174.

Eliot 1927: qu above p 175.

Dent 1933: p 4 above. "There comes every now and then in
  the history of most peoples a time when some writer appears
  who sums up in his work most of the characteristics of his
  predecessors, and who transcends them all by the universalit
  of his genius. This has happened at least twice in the
  history of the English people. It happened with
  Shakespeare; it happened with Dickens... It is not so
  much that Shakespeare and Dickens excel in every particular
  all other writers, though at their most exalted moments
  they do; it is rather that whereas the other writers excel
  only in isolated particulars, Shakespeare and Dickens rise
  at times to excellence in all particulars..." (p 481 1935
  edn; whole context of ch 16 is relevant. Dent was saying
  in 1933 what Edmund Wilson came to say in 1939-41 and F.R.
  Leavis not till 1970.)

Leacock 1933: qu above p 210 - probably only instance of a
  critic asserting that Dickens is superior to Shakespeare.

Duffield 1934: p 120 above.

Churchill 1937-42: qu above p 181.

Wilson 1939-41: qu above p 154.

Evans 1940: p 27 above. "He invented character and situation
  with a range that had been unequalled since Shakespeare"
  (p 182 1963 edn.)

Dickens and Shakespeare, cont.

Sampson 1941: p 28 above.   "With Shakespeare, Dickens is the
   most English of writers, and like Shakespeare he has
   conquered the world..." (pp 629-30 1970 edn.)

Stoll 1942: p 176 above.

Leavis 1947: qu above p 166.

Pearson 1949: qu above p 44.

Brown 1949: qu above p 206.

Churchill 1950: p 29 above.   "Each writer...bestrode his age
   like a colossus... Shakespeare...the most Dickensian of the
   Elizabethan writers... Dickens...the most Shakespearean
   writer among the Victorians..." (pp 111-13.)

Lindsay 1950: qu above p 155.

Churchill 1951: qu above p 166.

Trilling 1953: qu above p 103.

Maugham 1954: qu above p 177.

Churchill 1958: qu above pp 162, 182.

Churchill, R.C.   Shakespeare and His Betters.   London 1958;
   Bloomington Ind 1959.   Points out (pp 19n, 33) that Dickens
   has been wrongly described as a Baconian.

Kettle 1962: qu above p 116.

Fleissner, R.F.   Dickens and Shakespeare.   New York 1965.

Leavis 1970: p 36 above.   "He may be seen surely as the
   Shakespeare of the novel" (p xi.)   See also p 168 above.

Ryan 1970: p 58 above.

Wall 1970: p 7 above.   Incl comparisons with Lear, Merry Wives,
   etc and FitzGerald's letter to Fanny Kemble 25 Apr 1879 in
   which he calls Dickens "a little Shakespeare - a Cockney
   Shakespeare, if you will: but as distinct, if not so great,
   a piece of pure Genius as was born in Stratford" (p 210.)

Spencer 1972: p 121 above.   "...the greatest English writer
   after Shakespeare."

Dickens and Ben Jonson

Forster 1872-4: p 231 above.

Schelling, Felix E.   "Both were men of the people... Each
  knew the London of his time as few men knew it... Both men
  were at heart moralists... leaving the world the better for
  the art that they practised" (intn Complete Plays of Ben
  Jonson, EL 1910 p xxi.)

Thorndike, A.H.   "Not only... specific resemblances, as
  between Zeal-of-the-land Busy and Stiggins, but Dickens's
  comic invention and characterisation are often strikingly
  Jonsonian in method and effect" (Ben Jonson, CHEL vol VI,
  1910, p 28 1932 edn.   Cf Churchill and Knights below.)

Saintsbury 1916: qu above p 173.

Quiller-Couch 1922-5: qu above p 229.

Churchill 1937-42: p 26 above; pp 361, 363.

Simpson, E.   Jonson and Dickens: A Study in the Comic Genius
  of London.   Essays & Studies 29 1944.   Cf Schelling above
  and see further above under "Dickens's London".

Pritchett 1946: p 28 above.   "While the word Dickensian
  lasts, the English novel will be suffocated.   For the
  convivial and gregarious extravagance and the picaresque
  disorder which are supposedly Dickensian are not Dickens's
  especial contribution... They are his inheritance from
  Sterne, Smollett and...Richardson, an inheritance which
  may be traced back to the comedy of Jonson..."

Wilson, Edmund.   Morose Ben Jonson.   The Triple Thinkers,
  1952; pp 257-8 PB edn.

Knights, L.C.   Ben Jonson, Dramatist.   PGEL 2 1955 pp 305,
  317.

Churchill 1958: qu above p 182.

Hussey, Maurice.   Intn Bartholomew Fair.   New Mermaid edn
  1964 p xvii.

Hodgart 1969: p 103 above; p 121.

Hardy, Barbara.   In Slater 1970: p 8 above; p 39.
  Pecksniff, Quilp, Volpone "allowed libido as well as
  mercenary humour, and this expands caricature in the
  direction of life."

Dickens and Webster

Cecil 1931-4: p 25 above.   "Dickens's poetry...an Elizabethan
sort of poetry...akin to...the quips and cranks, part
comic, part macabre, part beautiful, with which Webster
and Tourneur and Ford have let their fancies play round
the drama of life and death" (p 42 FL edn.)

Dickens and Molière

Swinburne 1902: qu above p 94.

Swinburne 1908: qu above p 229.

Quiller-Couch 1922-5: p 23 above; p 27.

Dickens and Bunyan

Trilling 1953: p 103 above.   "The imagination of Little
Dorrit...is...akin to that which created Piers Plowman and
Pilgrim's Progress...akin to the imagination of The Divine
Comedy..." (see further above under "Dickens and Dante" and
"Dickens and Langland".)

Leavis, F.R.   Afterword to SC edn Pilgrim's Progress 1964;
rp Anna Karenina and Other Essays 1967 p 38.

Welsh 1971: p 36 above.

Dickens and Defoe

Dickens 1847: p 2 above.   Crusoe among his youthful reading.

Bagehot 1858: p 13 above; p 185 EL edn 1911.

Forster 1872-4: p 2 above; bk 2 ch 1.   Qu letter from
Dickens 3 Nov 1837 praising Defoe's History of the Devil:
"What a capital thing it is!"   (See further below under
Law 1925.)

Swinburne 1902: qu above p 65.

Dickens and Defoe, cont.

Saintsbury 1916: p 22 above. "Improving immensely upon the
lines of Defoe and Smollett, and adding to them an
imagination of which Defoe had nothing and Smollett not
very much..." (p 314 1932 edn.)

Quiller-Couch 1922-5: p 23 above; p 79.

Law, M.H. The Indebtedness of Oliver Twist to Defoe's
History of the Devil. PMLA 40 1925. Cf Forster above.

Dickens and Swift

Dickens 1847. "...it is never out of season to protest
against...the confounding of Christianity with any class of
persons who, in the words of Swift, have just enough
religion to make them hate, and not enough to make them
love, one another" (pref cheap edn Pickwick; see further
above under "Dickens and Religion".)

Spectator 1869: qu above p 223. Cf Lewes 1837 qu Collins
1971 p 67.

Hardy 1970: p 234 above. "...what we often feel as the
disappearance of the old free, wild humour from middle and
late Dickens is a sign of his control of humour. It is
there, but it is combined with seriousness in a way...
we are quite used to - as was Dickens - in Ben Jonson and
Swift" (p 37.)

Dickens and Richardson

Wilkie 1839: qu above p 10.

Forster 1927: p 24 above. "Good but imperfect novelists
like Wells and Dickens...are quite different from the
perfect novelist...who seems to pass the creative finger
down every sentence and into every word. Richardson,
Defoe, Jane Austen, are perfect in this particular way;
their work may not be great but their hands are always
upon it..." (p 80 PB edn.)

House 1941: p 27 above. Pamela, Emily, Lizzie Hexam (pp
162-3).

Carroll, John (ed). Selected Letters of Samuel Richardson.
Oxford 1971. Early letters show that Richardson shared

Dickens and Richardson, cont.

Dickens's (and David Copperfield's) faculty for story-
telling in boyhood.

Higbie, Robert Griggs.   Characterization in the English
Novel: Richardson, Jane Austen, and Dickens.   Ann Arbor
Mich 1973.

Churchill 1974: p 79 above.   Amplifies Wilkie 1839.

Basch 1974: p 192 above; p 265.

Dickens and Hogarth

Smith, Sydney.   "...the soul of Hogarth has migrated into
the body of Mr Dickens" (letter Sep 1837 qu House 1965
p 431n.)

Lister 1838: p 9 above.   "What Hogarth was in painting, such
very nearly is Mr Dickens in prose fiction."

Horne 1844: qu above p 170.

Emerson 1848: p 12 above.   "...a painter of English details,
like Hogarth; local and temporary in his tints and style, and
local in his aims."

Forster 1872-4: p 2 above; bk 6 ch 3.

Gissing 1898: p 17; ch 5.

Pinto, V.de S.   William Hogarth.   PGEL 4 1957, p 285.

Dickens and Fielding

Talfourd, Thomas Noon.   "...the most genial delineator of
human manners and affections who has arisen among us since
the days of Fielding" (letter to Dickens 16 Aug 1837 qu
House 1965 p 685.)

Lister 1838: qu above p 9.   Cf James Hannay 1866 qu Collins
1971 p 477.

Sun 1839: qu above p 49.

Dickens 1847: p 2 above. Tom Jones among his youthful reading.
"I have been Tom Jones (a child's Tom Jones, a harmless
creature) for a week together". Cf Copperfield ch 4 and
Dickens to Forster below.

Dickens to Forster 1849. Reporting birth of his sixth son
16 Jan 1849 "whom at first he meant to call by Oliver
Goldsmith's name, but settled afterwards into that of
Henry Fielding...in a kind of homage to the style of work"
- in Copperfield - "he was now so bent on beginning"
(Life bk 6 ch 6.)

Lewes 1872: p 15 above. "Compared with that of Fielding or
Thackeray, his was merely an _animal_ intelligence, i.e.
restricted to perceptions." See Forster below.

Forster 1872-4: p 2 above. Tom Jones and Little Dorrit
(bk 8 ch 1). Fielding and Dickens compared with ref to
criticisms by Taine and Lewes (bk 9 ch 1.)

Swinburne 1882: qu above p 16.

Harrison 1894-5: qu above p 145.

Wilson, F.W. Dickens in seinen Beziehungen zu den Humoristen
Fielding und Smollett. Leipzig 1899.

Swinburne 1902: p 19 above. Tom Jones and Copperfield
(pp 33-5 1913 edn.)

Quiller-Couch 1922-5: p 23 above; pp 72, 97.

Churchill 1937-42: qu above p 114.

Fraser 1953: qu above p 176.

Klingopulos 1958: p 32 above under Ford; pp 71-2.

Allott 1959: p 7 above. "We can always distinguish a
novelist's 'moral fable' from the abstract thinker's.
Jonathan Wild and Hard Times are novelists' fables;
Rasselas is not. All are genuine expressions of what
Johnson calls 'felt life', but the first two are vivid with
a sense of place and character..." (pp 207-8; cf pp 165, 179

Robinson, Roger. The Influence of Fielding on Barnaby Rudge.
AUMLA no 40 Nov 1973. See DSN 5 p 63.

Dickens and Sterne

Thackeray, W.M.   Compares Sterne's "dreary double entendre/
with "the innocent laughter and the sweet and unsullied
page which the author of David Copperfield gives to my
children" (English Humorists of the Eighteenth Century,
1851-3; EL edn 1912 pp 239-40.)

Forster 1872-4: p 2 above.   "Sterne did not more incessantly
fall back from his works upon himself than Dickens did, and
undoubtedly one of the impressions left by the letters is
that of the intensity and tenacity with which he recognized,
realized, contemplated, cultivated, and thoroughly enjoyed,
his own individuality in even its most trivial
manifestations..." (bk 11 ch 3).   Dickens, in fact, the
first Dickensian, as has been observed by many later critics
and biographers.

Swinburne 1882: qu above p 16.

Traill, H.D.   "...compare Uncle Toby's manly and dignified
gentleness of heart with the unreal 'gush' of the Brothers
Cheeryble or the fatuous benevolence of Mr Pickwick...
Captain Shandy is reality itself" (Sterne.   EML 1882;
p 169 1889 edn.)

Saintsbury 1916: p 22 above.   "Dickens had quite a different
manner of handling the pocket-handkerchiefv from that of
'the gentleman in the black silk smalls'" (p 319n 1932 edn.)

Phelps 1916: p 22 above.   "Of all British novelists, none has
been more purely creative than Dickens; his tears flow from
the great source, the sentimental novel of the eighteenth
century, the only link between him and Sterne..." (pp 106-7).

Jefferson, D.W.   "...Uncle Toby is a more real person than
the great Dickens creations.   He is of Shakespearian
quality..." (Laurence Sterne.   BCB 1954 pp 23-4.   Cf Traill
above.)

Hardy 1970: p 234 above.   "His art is a heterogeneous one,
but not in the way that Sterne's Tristram Shandy or Joyce's
Ulysses are heterogeneous..." (pp 30-1.)

Wilson 1970: ibid p 8 above.   Shandy and Copperfield as
studies of childhood (p 220.)

Dickens and Smollett

Lister 1838: qu above p 9.

Dickens 1847: p 2 above. Roderick Random, Peregrine Pickle and Humphrey Clinker among his youthful reading. "I have sustained my own idea of Roderick Random for a month at a stretch... I have seen Tom Pipes go climbing up the church steeple... "

Forster 1872-4: p 2 above. "When he resolved that Sam Weller should be occupant of the prison with Mr Pickwick, he was perhaps thinking of his favourite Smollett, and how, when Peregrine Pickle was inmate of the Fleet, Hatchway and Pipes refused to leave him..." (bk 2 ch 1). Smollett and Copperfield (bk 6 ch 7).

Child, Harold. Fielding and Smollett. CHEL vol X 1913; p 45 1932 edn.

Chesterton 1913: p 21 above. "Smollett was coarse; but Smollett was also cruel. Dickens was frequently horrible; he was never cruel" (p 51 OPUS edn.)

Wierstra, F.D. Smollett and Dickens. Amsterdam 1928.

Shaw 1937: qu above p 231.

Orwell 1939-40: p 26 above. "Even by the standards of his time Dickens was an exceptionally artificial writer... His characters are even more distorted and simplified than Smollett's "(p 51 1946 edn.)

Jones, Howard Mumford. Intn Humphry Clinker. EL edn 1943 p xi.

Allen 1954: p 30 above; p 75 PB edn.

Maugham 1954: p 30 above; p 147 PB edn.

Allott 1959: p 7 above; p 12.

Allen, Walter. In Slater 1970: p 8 above; pp 6-8, 14-15. Cf Chesterton 1913 above and Phelps 1916 p 69: "No two novelists in English literature are more unlike than Smollett and Dickens".

Dickens and Goldsmith

Dickens 1847: p 2 above.   Vicar of Wakefield among his
   youthful reading.

Dickens 1847.   "'Boz', my signature in the Morning
   Chronicle...was the nickname of...a younger brother,
   whom I had dubbed Moses, in honour of the Vicar of
   Wakefield; which being facetiously pronounced through
   the nose, became Boses, and being shortened, became Boz.
   'Boz' was a very familar household word to me, long before
   I was an author..." (pref cheap edn Pickwick.)

Forster 1872-4: p 2 above.   Bk 2 ch 6.

Swinburne 1882: qu above p 16.

Shaw 1937: p 86 above.

Ford, Boris.   Oliver Goldsmith.   PGEL 4 1957 p 377.

Churchill 1958: qu above p 182.

House 1965: p 6 above.   Dickens's letters and editors' notes
   give details of influence of Goldsmith's Bee and Citizen
   of the World on Master Humphrey's Clock.   See particularly
   pp 563-5.

Blount 1968: qu above p 52.

Dickens and Blake

Lewes 1872: p 15 above.   "He was a seer of visions; and his
   visions were of objects at once familiar and potent...
   in no other perfectly sane mind (Blake, I believe, was not
   perfectly sane) have I observed vividness of imagination
   approaching so closely to hallucination."

Orwell 1939-40: p 26 above; p 21 1946 edn.

Lucas 1970: qu above p 68.

Leavis 1970: p 36 above.   "He is indeed the Blake as well
   as the Shakespeare of the novel".   See ch on Little Dorrit.

Williams 1970: p 78 above; pp 22-3.

Gold 1974: p 37 above.   Cf DSA 1971 on Nickleby: "a Blakean
   song of innocence and experience".

Dickens and Cobbett

Chesterton 1913: p 21 above. "...he represents the return
of Cobbett...proud of being the ordinary man... Dickens...
liked the things that Cobbett had liked...hated the things
that Cobbett had hated: the Tudors, the lawyers, the
leisurely oppression of the poor..." (pp 36-7 OPUS edn.)

Churchill 1937-42: p 26 above. "...It is this insistence on
the personal, this hatred of the institution for ignoring
the human element...that is typical of all Dickens's
writing on social justice. Like Cobbett, he was concerned
not only for the welfare of the poor but for their
dignity..." (p 374.)

House 1941: p 27 above; p 135.

Williams 1958: p 97 above; p 37 PB edn.

Dickens and Wordsworth

Wordsworth 1842: qu above p 125.

Horne 1844: p 163 above. Considers Dickens's unconscious
"blank verse" in Old Curiosity Shop "worthy of the best
passages in Wordsworth, and thus, meeting on the common
ground of a deeply truthful sentiment, the two most unlike
men in the literature of the country are brought into the
closest approximation" (p 68; cf Bagehot below.)

Bagehot 1858: p 13 above. "Mr Dickens has...no feeling
analogous to the nature-worship of some other recent
writers. There is nothing Wordsworthian in his bent..."
(p 175 EL edn 1911.)   Cf Chambers's Journal 1846 qu p 70
                                                    above.
Forster 1872-4: p 2 above; bk 9 ch 8 para 2-3.

Trilling 1953: p 103 above. Wordsworth and Little Dorrit.

Coveney 1957: p 207 above. Considers Dickens's novels as
heirs to Wordsworth's poems in their treatment of childhood

Wilson, Angus. In Slater 1970: p 8 above. "...the heir of
the Wordsworthian romantic tradition, and especially in
what concerned memory, dreams, childhood influence, fancy
as a superior force to reason..." (pp 219-20.)

Williams 1970: p 78 above. Prelude, Dombey, Little Dorrit
(p 23.)

Dickens and Wordsworth, cont.

Speirs, John. Poetry Towards Novel. 1971. Shows in detail
    how in The Prelude and other poems Wordsworth originated
    theme of "growing up", later one of main themes in Dickens
    and other Victorian novelists. Cf Coveney above.

Churchill, R.C. The Heirs of Wordsworth. Use of English
    Winter 1972. Review of Speirs above.

Dickens and Scott

Lytton 1841: qu above p 57.

Bagehot, Walter. Compares Scott's "lifelike description of
    poor persons" with Dickens's "delineation" of "mean manners
    and mean vices" to which he has "been led by a sort of pre-
    Raphaelite cultus of reality" (The Waverley Novels, 1858;
    rp Literary Studies 1879, pp 142-4 EL edn 1911.)

Flaubert 1872: qu above p 42.

Watt 1880: p 16 above.

Ruskin 1880-1: p 16 above. Old Mortality and Bleak House.

Harrison 1894-5: qu above pp 145, 180.

Gissing 1898: p 17 above. Scott and Barnaby Rudge (ch 5.)

James 1899: qu above p 224.

Henderson, T.F. Sir Walter Scott. CHEL XII 1914; p 25 1932
    edn.

Phelps 1916: qu above p 142.

Cecil 1931-4: p 25 above. "Effie Deans' lapse from virtue is
    referred to without any of that atmosphere of drawing the
    blinds and lowering the voice...in which Dickens has seen
    fit to enshroud the similar fate of little Em'ly" (p 26
    FL edn; cf Allott 1959 pp 36-7 where a similar comparison
    is made between Em'ly and Stendhal's Gina.)

Leavis 1948: p 29 above. Neither Scott nor Dickens, for
    reasons explained in ch 1, worthy of inclusion "in the line
    of great novelists" represented by Jane Austen, George
    Eliot, Henry James, Conrad and D.H. Lawrence. Cf Leavis
    1970 for revised opinion.

Dickens and Scott, cont.

Pearson 1949: p 4 above. Shakespeare and Scott: "the only two writers in English who are in Dickens's creative class" (p 250.)

Anon (R.C.Churchill). The Disinherited Baronet. TLS 20 Jun 1952. See closing paras.

Marcus 1964: p 34 above. Sketches by Boz and The Heart of Midlothian (p 76.)

Anon. The Slow Resuscitation of Sir Walter Scott. TLS 15 Jan 1970. See opening paras and cf Churchill 1952 above.

Dickens and Jane Austen

Forster 1872-4: qu above p 49. Nickleby and Emma.

Howells, William Dean. "The art of fiction, as Jane Austen knew it, declined from her through Scott, and Bulwer, and Dickens...because the mania of romanticism had seized upon all Europe" (Essay on Mark Twain, c1890, qu Robert E. Spiller, The Cycle of American Literature, 1955, pp 116-17 MB edn.)

Quiller-Couch 1922-5: p 23 above; pp 301, 71.

Forster 1927: qu above p 236.

Cecil 1931-4: p 25 above; pp 32, 47.

Churchill, R.C. The Regency Jane. Tribune 18 May 1945.

Leavis 1948: qu above p 243.

Kettle 1951: p 30 above. "...we do not become involved in the world of Oliver Twist in the way we become involved in the world of Emma..." (pp 124-5.)

Allen 1954: p 30 above. "Dickens recognizes no limits at all; the art of Jane Austen is made possible precisely by the recognition of limits" (p 109 PB edn; cf Cecil and E.M.Forster above.)

Garis 1965: p 34 above.

Holloway 1970: p 8 above under Slater; pp 73-4.

Dickens and Washington Irving

Hogarth 1836: qu above p 38. Cf Charles Buller, Westminster
Rev Jul 1837 (qu Collins
Saintsbury 1916: qu above p 216.   1971 p 53).

Brooks 1944: p 64 above under Coombes.

House 1969: qu above p 40.   Cf Pacey 1945: p 134 above.

Dickens and Leigh Hunt

Dickens.   Leigh Hunt: A Remonstrance.   All the Year Round
24 Dec 1859.   Tribute to Hunt after his death, claiming
he had not anticipated (as some newspapers had hinted
regarding Skimpole in Bleak House) that "the admired
original would ever be charged with the imaginary vices
of the fictitious creature" (rp Dickens 1892: p 17 above).
Cf Forster 1872-4 bk 6 ch 7; James Payn, Cornhill Mag
Mar 1884; Quiller-Couch 1922-5 pp 90-2; and L.A.Brewer,
Leigh Hunt and Dickens: the Skimpole Caricature, Cedar
Rapids Iowa 1930.

Clarke 1878: p 2 above.

Saintsbury, George.   The Landors, Leigh Hunt, De Quincey.
CHEL vol XII 1914.   Hunt's influence on Sketches by Boz
and Household Words (p 221 1932 edn; cf Saintsbury 1916
pp 307-8, 328.)

Dickens and Carlyle

Carlyle: qu above pp 41, 62.

Dickens 1859: qu above p 105.

Forster 1872-4: p 2 above.   Qu Dickens on Carlyle (bk 11 ch 3).

Davey, S.   Darwin, Carlyle and Dickens.   1875.

Trollope 1883: qu above p 164.

FitzGerald 1889: qu above p 16.

Dickens and Carlyle, cont.

Lilly 1895: p 17 above.

Aronstein, P. Dickens und Carlyle. Anglia 18 1896.

Matz, B.W. Two Great Victorian Writers. 1905.

Chesterton 1907-11: qu above p 95.

Chesterton 1913: p 21 above. "...Carlyle a man who saw...
Arnold a man who knew... Dickens a man who...felt..."
(p 35 OPUS edn.)

Quiller-Couch 1922-5: p 23 above. "Carlyle never said an
unjuster thing... than when he accused Dickens's theory of
life as entirely wrong... Dickens had a keener eye for sin
than Carlyle ever had..." (p 40.)

Young 1936: qu above p 201.

House 1941: qu above p 124. See also House on The Chimes:
"the story obviously owes a good deal to Carlyle..." (p 72).

Pope-Hennessy 1945: p 4 above; ch 10.

Christian, M.G. Carlyle's Influence upon the Social-Theory
of Dickens. Trollopian 1-2 1946-7.

Williams 1958: p 97 above; p 91 PB edn.

Klingopulos 1958: p 32 above under Ford. "Carlyle and
Dickens dominate the first half of Victoria's reign..."
(pp 26-7.)

Lucas 1970: qu above p 68.

Snow 1970: p 104 above. Little Dorrit and Latter-Day
Pamphlets (p 132n.)

Dunn, Richard J. David Copperfield's Carlylean
Retailoring. DSA 1971.

Oddie 1973: p 98 above. And qu above p 168. See review
by G.B.Tennyson DSN Mar 1974.

Goldberg, Michael. Carlyle and Dickens. Athens Ga 1973.

Campbell, Ian. Thomas Carlyle. 1974. pp 107-8, 120-1.

Dickens and Thomas Hood

Hood 1840: qu above pp 51, 53.

Thackeray 1852: p 150 above; p 283 EL edn 1910.

Reid, J.C. Thomas Hood. 1963. Points out similarities
between murder scenes in Dickens and Hood's poem The Dream
of Eugene Aram (1826).

House 1965-74: p 6 above. Letters to Hood and editorial
notes on their friendship.

Slater, Michael. In Slater 1970: p 8 above; pp 104, 107.

Dickens and Balzac

Belinsky 1844-8: p 141 above. Put Dickens above Balzac,
an opinion based on a reading of the earlier novels.
Cf Frenssen qu Pope-Hennessy 1945 p 321 who found Balzac
"rather hollow" compared with Dickens.

Taine 1856: p 13 above.

Dickens. Letter to Forster 15 Aug 1856 on alleged
uninteresting nature of English fictional heroes compared
with those of Balzac and George Sand (qu Forster bk 9 ch 1).

James 1865: p 14 above.

Harrison 1894-5: p 17 above. "...Dickens does not look on
the mean and the vile as do Balzac and Zola, that is, from
without, like the detective or the surgeon. He sees things
more or less from their point of view..." (p 133.)

Gissing 1898: p 17 above. "One finds in Balzac a stronger
intellect, but by no means a greater genius... I doubt
whether he ever imparts his vision with the vividness of
Dickens at his best" (pp 210-11 1926 edn.)

Brownell 1900: qu above p 165.

Swinburne 1902: p 19 above. "...nothing in the work of
Balzac is newer and truer and more terrible than the
relentless yet not unmerciful evolution of the central
figure" in Little Dorrit "...the Father of the Marshalsea
..." (pp 45-6 1913 edn.)

Saintsbury 1916: p 22 above. "He has constantly been
compared with Balzac, and the comparison has some solid

247

Dickens and Balzac, cont.

foundations. But it must be a strange taste which would
take in exchange even the great Frenchman for our English
Dickens" (p 339 1932 edn.)

Zweig 1920: p 23 above.

Lubbock 1921: p 23 above. "...Dickens manages it far more
artfully than Balzac, because his imagination is not, like
Balzac's, divided against itself..." (qu fully in Wall 1970
pp 269-70.)

Quiller-Couch 1922-5: p 23 above. "...like Balzac, he has a
world of his own and can at call dispense to us of its
abundance" (p 33.)

Orwell 1939-40: p 26 above. "D.H.Lawrence once said that
Balzac was 'a gigantic dwarf', and in a sense the same is
true of Dickens..." (pp 51-2 1946 edn.)

Monod 1953: qu above p 155; cf Quiller-Couch above.

Trilling 1953: p 103 above. Blandois and Vautrin.

Maugham 1954: qu above p 188.

Allott 1959: p 7 above. "...when Dickens creates figures
which he intends to be taken seriously - Quilp, let us say,
or Bradley Headstone - we respond to the vibrations of the
author's own tremendous vitality but miss the deeper
springs of creative life from which Dostoevsky's Smerdyakov
or Balzac's Père Goriot derive their tragic fulness of
stature" (p 203.)

Snow 1970: p 104 above. Little Dorrit and Les Employés
(pp 125-6, 146.)

Dickens and Victor Hugo

Hogarth 1836: p 38 above. Compares A Visit to Newgate with
Victor Hugo.

Poe 1842: p 57 above. Compares Barnaby Rudge with Hugo's
Notre Dame, to Dickens's disadvantage in point of
"concentration or unity of place" (qu fully Collins 1971
p 110.)

Dickens and Victor Hugo, cont.

Anon. Christian Remembrancer Jan 1845. "...the influence of the chimes, and the leading idea of the story, is taken from Schiller's Song of the Bell; the mysterious affection and attraction between the Bells and Toby Veck may be traced to Quasimodo in Victor Hugo's Notre Dame de Paris" (qu Collins 1971 p 161.)

Anon. Illustrated London News 18 Jun 1870. "Dickens is always a great writer; but he is a most successful creator in the department of quaint figures and odd habits, curious bits of human life... In this department he excels Balzac and Victor Hugo..." (qu fully Collins 1971 p 516.)

Swinburne 1902: qu above p 101. Little Dorrit and Les Misérables.

Leacock 1933: qu above p 137.

Dickens and Bulwer Lytton

Anon. Westminster Rev Jun 1844. Oliver Twist and Pickwick contrasted with Bulwer's Paul Clifford. "Dickens is a Londoner, Bulwer is a cosmopolite" (qu fully Collins 1971 p 152.)

Illustrated London News 1870: see above under Hugo. "He was inferior to Bulwer-Lytton, George Eliot, and Charles Kingsley, in the art of composing a narrative plot, and of preserving and enhancing its dramatic interest; while his perception of the delicate shades of character...which belong to the comedy of polite life...was far below that of Bulwer-Lytton, Thackeray or Trollope."

United States Mag 1853: p 87 above. Review of Bleak House and My Novel, ending with exhortation: "Get up, some one, and write a snatch against Bulwer and Dickens.' In sober earnest, it is not half so difficult as it looks" (qu Dickens 1892: p 17 above.)

Dickens 1861: qu above p 108.

Forster 1872-4: p 2 above; bk 9 ch 3.

Anon. Bulwer and Dickens: A Contrast. Temple Bar Jan 1875.

Watt 1880: p 16 above.

Dickens and Bulwer Lytton, cont.

Harrison 1894-5: qu above p 164.

Chesterton 1913: p 21 above; pp 59-60 OPUS edn.

Lindsay 1950: p 186 above.

Bayley 1962: qu above p 111.

Hollingsworth 1963: p 48 above.

Dickens and Disraeli

Harrison 1894-5: qu above p 164.

House 1941: p 27 above. "...his imagination was as
   different from Dickens's as it could be..." (p 12.)

Aldington 1948: p 4 above.

Kettle 1958: p 32 above under Ford.

Williams 1958: p 97 above; p 108 PB edn.

Williams 1970: p 8 above under Slater; p 85.

Slater 1970: ibid. The Chimes and Coningsby (pp 110-11.)

Dickens and Edgar Allan Poe

Leacock 1933: p 57 above under Poe.

Sayers, Dorothy L. Intn Tales of Detection. EL 1936.
   Compares Dupin stories with English "sensational novel"
   of Dickens, Collins and Le Fanu (pp viii-ix.)

Mason, L. A Tale of Three Authors. 1940. Dickens,
   Ainsworth, Poe.

Brooks, Van Wyck. "Some of the tales were humorous, and
   these were perhaps the most sinister of all, for one seldom
   felt any warmth in the humour of Poe, although Dickens was
   ond of his favourite writers" (The World of Washington
   Irving, 1944, p 279.)

Dickens and Poe, cont.

Nisbet, Ada C.   New Light on the Dickens-Poe Relationship.
NCF 5 1951.

Grubb, Gerald G.   The Personal and Literary Relationships
of Dickens and Poe.   NCF 5 1951.

House 1974: p 6 above.   Letters to Poe and editorial notes
on their relationship.   Cf Nicoll 1923 pp 221-44 and
Pope-Hennessy 1945 pp 174-5.   Poe's poem The Raven (1844)
was partly inspired by Barnaby Rudge.

Dickens and Gogol

Pritchett 1946: p 28 above.   "...What Dickens really
contributed may be seen by a glance at the only novelists
who have seriously developed his contribution - in
Dostoevsky above all and, to a lesser degree, in Gogol"
(see further below under "Dickens and Dostoevsky".)

Futrell, M.A.   Gogol and Dickens.   Slavonic Rev 34 1956.

Priestley 1960: p 33 above.   "There is of course more than a
reminder of Dickens in this comic-grotesque imagination of
Gogol's... but this is only one side, though a not
inconsiderable side, of Dickens, a far more positive and
stronger character" (p 188 PB edn.)

Gifford 1968: p 144 above.

Dickens and Mrs Gaskell

Mrs Gaskell.   Cranford.   1853.   Capt Brown and Miss Jenkyns
in ch 1 discuss the rival merits of Boz and Dr Johnson as
writers of fiction - the latter being (ironically)
triumphant.

Stephen 1857: p 13 above.

Ward, Sir A.W.   The Political and Social Novel.   CHEL vol
XIII 1916; pp 375-7 1932 edn.

Quiller-Couch 1922-5: p 23 above; pp 211-12.

Dickens and Mrs Gaskell, cont.

House 1941: p 27 above.   Mary Barton and Hard Times (pp 204-5)

Hopkins, A.B.   Dickens and Mrs Gaskell.   HLQ 9 1946.

Williams 1958: p 97 above.   Hard Times, Mary Barton, North
and South (ch 5.)

Klingopulos 1958: p 32 above under Ford; p 106.

Kettle 1958: ibid.

Carnall 1964: p 97 above.

Williams 1970: p 8 above under Slater; pp 85-6.

Basch 1974: p 192 above; pp 66, 83, 175.

Dickens and Thackeray

Sterling, John.   "I got hold of the first two numbers of the
Hoggarty Diamond; and read them with extreme delight... The
man is a true genius... There is more truth and nature in
one of these papers than in all Dickens's novels together"
(letter to his mother 11 Dec 1841 qu Carlyle, Life of John
Sterling, pt 3 ch 3.)

Bon Gaultier (Theodore Martin).   Tait's Edinburgh Mag Apr 184[
"...I'll back Michael Angelo Titmarsh against him, in his ov
line, for a hundred pounds..." (qu fully Collins 1971 pp
172-3; cf Collins's comment p 172.)

Hayward, Abraham.   Letter to Thackeray on Vanity Fair Nov 184'
"...you have completely beaten Dickens out of the inner
circle already" (qu Pope-Hennessy 1945 p 276.)

Carlyle, Jane.   Letter on Vanity Fair 1847.   "Very good indee(
Beats Dickens out of the world" (ibid). For Thomas Carlyle
on Dickens and Thackeray see Collins 1971 p 204.)

Macready, W.C. on Vanity Fair 1849.   "...second to none of
the present day, which is an admission I make almost
grudgingly for Dickens's sake, but the truth is the truth"
(qu Collins 1971 p 3.)

Thackeray 1849: qu above p 80.   Copperfield "beats" Pendennis
"hollow".

252

Anon (David Masson). Pendennis and Copperfield: Thackeray
  and Dickens. North British Rev May 1851. "Thackeray and
  Dickens...the two names now almost necessarily go together
  ...But...differences are certainly very great..." (qu
  fully in Collins 1971 pp 249-59.)

Thackeray to Masson 1851: qu above p 150.

Anon (Samuel Phillips). David Copperfield and Arthur
  Pendennis. Times 11 Jun 1851. "...Mr Dickens touches a
  higher key... The epic is greater than the satire..."
  (qu Collins 1971 pp 261-3 and see comment by Collins p 261).

Dickens 1858: qu above p 187. Tribute to Thackeray qu Forster
  1872-4 bk 7 ch 2 and Wall 1970 p 120. "...the well-thumbed
  pages of Mr Thackeray's books...how full of wit...how full
  of wisdom... paying my little due of homage and respect to
  them... to have such a writer as my friend..." (cf Dickens
  1864 below.)

Bagehot 1858: p 13 above. "Mr Thackeray without doubt
  exercises a more potent and plastic fascination within his
  sphere, but that sphere is limited..." (p 165 EL edn 1911.)

Brown, Dr John. "John Brown of the Horae Subsecivae (1858-82)
  was strong against Dickens, the hard and shrill, and eager
  for Thackeray, the true and tender-hearted" (Sampson 1941:
  p 28 above; p 767 1970 edn.)

Masson 1859: qu above p 164. See also p 129 above.

Dickens 1864. "I thought that he too much feigned a want of
  earnestness and that he made a pretence of undervaluing his
  art, which was not good for the art that he held in trust"
  (obituary Cornhill Mag Feb 64 qu Forster bk 8 ch 7; Pope-
  Hennessy 1945 p 438; Pearson 1949 p 273; Leavis D.H.
  Lawrence PB edn p 311.)

Austin 1870: p 15 above. "With a Thackeray, a Lytton, an
  Eliot, on the course, we cannot say that Dickens was first
  and the rest nowhere; but though...men might momentarily
  think that these would overtake and even outstrip him,
  they never did so..." (qu Collins 1971 pp 533-6.)

Anon. Two English Novelists: Dickens and Thackeray.
  Dublin Rev Apr 1871. See Collins 1971 pp 551-4.

Trollope 1879: qu above p 126.

FitzGerald 1879: p 233 above under Wall. "...had I to choose

but one of them, I would choose Dickens's hundred
delightful Caricatures rather than Thackeray's half-dozen
terrible Photographs. "

Watt 1880: p 16 above.

Trollope 1883: p 164 above.   "...I do not hesitate to name
Thackeray the first..."

James 1884: qu above p 151.

Harrison 1894-5: qu above p 164.

Lilly 1895: p 17 above.

Gissing 1898: p 17 above.   Pendennis, Dombey: "comparisons
arise..." (ch 5.)

Brownell 1901: qu above p 165.

Canning, A.S.G.   Dickens and Thackeray Studied in Three
Novels.   1911.   Pickwick, Nickleby, Vanity Fair.

Dickens, Kate, Mrs Perugini.   Thackeray and my Father.
Pall Mall Mag Aug 1911.   Cf Anne Thackeray, Lady Ritchie,
Dickens as I remember him, Pall Mall Mag Mar 1912.

Mair 1911: p 21 above; pp 226-7, 228.

Chesterton 1913: p 21 above.   "Thackeray...was too Victorian
to understand the Victorian epoch... Dickens, being in
touch with the democracy, had already discovered that the
country had come to a dark place of divided ways and
divided counsels.   In Hard Times he realized Democracy at
war with Radicalism... In Our Mutual Friend he felt the
strength of the new rich..." (pp 55-7 OPUS edn.)

Thompson, A.Hamilton.   "...his range of character was limited
compared with that of Dickens and Balzac... But...he kept
more closely...to the observation of the life that lay
immediately beneath his notice" (Thackeray in vol XIII
CHEL 1916; p 301 1932 edn.)

Phelps 1916: p 22 above.   "Thackeray's mind was more critical
than that of Dickens..." (pp 111-12.)

Lubbock 1921: p 23 above; pp 216-17.

Santayana 1921-2: p 23 above. "It is usual to compare
  Dickens with Thackeray, which is like comparing the grape
  with the gooseberry; there are obvious points of
  resemblance, and the gooseberry has some superior qualities
  of its own; but you can't make red wine of it."

Quiller-Couch 1922-5: p 23 above; pp 126-30.

Elton, Oliver. Dickens and Thackeray. 1925.
  rv from ch in A Survey of English Literature 1830-80,
  2 vols 1920.

Cecil 1931-4: p 25 above. "...two entirely different species
  of writer... the nature of their inspiration is wholly
  different..." (p 59 FL edn.)

O'Faolain 1936: p 26 above.

Shaw 1937: p 26 above. "...Trollope and Thackeray could see
  Chesney Wold; but Dickens could see through it..."

Orwell 1939-40: p 26 above. "Vanity Fair is a full-length
  version of what Dickens did for a few chapters in Little
  Dorrit" (pp 24-5 1946 edn.)

Williams, C.R. The Personal Relations of Dickens and
  Thackeray. Dickensian 35 1939.

Maly-Schatter 1940: p 27 above.

Stevenson, Lionel. The Showman of Vanity Fair. New York 1947.

Pearson 1949: p 4 above. "Gowan-Thackeray" (p 263): an
  identification also made by Leavis 1954 below, but should be
  taken cautiously, despite Dickens 1864 qu above, in view of
  the fact that Thackeray, unlike Gowan, worked very hard both
  as writer and artist (Saintsbury's edn runs to 17 vols) and
  that his claim to be a gentleman-amateur like Congreve, not
  a professional writer, was not meant to be taken very
  seriously. Dickens 1858 qu above saluted a fellow craftsman.

Anon (R.C.Churchill). The Sentimental Satirist. TLS 4 Aug
  1950. Review of J.Y.T.Greig, Thackeray: A Reconsideration.
  Incl some comparisons with Dickens.

Tillotson 1954: p 30 above.

Allen 1954: p 30 above.

Maugham 1954: qu above p 146.

Dickens and Thackeray, cont.

Tillotson, Geoffrey. Thackeray the Novelist. Cambridge 1954.
See review by V.S.Pritchett New Statesman 7 Dec 54 and
letter by F.R.Leavis 11 Dec rp Letters in Criticism ed
John Tasker 1974 p 43.

Klingopulos 1958: p 32 above under Ford. "Thackeray appears
a substantial writer, but he is decidedly not of the same
order of genius as Fielding, Jane Austen, Scott, or
Dickens" (p 106.)

Betsky, Seymour. Society in Thackeray and Trollope.
PGEL 6 1958 as above. "Thackeray...fails entirely to see
...the alignment (as Dickens saw in Hard Times) of
industrialism and utilitarianism" (p 145; cf Chesterton
1913 qu above.)

Allott 1959: p 7 above.

Hollingsworth 1963: p 48 above.

Mauskopf, Charles. Thackeray's Attitude towards Dickens's
Writings. NCF 21 1966.

Flamm, Dudley. Thackeray's Critics: An Annotated
Bibliography of British and American Criticism 1836-91.
Chapel Hill 1967. Incl many comparisons with Dickens.

Tillotson, Geoffrey and Donald Hawes (ed). Thackeray:
The Critical Heritage. 1968. Many Dickens comparisons.

Collins 1971: p 8 above; pp 3, 242, 249 etc.

Basch 1974: p 192 above; pp 263-4.

Dickens and Henry Mayhew

Mayhew 1861: p 130 above.

Churchill 1958: p 32 above under Ford; pp 345-6, 350. See
also Tribune reviews by Churchill 1948-9 of modern Mayhew
selections.

Bradley, John L. Intn WC selection 1965.

Nelson, H.S. Our Mutual Friend and Mayhew's London Labour
and the London Poor. NCF 20 1966.

Dickens and Henry Mayhew, cont.

Anon. TLS 27 Jun 1968. Mayhew's London. Review of 1968 rp.

Chesney 1970: p 132 above.

Leavis 1970: p 36 above; pp 184-6. Cf Churchill 1958 above.

Basch 1974: p 192 above; pp 195-208.

Dickens and Charles Reade

Stephen 1857: p 13 above. "They tend to beget hasty
  generalizations and false conclusions. They address
  themselves almost entirely to the imagination upon subjects
  which properly belong to the intellect..." (qu Snow 1970,
  more fully Collins 1971.)

Phillips, Walter C. Dickens, Reade and Collins: Sensation
  Novelists. New York 1919.

Quiller-Couch 1922-5: p 23 above; p 59.

Orwell 1939-40: p 26 above; pp 9, 42-3 1946 edn.
  Hard Cash and Nickleby.

Churchill 1958: p 32 above under Ford. Cf Orwell above.

Klingopulos 1958: ibid; p 103.

Dickens and Trollope

Harrison 1894-5: qu above p 164.

Chesterton 1913: qu above p 52.

Quiller-Couch 1922-5: p 23 above; pp 228-30.

Shaw 1937: qu above p 255.

Orwell 1939-40: p 26 above; pp 24, 31-2, 36 1946 edn.

Boll, E. The Infusion of Dickens in Trollope.
  Trollopian 1 1946.

Dickens and Trollope, cont.

Booth, B.A.   Trollope and Little Dorrit.   Trollopian 2 1948.

Allen 1954: p 30 above.   Compares Our Mutual Friend and The
   Way We Live Now as studies of "the role of money in
   society" (p 207 PB edn.)

Fielding 1958: p 5 above.   Compared with novels by Trollope
   and Disraeli, Dickens's are not "a mirror of his times;
   his relationship with society was a creative one."
   Cf Dickens 1858 qu above p 187: "...that great mirror which
   he holds up to nature."

Snow in Slater 1970: p 8 above.   Little Dorrit and The Three
   Clerks (pp 125, 131, 139, 144.)

Johnson: ibid.   Little Dorrit and The Eustace Diamonds
   (pp 179-80); Dombey and The Duke's Children (pp 186-9.)

Collins 1971: pp 17, 481, 517, 542.

Skilton, David.   Anthony Trollope and his Contemporaries:
   A Study in the Theory and Conventions of Mid-Victorian
   Fiction.   1972.

Basch 1974: p 192 above; pp 75-6.

Dickens and the Brontës

McCarthy 1864: p 14 above.   Contrasts variety of Charlotte
   Brontë's heroes with the dull sameness of Dickens's.
   "There is just one exception to the triviality of his
   heroes.   David Copperfield has some marks of life about
   him".   Cf Orwell pp 36, 40 1946 edn.

Quiller-Couch 1922-5: p 23 above; p 72.

Cecil 1931-4: p 25 above.   "The first quarter of Jane Eyre,
   with the first quarter of David Copperfield, is the most
   profoundly-studied portrait of childhood in English"
   (pp 108-9 FL edn; cf pp 101, 135.)

Orwell 1939-40: p 26 above.   "...not a trace in him of the
   feeling that one finds in Manon Lescaut, Salammbo, Carmen,
   Wuthering Heights" (p 51 1946 edn.)

Mason, L.   Jane Eyre and David Copperfield.   Dickensian 40
   1944.

Craig, G.A.   Jane Eyre and Bleak House.   Society and the
    Self in the Novel, ed Schorer, New York 1956.

Williams 1970: p 78 above; p 12.

Dickens and George Eliot

Hutton 1862: p 32 above under Stang.   Considered Dickens and
    George Eliot to be best of contemporary novelists.

Stott 1869: p 14 above.   "...while George Eliot weaves her
    stories without seeming anxiety as to their moral effect...
    with Mr Dickens the doctrines are not only latent in the
    stories, they are their formative principle..." (qu more
    fully Collins 1971 pp 493-4.)

Lewes 1872: p 15 above.   Implied contrast with George Eliot
    (in opinion of Forster and other defenders of Dickens.)

Acton, Lord.   "I am ashamed to think how much more often
    I return to Dickens than to George Eliot..." (letter qu
    Collins 1971 pp 2-3.)

Harrison 1894-5: qu above p 164.

Lilly 1895: p 17 above.

Bennett to George Sturt 6 Feb 1898: p 16 above under Hepburn.
    "Of Dickens...I know nothing.   About a year ago...I picked
    up The Old Curiosity Shop, and of all the rotten vulgar
    un-literary writing! Worse than George Eliot's..."

Stephen 1902: p 213 above.   "Dickens's appreciation" of
    Scenes of Clerical Life "is the more creditable to him
    because the work is conspicuous by its freedom from his
    besetting faults.   The humour is perfectly unforced and
    ...without a touch of grotesque extravagance" (pp 61-2.)

Phelps 1916: p 22 above; p 113.

Quiller-Couch 1922-5: p 23 above; p 72.

Cecil 1931-4: p 25 above.   "...inferior to him in creative
    imagination..." (p 247 FL edn.)

Maly-Schatter 1940: p 27 above.

Dickens and George Eliot, cont.

Dodds, M.H. George Eliot and Charles Dickens. Notes &
Queries 6 Apr 1946.

Churchill, R.C. Dickens and George Eliot. John o'London's
Weekly 7 Feb 1947.

Leavis 1948: qu above p 243.

Maugham 1954: p 30 above. "...It may be that it is because
this high seriousness is lacking in Dickens's novels that,
for all their great merits, they leave us faintly
dissatisfied. When we read them now with the great French
and Russian novels in mind, and not only those, but George
Eliot's, we are taken aback by their naïveté. In comparison
with them, Dickens's are scarcely adult" (p 145 PB edn.)

Leavis, Q.D. A Note on Literary Indebtedness: Dickens,
George Eliot, Henry James. Hudson Rev 8 1955.

Garis 1965: p 34 above.

Williams 1970: p 78 above. "...it is the contrast – the
profound contrast – between Dickens and George Eliot that
is the beginning of any important critical understanding
of the English nineteenth-century novel" (p 14; cf
Churchill 1947 above.)

Williams in Slater 1970: p 8 above; pp 86-7.

Q.D.Leavis 1970: p 36 above. Dickens has "a far better idea
of how speech occurs and of the laws of association which
direct thought than either George Eliot or Tolstoy".

Basch 1974: p 192 above; pp 57-8, 251. Ruth Pinch and Mrs
Amos Barton; Edith Dombey and Hetty Sorrel.

Dickens and Walt Whitman

Whitman 1842: qu above p 11.

Whitman 1857: see Collins 1971 p 358.

Santayana 1921-2: p 23 above. "In his love of roads and
wayfarers, of river-ports and wharves and the idle or
sinister figures that lounge about them, Dickens was like
Walt Whitman... The spirit of Dickens would be better able
to do justice to America... Whitman had a sort of

Dickens and Walt Whitman, cont.

transcendental philosophy which swallowed the universe
whole... Dickens was innocent of any such clap-trap...
Whitman, in his comprehensive democratic vistas, could
never see the trees for the wood, and remained incapable,
for all his diffuse love of the human herd, of ever
painting a character or telling a story: the very things
in which Dickens was a master."

Brooks 1947: p 134 above; pp 101-2.

Dickens and Herman Melville

Brooks 1947: p 134 above; pp 120n, 208.   Chuzzlewit and
   Mardi; Bartleby and Dickens.

Trilling 1953: p 103 above.   Bartleby and Little Dorrit.

Cunliffe 1954: p 135 above.   Bartleby and Bleak House
   (p 120 1967 edn.)

Dickens and Dostoevsky

Dostoevsky 1846-8: p 54 above.

Vvedensky 1848: p 141 above.

Druzhinin 1849: p 141 above.

Gissing 1898: p 17 above.   The two novelists spiritually
   akin.   "With a change of birth and breeding" Dickens
   "might well have written" Crime and Punishment.

Bourne, Randolph.   The History of a Literary Radical,
   ed Van Wyck Brooks, New York 1920, from articles written
   c1913-18.   Dostoevsky appealed to Bourne as "a forerunner
   of the modern mind" who felt those "irrational turns of
   human thought" that had come to make novelists like
   Dickens and Balzac "seem too simple."

Phelps 1916: pp 22 and 142 above.   "Although Dickens had an
   enormous influence on the literature of the Continent,
   the only foreign novelist who resembled him both in genius
   and in temperament was Dostoevsky.   The title of one of
   the latter's stories, The Insulted and Injured, might
   almost be taken as the subject of the complete works of

Dickens and Dostoevsky, cont.

both writers. Both had suffered terribly in earliest
youth; both knew the city slums; both knew the very worst
of which humanity is capable; both loved humanity with a
love that survived every experience; both were profoundly
spiritual, intensely religious, and thoroughly optimistic.
For the great artists who have known suffering and
privation are more often optimists than those whose lives
have been carefully sheltered..." (pp 107-8.)

Grossman 1919: qu above p 142.

Zweig 1920: p 23 above.

Radlov 1922: p 143 above.

Quiller-Couch 1922-5: p 23 above; p 75.

Huxley 1930: p 55 above. "A child, Ilusha, suffers and dies
in Dostoevsky's Brothers Karamazov. Why is this history so
agonizingly moving, when the tale of Little Nell leaves us
not merely cold, but derisive? Comparing the two stories,
we are instantly struck by the incomparably greater
richness in factual detail of Dostoevsky's creation..."

Wilson, Edmund. Axel's Castle. 1931. "...if we ask
ourselves why even so great a novelist as Dickens does not
make upon us so profound an impression as Dostoevsky,
we realize that it is because...Dickens, wide and varied
as the world of his novels is...is not sufficiently
conscious of the significance of what happens there, so
that, except in the very best of them, he has admitted a
larger conventional element than the greatest novelists
ordinarily allow..." (p 144 FL edn.)

Yelizarova 1934: p 143 above.

Wilson 1939-41: p 27 above. "The Bloomsbury that talked
about Dostoevsky ignored Dostoevsky's master, Dickens"
(p 1 UP edn; cf p 45 and Wilson 1931 qu above.)

Pritchett 1946: qu above p 251. Cf Gide 1923 and Wilson
1939-41.

Katkov, G. Steerforth and Stavrogin: On the Sources of
The Possessed. Slavonic Rev 27 1949.

Symons 1951: p 5 above. Comparison "terribly damaging"
to Dickens. Cf Gide 1923 qu above p 158 and Wilson 1931.

Dickens and Dostoevsky, cont.

Trilling 1953: p 103 above. "The influence of Dickens upon
Dostoevsky is perhaps nowhere exhibited in a more detailed
way than in the similarities between Blandois and the
shabby-genteel devil of The Brothers Karamazov, and also
between him and Smerdyakov of the same novel..."

Allen 1954: p 30 above; pp 174, 219 PB edn.

Maugham 1954: qu above p 188.

Futrell, M.S. Dickens and Dostoevsky. English Miscellany 7
Rome 1956.

Allott 1959: p 7 above. "War and Peace and Crime and
Punishment, both contemporary with Our Mutual Friend,
are obviously achievements of quite a different order...
Dostoevsky...depicts in Crime and Punishment, as in his
other novels, regions of spiritual suffering which are
outside Dickens's conception" (p 34.)

Katarsky 1960: p 5 above.

Priestley 1960: p 33 above.

Wexler, A. Dickens und Dostojewski. Deutsche Rundschau 88
1962.

Bayley 1962: p 48 above. Oliver Twist and Crime and
Punishment.

Fanger, D. Dostoevsky and Romantic Realism: A Study of
Dostoevsky in relation to Balzac, Dickens and Gogol.
Cambridge Mass 1965.

Katarsky 1966: p 144 above.

Gifford 1968: qu above p 144.

Anikst 1970: p 144 above

Wall 1970: p 144 above.

Wilson, Angus. Dickens and Dostoevsky. Dickens Memorial
Lecture 1970.

Lary, N.M. Dostoevsky and Dickens: A Study of Literary
Influence. 1973.

Anon. TLS 10 Aug 1973. Was Myshkin Pickwick?
Review of Lary above.

263

Dickens and Flaubert

Bagehot 1858: qu above p 163.   Dickens and le mot juste.

Flaubert 1872: qu above p 42.

Maupassant, Guy de.   "M.Flaubert is...first and foremost an
  artist: that is, an objective writer.   I defy anyone, after
  having read all his works, to make out what he is in private
  life, what he thinks... One knows what Dickens must have
  thought, what Balzac must have thought.   They appear all the
  time in their books..." (Gustave Flaubert, 1876, qu Allott
  1959 p 272.)

James 1884: p 16 above.   "...you have only to remember that
  talents so dissimilar as those of Alexandre Dumas and Jane
  Austen, Charles Dickens and Gustave Flaubert, have worked in
  this field with equal glory" (p 97 PB edn.)

Gissing 1898: p 17 above.   "...not one page of Flaubert gives
  proof of sight and grasp equal to that evinced in a thousand
  of Dickens" (p 181 1926 edn.)

Swinburne 1908: p 20 above.   "...the noble simplicity and
  selfless devotion of Agnes Wickfield and Esther Summerson...
  there are still some who prefer the type...to the type of
  Emma Bovary...with all due reverence to the unique genius
  of Flaubert" (p 10 1913 edn.)

Cecil 1931-4: p 25 above; p 47 FL edn.

Maugham 1948: qu above p 82.

Wilson, Edmund.   The Triple Thinkers.   1952.   Our Mutual Friend
  and L'Education sentimentale (pp 7-8 PB edn.)

Allen 1954: p 30 above; p 235 PB edn.

Stang 1959: qu above p 32.

Priestley 1960: p 33 above.   "Flaubert...retired into his
  study...as other men have retreated into monasteries.
  Perhaps some of his later admirers, who set him above
  Tolstoy, Dickens, Balzac, are secretly more impressed by
  this retreat than by the work that came out of it" (p 268
  PB edn.)

Bayley 1962: qu above p 111.

Leavis, F.R. "I will say here, what I have found myself
   saying in discussion, that (if one can imagine oneself
   faced with such a choice) I would without hesitation
   surrender the whole oeuvre of Flaubert for Dombey and Son
   or Little Dorrit" (letter to Spectator 4 Jan 1963 rp
   Letters in Criticism 1974 p 96). Cf Leavis 1948: "There is
   only one Hard Times in the Dickensian oeuvre" (PB edn 1962
   p 30).

Basch 1974: p 192 above; p 228. Emma Bovary and Dickens's
   "fallen women".

Dickens and Wilkie Collins

Collins 1874: qu above pp 80, 118, 226.

Reade 1887. Memoirs of Charles Reade (1887) qu Robinson 1951
   below (p 253 1974 edn) records that Reade ranked Collins
   next to Dickens among contemporary novelists.

Hutton 1892: p 5 above.

Swinburne, Algernon Charles. Wilkie Collins. Studies in
   Prose and Poetry, 1894.

Chesterton 1906: p 20 above. "In his capacity as editor
   Dickens made one valuable discovery. He discovered Wilkie
   Collins. Wilkie Collins is the one man of unmistakable
   genius who has a certain affinity with Dickens... No two
   men would have more contempt for superstitions; and no two
   men could so create the superstitious thrill" (cf Chesterton
   1913 pp 56-7 OPUS edn.)

Swinburne 1908: p 20 above. "It is a crowning feather in the
   cap of Mr Wilkie Collins that he alone should have been able
   to give us in the person of Sergeant Cuff a second detective
   officer worthy to be named" with Mr Bucket (pp 11-12 1913 edn)

Saintsbury 1916: p 22 above. "It has been justly and acutely
   remarked that, though Wilkie Collins was, undoubtedly,
   Dickens's pupil, the pupil had a good deal of reflex
   influence on the master, not always for good" (p 336 1932
   edn; cf W.T.Young, Lesser Novelists, ibid p 438.)

Phillips, Walter C. Dickens, Reade and Collins: Sensation
   Novelists. New York 1919.

Eliot 1927: qu above pp 89, 187.   Bleak House and The Moonstone

Duffield 1930: p 120 above.   Edwin Drood and The Moonstone.

Sayers 1936: p 250 above.

Dexter 1938: p 6 above.

Milley, H.J.W.   Wilkie Collins and A Tale of Two Cities.
   MLR 34 1939.

Pope-Hennessy 1945: p 4 above; ch 22 Arctic Concerns.
   The Frozen Deep.   Cf Eliot 1927.

Davis, E.R.   Dickens and Wilkie Collins.   University of
   Wichita Studies no 16 1945.

Ashley, R.P.   Wilkie Collins Reconsidered.   NCF 4 1950.

Robinson, Kenneth.   Wilkie Collins.   1951; rv 1974.   "The
   references to Collins in Forster's Life are deliberately
   reduced to a minimum, and do scant justice to the part he
   played in the last twenty years of Dickens's life... Later
   biographers... seem to have taken their cue from Forster and
   are content to deplore instead of trying to explain the
   undoubted influence of Collins on the other novelist.
   Insofar as this influence extended to Dickens's writing,
   it may have been detrimental - although this is a matter of
   opinion; but there is little doubt that in Collins's
   company he spent some of the happiest periods of his life"
   (p 59 1974 edn; cf pp 61, 71-9, 88-93, 99-101, 221-4 and
   Johnson 1952 below.)

Booth, B.A.   Collins and the Art of Fiction.   NCF 6 1951.

Johnson 1952: p 5 above.   Does justice to Collins (cf
   Robinson above) as does Pearson 1949 on a smaller scale.

Davis, Nuel P.   The Life of Wilkie Collins.   Urbana Ill 1956.

Allott 1959: p 7 above; p 179.

Brannan 1970: p 192 above.

Buchloh, Paul G.   Der viktorianische Detektivroman: Dickens
   und Collins.   Der Detektivroman, by Buchloh and Becker,
   Darmstadt 1973.

Dickens and Wilkie Collins, cont.

Stewart, J.I.M.   From Mystery to Mission.   TLS 6 Sep 1974.
  Review of Norman Page, Wilkie Collins: The Critical
  Heritage, 1974.

See also above under "Household Words", "Christmas Stories",
  "Stage and Platform" etc.

Dickens and Tolstoy

Tolstoy 1852-1903: qu above pp 19, 142.

Cockerell 1903: p 19 above.

Swinburne 1903: qu above p 19.   Cf Quiller-Couch below.

Phelps 1916: qu above p 142.

Quiller-Couch 1922-5: p 23 above.   "...Things happen to Mr
  Pecksniff, to Little Nell, to Mr Micawber, to Mr Dombey...
  but, as the rule, these things do not happen within them,
  as such things happen in the soul of any protagonist in a
  novel by Tolstoy or Dostoevsky..." (p 75).   "I conclude
  these lectures on Dickens with a word or two casually
  uttered in conversation by a great man...of the generation
  that succeeded Dickens; himself a superb novelist, and a
  ruthless thinker for the good of his kind..."   Q then
  records Cockerell and Swinburne above and concludes:
  "Tolstoy to Dickens: that is how the tall ships, the
  grandees of literature, dip their flags and salute as they
  pass.   Gentlemen, let us leave it at that." (p 100.)

Apostolai, N.   Tolstoy and Dickens.   Family Views of Tolstoy,
  ed Aylmer Maude, 1926.

Cecil 1931-4: p 25 above.   "Tolstoy - and who should know
  better than he - thought Dickens one of the few supreme
  novelists that had ever lived" (p 54 FL edn.)

Dent 1933: p 4 above; p 332.

Orwell 1939-40: p 26 above.   "If I were forced to compare
  Tolstoy with Dickens, I should say that Tolstoy's appeal
  will probably be wider in the long run, because Dickens is
  scarcely intelligible outside the English-speaking culture;

Dickens and Mark Twain

Shaw 1924: qu above p 89.

Leacock 1933: p 4 above. Pickwick and Huckleberry Finn
(qu above p 43). American Notes and Huck (Leacock p 93);
Pictures from Italy and The Innocents Abroad (pp 114-15).
See also below.

Leacock, Stephen. Two Humorists. Yale Rev 24 1934.

Brooks 1944: p 64 above under Coombes. See p 293.

Auden, W.H. Huck and Oliver. Listener 1 Oct 1953.

Cunliffe 1954: p 135 above; pp 170, 176 1967 edn.

Blair, W. The French Revolution and Huckleberry Finn.
MP 55 1958. Compares Tale of Two Cities.

Brunner 1959: p 141 above.

Ridland, J.M. Huck, Pip and Plot. NCF 20 1966.

Churchill, R.C. The Literature of the United States.
In Sampson 1970: p 28 above. Chuzzlewit and Twain's
Mississippi (pp 820-1). Cf Churchill 1974: p 65 above.

Dickens and Zola

Phelps 1916: p 22 above; pp 133-6.

Leacock 1933: qu above p 73.

Atkins, S. A Possible Dickens Influence in Zola. MLQ 8 1947.

Holloway, John. The Literary Scene. In The Modern Age,
PGEL 7 1961. Treatment of common life in Dickens and Zola
according to characters in Gissing's New Grub Street ch 10
(p 58; see further below under "Dickens and Gissing".)

Dickens and Daudet

James 1888: p 142 in 1968 edn. Cf Munro 1908.

270

simple people,
can cross a
igarette-card.
n them than
es barely

y; it was quite
man's struggles

Anna Karenina

as
ms of adult
l to suffer,
intelligent
l Edith Dombey
ovelette" (p 37;

ible level of
his age are
immense
rld" (p 197

513-16.

eld. CQ Autumn

Dickens's
Allott 1959.

Dickens and Hardy

Quiller-Couch 1922-5: p 23 above. "...No one seeks in Jane
Austen for examples of strength: and you will find none in
Dickens to compare with Othello or Cleopatra or (say) with
Mr Hardy's Mayor of Casterbridge..." (p 30.)

Liddell 1947: p 28 above. "...Dickens's people are big
enough to set against their background, while Hardy's are
apt to get lost on Egdon Heath..." (p 115.)

Leavis 1948: p 29 above. Neither Dickens nor Hardy thought
fit to be included in the line of great novelists from Jane
Austen to D.H.Lawrence. Hardy dismissed in a quotation from
Henry James about "the good little Thomas Hardy" (p 33 PB edn)
and Dickens relegated to an appendix on the strength of Hard
Times. Leavis 1970 reverses Leavis 1948 in regard to
Dickens, but Hardy remains outside "the great tradition"
up to the spring of 1975. Cf Howells 1891 below.

Churchill 1951: p 30 above; p 101.

Wing 1973: p 121 above. Drood and Desperate Remedies.

Furbank, P.N. Intn Tess of the d'Urbervilles. New Wessex edn
1974, pp 11-13.

Hardy, Barbara. Intn The Trumpet Major, ibid pp 13-14.

Bayley, John. Intn Far from the Madding Crowd, ibid pp 23-4.

Dickens and Henry James

James 1865, 1884, 1913: pp 14, 16, 22 above.

Howells 1891: p 17 above. Line of the novel runs to James
from Hawthorne and George Eliot, not through the slack and
untidy work of Dickens and Thackeray (qu Cunliffe 1954 p 229
1967 edn; cf Leavis 1948 above.)

Phelps 1916: p 22 above. "Henry James was a specialist in art
... Dickens was what I should call a general practitioner...
(pp 318-20; this ch first appeared in Yale Rev Jul 16.)

Pound, Ezra. "He had most assuredly a greater awareness than
was granted to Balzac or to Mr Charles Dickens..." (Henry
James, Little Rev Aug 1918, rp Literary Essays 1954, p 301
1960 edn.)

Dickens and Henry James, cont.

Eglington, John. See above p 24 under Moore 1924.

Eliot 1927: p 24 above; final para (pp 431-2 1934 edn.)

Leavis 1948: p 29 above. Roderick Hudson and Chuzzlewit:
"...This passage...of course couldn't possibly have been
written by Dickens: something has been done to give the
Dickensian manner a much more formidable intellectual edge.
We feel a finer and fuller consciousness behind the ironic
humour, which engages mature standards and interests such as
Dickens was innocent of" (p 147 PB edn). Dickens and The
Bostonians: "...the un-Dickensian subtlety...the implicit
reference to mature standards and interests... We are a long
way from Dickens here... he gives us Martin Chuzzlewit
redone by an enormously more intelligent and better
educated mind... a force so much surpassing Dickens's...
because of the so much greater subtlety of James's art"
(pp 150-3; cf Leavis 1970 below for an almost exactly
contrary opinion.)

Leavis, F.R. What Maisie Knew. Scrutiny Summer 1950; rp
Anna Karenina and Other Essays, 1967, pp 80-2. Maisie and
Copperfield.

Fraser 1953: qu above p 176.

Stang 1959: qu above p 32.

Engel 1959: qu above p 32.

Churchill, R.C. The Comedy of Ideas. PGEL 7 1961 pp 225-6.

Garis 1965: p 34 above

Leavis 1970: p 36 above. "James's assured critical bent is
that of the decidedly less great artist" (p 227); "Dickens
is not only a different kind of genius from James, but a
genius of a greater kind... Dickens is certainly no less a
master than James of the subtleties of the inner life"
(p 248; cf Leavis 1948 above.)

Leavis, F.R. "That The Princess Casamassima has this kind of
radical dependence on Little Dorrit is made plain by the
elaborate but feeble complex of borrowings and echoings that
we have to recognize when we compare the two novels"
(letter to TLS 5 Mar 1971 rp Tasker 1974 p 141.)

272

Dickens and Bernard Shaw

Shaw 1897: qu above p 101. Little Dorrit and The Devil's Disciple.

Shaw 1914: p 22 above.

Swinnerton, Frank. "Shaw has told the world that his ideas were derived from Wagner, Ibsen, Samuel Butler, and Nietzsche, and that his characters were stolen from Dickens. There is not a word of truth in all this..." (The Georgian Literary Scene, 1935; p 38 EL edn.)

Shaw 1937: p 26 above.

Wilson 1939-41: p 27 above. Shaw insisted on his own debt to Dickens "at a time when it was taken for granted that he must derive from such foreigners as Ibsen and Nietzsche" (pp 2-3 UP edn.)

Pearson 1942: qu above p 131.

Johnson, Edgar. Dickens and Shaw: Critics of Society. Virginia Quarterly Rev 33 1957.

Barnes, T.R. Shaw and the London Theatre. PGEL 7 1961 p 215.

Churchill 1961: p 272 above; pp 225-30.

Brooks, H.F.and J.R. Dickens in Shaw. Dickensian 59 1963.

Basch 1974: p 192 above; pp 227-8.

Dickens and Gissing

Gissing 1901: p 19 above.

Seccombe, Thomas. The Work of George Gissing. Intn The House of Cobwebs, 1906; pp vii-ix, xi-xiii, xvi-xix, xxxiv, xliv 1931 edn.

Young, W.T. Meredith, Butler, Gissing. CHEL XIII 1916. "The differences in attitude between Dickens and his disciple are profound..." (p 458 1932 edn.)

Quiller-Couch 1922-5: 1923 above. See pp 98-100.

Anon (R.C.Churchill). The Gissing Legend. TLS 30 Jan 1953.

Dickens and Gissing, cont.

Churchill 1958: p 269 above; p 343.

Anon. TLS 22 Jun 1968. "...if we are really going to
understand Gissing we had better get him off the
European Dostoevsky-Schopenhauer axis altogether and put
him on the Home Counties Dickens-E.M.Forster axis...His
heroes look back on the one hand to Copperfield and
forward on the other to Leonard Bast" (review of Gissing
reprints.)

Coustillas 1969: p 19 above.

Choudhury, M.K. The Influence of Dickens on George Gissing.
Indian Journal of English Studies 14 1973.

Allen, Walter. Intn The Nether World. EL 1973.

Tindall, Gillian. The Born Exile. 1974. Describes New
Grub Street as "a key book in the development away from
the Dickensian theme of the individual versus circumstances
and towards the twentieth-century image of the individual
grappling with himself."

Dickens and Conrad

Conrad 1912: qu above p 89.

Phelps 1916: p 22 above. "...while Dickens is a refracting
telescope, Conrad is a reflector..." (pp 215-16.)

Dybowski 1936: p 4 above.

Leavis 1948: qu above p 188.

Warner, Oliver. "Nicholas Nickleby in Polish was his first
introduction to English literature. He retained his
affection for Dickens when he came to know the originals,
particularly for Bleak House" (Joseph Conrad, BCB 1950,
p 16 1954 edn.)

Brown, Douglas. An Approach to Conrad. PGEL 7 1961; p 129.

Dickens and H.G.Wells

James, Henry.   Letter to Wells 19 Nov 1905.   "You have for
   the very first time treated the English 'lower middle' class
   etc without the picturesque, the grotesque, the fantastic and
   romantic interference of which Dickens...is so misleadingly...
   full" (qu Henry James and H.G.Wells, ed Leon Edel and Gordon
   N.Ray, 1958, p 105.)

Wells 1915: p 22 above.   See also p 52 above.

Phelps 1916: qu above p 142.

Forster 1927: p 24 above.   "...neither of them has much taste:
   the world of beauty was largely closed to Dickens, and is
   entirely closed to Wells.   And there are other parallels –
   for instance their method of drawing character..." (pp 24-5
   PB edn; cf p 80.)

Swinnerton 1935: p 273 above.   "...one side of Wells's genius
   ...has kinship with the comic genius of Dickens, his
   favourite author" (pp 56-7 EL edn; cf pp 62-3 on Copperfield
   and Tono-Bungay.)

Shaw 1937: p 26 above.   "...Compare the case of H.G.Wells,
   our nearest to a twentieth-century Dickens..."

Orwell 1939-40: p 26 above; pp 22-3, 40 1946 edn.

Murry, John Middleton.   H.G.Wells.   Adelphi Oct 1946; rp
   Little Reviews Anthology 1947-8, 1948, p 188.

Churchill, R.C.   Wells the Novelist.   Tribune 20 Oct 1950.
   Copperfield and Tono-Bungay; Great Expectations and Mr Polly.
   Cf Shaw and Orwell above.

Allen 1954: p 30 above; p 316 PB edn.

Ford 1955: p 31 above.   "There is a sense in which James and
   Conrad can be regarded as being much closer to the essential
   nature of Dickens's work than are Bennett and Wells," in
   spite of "the obvious Dickensisms" of the latter two (p 221.)

Bergonzi, Bernard.   The Early H.G.Wells.   Manchester 1961.

Meckier 1972: qu above p 98.

Dickens and Proust

Cor, R.   Un romancier de la vertu et un peintre du vice:
Dickens-Proust.   Paris 1928.

Wilson, Edmund.   "...in the social scenes...we shall look
in vain for anything like them outside the novels of
Dickens... And there even seems distinguishable in the
Verdurin circle an unconscious reminiscence of the
Veneerings of Our Mutual Friend..." (Axel's Castle, 1931,
pp 114-16 FL edn.)

Wilson, Angus.   In Slater 1970: p 8 above.   Dickens's David
and Proust's Marcel (p 225.)

Dickens and G.K.Chesterton

Chesterton 1903, 1906, 1907, etc: pp 3, 20...above.

Maury 1911: p 136 above.

Chesterton 1929: p 143 above.

Teranishi Takeo.   Chesterton and Dickens.   1936.   See Peter
Milward, Chesterton in Japan, in G.K.Chesterton: A
Centenary Appraisal, ed John Sullivan 1974 p 228.

Orwell 1939: qu above p 131.

Ward, Maisie.   Gilbert Keith Chesterton.   1944; pp 45-6,
127-8 PB edn.

Allen 1970: p 8 above under Slater.   "Recent interpretations
of Dickens that stress his affinities with Dostoevsky and
Kafka, interpretations that, once made, seem self-evident,
do not negate the truths contained in Chesterton's
interpretation.   Both are right, and they are not
incompatible" (p 27.)

Robson, W.W.   "...all these writers - Chesterton, Stevenson,
Doyle - are disciples of Dickens, the great master of the
unfamiliar in the familiar.   But Chesterton was perhaps
the closest of them all to the detective story side of
Dickens... The quality of Chesterton's work at its best,
in the Father Brown stories, is comparable to that of
Edwin Drood" (Father Brown and Others, in Sullivan 1974
above, p 61; cf Robson, Southern Rev Summer 1969.)

Dickens and G.K.Chesterton, cont.

Churchill and Monod 1974: p 92 above.

Dickens and James Joyce

Lewis, Wyndham.   Mr Jingle and Mr Bloom.   The Art of Being
Ruled, New York 1926, pp 413-16.

Gorman, Herbert.   Intn A Portrait of the Artist... New York
1928.

Wilson 1939-41: qu above p 169.

Pritchett 1946: p 28 above.   "There is more of Dickens, to
my mind, in James Joyce's Ulysses than in books like
Kipps or Tono Bungay" (p 78.)

Edel, Leon.   The Psychological Novel 1900-50.   New York 1955.

Freidman, Melvin.   Stream of Consciousness: A Study in
Literary Method.   New Haven 1955.

Stone 1958: qu above p 167.

Allott 1959: qu above p 167.

Stone 1959: qu above p 121.

Kettle, Arnold.   The Consistency of James Joyce.   PGEL 7
1961, pp 305-6.

Gross, John.   "Among English novelists...there were no major
precedents at the time Joyce was writing - unless one goes
all the way back to Dickens, an even more original poet of
the city, who in this respect as in many others
anticipated his kaleidoscopic and impressionistic
techniques" (Joyce.   Modern Masters series 1971 p 55.)

See also Ulysses (1922) parody of Dickens in Oxen of the Sun
episode; and Finnegans Wake (1939) ref to "Mr Jinglejoys"
p 466.   Cf Stone 1959 qu Wall 1970 p 423n.

Dickens and Kafka

Kafka 1917: qu above p 81.

Wilson 1939: qu above p 169.

Pascal, Roy.   Dickens and Kafka.   Listener 26 Apr 1956.

Spilka, M.   Dickens and Kafka.   Bloomington Ind 1962.

Stoehr 1965: p 34 above.

Allen 1970: qu above p 276.

Snow 1970: p 8 above under Slater; pp 147-8.

Dickens and D.H.Lawrence

E.T.(Jessie Chambers).   D.H.Lawrence: A Personal Record.
1935.   Describes their early reading of Dickens c1900-05
as "a widening and enlargement of life."

Leavis 1948: p 29 above.   "The ironic humour and the
presentation in general" in the first part of The Lost Girl
"bear a clear relation to the Dickensian, but are
incomparably more mature and belong to a total serious
significance" (p 31 PB edn.)

Leavis, F.R.   D.H.Lawrence: Novelist.   1955.   "The Lost Girl
...suggests the work of an unsentimental, more subtle and
incomparably more penetrating Dickens..." (pp 31-2 PB edn.)

Bayley 1962: p 48 above.   "The Dickens of Hard Times, whom
Dr Leavis admires, manipulates symbolic meaning in a manner
that reaches its apotheosis with Clifford Chatterley sitting
in his motor-chair" (p 62).

Williams, Raymond.   The English Novel.   1970.

Williams 1970: p 8 above under Slater; pp 78-81.

Meckier 1972: p 98 above.   Hard Times and Lady Chatterley's
Lover.   Cf Bayley above.

McCullen 1974: p 98 above under Meckier.

Dickens and Sinclair Lewis

Brooks, Van Wyck. "In the range and variety of his types, in his fecundity, in his virility, Sinclair Lewis suggested another Dickens - the 'Dickens of America', the name to which the hotel-man's brother, the writer brother, aspired in Lewis's novel Work of Art" (The Confident Years, 1952, p 301.)

Cunliffe, Marcus. "Perry Miller has noted that Lewis adored Dickens... But perhaps the America of the 1920s held fewer resources for social satire than Dickens's England... Though Dickens had his faults, he never tried to pass Mr Podsnap off as Mr Pickwick. This is what Sinclair Lewis tends to do" (The Literature of the United States, 1954; p 282 1967 edn.)

Dickens and George Orwell

Braybrooke, Neville. "To contemporary readers, the figure which he cut was that of an English radical: he was in the tradition of Langland, Bunyan, Cobbett and Dickens. Indeed, one might be tempted to say that, with Chesterton, he stood for the end of a tradition; but this is not so. For in R.C.Churchill's work - a less prolific modern author - the same tradition is being continued; and if a definition of that tradition is wanted, then one can do no better than turn to Orwell's comments on Dickens. They are equally applicable to himself..." (George Orwell, Fortnightly Jun 1951.)

INDEX.

The Table of Contents gives the main references. This Index
  lists the chief critics and commentators from Dickens's
  time to the present day, with a few other names of
  relevant interest.

Auden, W.H.   44, 48, 215, 231, 270

Austin, Alfred   15, 212, 253

Axton, W.F.   34, 44, 77, 78, 187, 188, 191

Aylmer, Felix   121, 225, 228

Baetzhold, H.G.   64

Bagehot, Walter   13, 46, 123, 129, 160, 163, 171, 178, 179,
   196, 210, 223, 229, 235, 242, 243, 253, 264

Baillie-Saunders, Margaret   198

Baker, George P.   6

Baker, R.M.   120

Baldwin, Stanley, Earl   200

Barlow, G.   20

Barnes, A.W.   128

Barnes, J.   112

Barnes, T.R.   273

Barnett, C.Z.   66

Barrett, Elizabeth, Mrs Browning   61

Barrie, Sir James   232

Bartholomew, J.G.   128

Basch, Françoise   192, 203, 209, 222, 227, 228, 237, 256,
   257, 258, 260, 265, 268, 273

Bateson, F.W.   1, 14, 84, 99, 108, 113

Batho, Edith   26, 201

Bayley, John   7, 48, 111, 222, 263, 264, 271, 278

Beaumont, G.   33

289

INDEX, cont.

309